IN THE
SHADOW OF
DENALI

Praise for In The Shadow of Denali:

"A mountaineering classic, not only because it takes as its subject the nation's highest mountain but also because Waterman writes with unusual vision and spirit . . . Striking not a single false note . . . this is a strong, mature work by a gifted writer."—*Booklist*

"A fine writer with a profound appreciation of what towering mountains are . . . this is a book about the high mountains written by a real mountain man."—James Michener

"A magnificent book, beautifully written, a superb delineation, in the broadest sense, of one person's relationship to landscape."—Ann Zwinger

"Tales from the mean side of Denali, from a freelancer with a reputation for writing fine climbing stories . . . Arresting . . . A pleasure to read." —*Kirkus Reviews*

"Masterful storytelling . . . There is climbing in this book, but remarkably it is not a book about climbing, any more than *A River Runs Through It* was a book about fishing. Waterman the writer resembles that other Alaskan adventurer, Jack London. But in his storytelling, in the way he renders non-fiction close to fiction with its alien and thoughtful beauty, he descends more directly from Norman Maclean . . . He is our Ishmael, the eloquent witness to a profound journey."—Jeff Long, *Boulder Camera*

"Bewitching. It was an honor to read this eyes-open chronicle of being beaten to a psychological pulp and then reborn."—*American Alpine Journal*

"Poetic and powerful—a testimony to both the man and the mountain." —Dennis Eberl

"Taut understated prose captures the commitment of dedicated climbers." —*Publishers Weekly*

"Personal, intense, gripping . . . a compelling book. He is a serious writer, daring to take up the challenge of avoiding hackneyed prose in telling about fear, cold, wind and such wondrous beauty as the aurora shining on the mountain."—Bill Hunt, *Alaska*

IN THE SHADOW OF DENALI

Life and Death On Alaska's Mt. McKinley

JONATHAN WATERMAN

THE LYONS PRESS
Guilford, Connecticut
An imprint of The Globe Pequot Press

The Lyons Press is an imprint of The Globe Pequot Press.

10 9 8 7 6

ISBN 13 978-1-55821-726-3

Library of Congress Cataloging-in-Publication Data

Waterman, Jonathan.
   In the shadow of Denali / Jonathan Waterman.
      p. cm
   Originally published: New York: Dell Pub., c1994. With new introd.
   ISBN 1-55821-726-6
      1. Mountaineering—Alaska—McKinley, Mount—History.
   2. Mountaineering—Accidents—Alaska—McKinley, Mount—History.
   3. McKinley, Mount (Alaska)—History. I. Title.

GV199.42.A42M3276   1998
796.52'2'097983–dc21   98-16946
                                                                          CIP

Manufactured in the United States of America

Chequer'd shadow.

—Shakespeare,
Titus Andronicus

To that high Capitol, where kingly Death
Keeps his pale court in beauty and decay,
He came.

—Percy Bysshe Shelley,
Arethusa

IN THE
SHADOW OF
DENALI

Acknowledgments

I REMAIN INDEBTED TO MANY FRIENDS WHO HAVE HELPED ME breathe life into my work here and on other pages. Brad Washburn's inspiration and kindness over the years have helped to unveil the world that lurks behind a 20,320-foot mountain. My sincere thanks also go to: John Thackray, Lou Dawson, Ed Webster, Dave Hale, Steve Roper, Michael Kennedy, Michael Benge, Alison Osius, John Harlin, Dave Gretchell, Jim Chase, Jed Williamson, James Michener, George Bracksiek, Will Glad, Nancy Prichard, Ralph Bovard, Charlie Houston, Carolyn Hines, Paul Konrad, Steve Cassimiro, Greg Cliburn, Andrew Tillon, Mark Bryant, Al Steck, Greg Child, Kim Heacox, Jeff Long, Rick Ridgeway, John Wilcox, Scott Gil, Susan Golomb, Mitch Horowitz, Kerre Martineau, Bryan Oettel, and David Sobel. Like my accomplices on Denali, these people put forth incentive and, sometimes, the grubstake for my stories. Their examples as writers or editors or their specific advice incited me to slog through tedious rewrites, pulled me out of gaping non sequiturs, rescued me from dangling participles, then hauled me into fulfillment.

I would like to thank the surviving friends and family of: Dave Shoemaker, who dreamed of 20,320 feet but fell from grace in New Hampshire's Arctic Wind; Herb Atwater, who couldn't hold on any longer in the shadow of Denali; Chris Kerrebrock and Mugs Stump, to whom crevasses became an exit from this life; Ray Genet, who loved the mountain as much as people; Johnny Waterman, who chose Denali as his tombstone; and Gretta Berglund, who came to the darkened ranger station after we pulled her corpse from the Sanctuary River. From my time on Denali I have deduced that when you die, you're not screwing yourself but the people you love.

My deepest bow of respect goes to the park rangers and mountain guides and Alaskan pilots who nearly traded their lives for those of fallen climbers—often strangers.

Foreword

ON MY ONE TRIP TO ALASKA, IN 1982, I WAS FLATTENED ON A glacier landing strip by a skiplane. My hip smashed off a piece of the plane's tail, and the tail nearly removed a piece of my hip. Though plane and climber flew and walked again, this imbroglio served as a fitting end to a disastrous climbing trip on which, despite high ambitions, I ascended nothing. Also on that trip, snow fell incessantly, bitter cold gnawed at me, and my partner and his girlfriend stressfully terminated their affair while we were tentbound in a two-week whiteout.

All this transpired on the Shadows Glacier in the Kichatna Spires (one of many Denali settings for this book). While we were flying out, Denali was a massive presence on the horizon. I was torn between a desire to return and climb it, and a feeling that I should avoid Alaska and its beautiful, cold mountains. While nursing my hip, I had the conviction—call it a premonition—that in Alaska only epics of discomfort and danger awaited me, so I stuck to Himalayan climbing and contented myself with being an armchair mountaineer on peaks Alaskan.

From this vantage, I found that the literature of Alaskan climbing comprises some of America's finest mountain writing. This is only fitting, for Alaska's mountains demand much from those who climb them. Of all these books, Jonathan Waterman's *In the Shadow of Denali* is stratospherically the finest of the genre. With this book, Waterman has earned a place alongside such great modern American mountain writers as David Roberts and Jon Krakauer, for Waterman writes in the intoxicating style of the inquiring modernist, rather than the nuts-and-bolts manner of the classic alpine storytellers.

These are vignettes about the people whose lives have been touched by—and sometimes taken by—Denali and its icy neighbors. Waterman has an encyclopedic knowledge of Alaskan climbing history that he has magically woven with his own encounters. His narrative commands authority, clarity, verve, poignancy, and not a little opinion of the many who climb in the Alaska Range. And he writes from many viewpoints: Climbing bum, park custodian, and rescuer—Waterman has been all of these.

Over the years, I came to know Jon Waterman through our mutual professions and passions, writing and climbing. When he was an editor at *Climbing* magazine, Jon was often on the other end of the phone, prying into some expedition of mine, prospecting nuggets of information for mountaineering news. I also relied on Jon's voluminous knowledge and his reliable pen for the Alaskan entries within my *Encyclopedia of Climbing*.

We also commiserate with each other about the fruitful penury of living to climb and writing to live. Once, in Italy, we drank each other under the table during a festive Chianti blowout that had something to do with climbing. In 1992, he poked into my life again to write a profile of me for *Climbing* magazine. As he became familiar with me, so did I create a portrait of my biographer: a steady-handed, soft-spoken, curious-minded, and articulate man—a natural reporter—as comfortable in cowboy boots as he is in cramponed double boots. Most recently, Jon's role as production manager of the American Alpine Club Press promises to be a positive move for American climbing writing.

Crafting a story is often described as something akin to squeezing a stone for a drop of blood—it is nothing but hard work. I look at stories as contraptions: They move, they have many parts, and it all needs constant adjustment. Built of words, this contraption is fueled by personal involvement and truth. Sometimes the contraption works, sometimes it is destined for the scrap heap; Waterman's work fairly purrs with well-oiled and seamless honesty. His collection of stories succeeds in one of the most difficult facets of storytelling: maintaining objective clarity while speaking from a deeply personal perspective. His are among the most personal pieces of climbing writing ever penned.

The mountain that is the setting for these stories is a cold and inhospitable place guaranteeing adventure for all and a promise of disaster for a few. As long as Denali stands, climbers will come, and some of them will die. It is an icon of American climbing, as identifiable as the Eiger Nordwand or Mount Everest. From Denali's rich, sometimes flamboyant history, Jon has distilled the essence of a mountain deeply rooted in the minds of American climbers, weaving his own encounters with Denali as mountaineer, guide, climbing ranger, historian, and environmentalist into the continuum of that history. He has achieved this not only by research but also by living and climbing himself in the shadow of Denali.

Waterman's Denali is conveyed through images as sharply defined as the wind-carved facets of the mountain. At times this Alaska and its *dramatis personae* is a bleak world of "stifling black winters, high suicide rates, eccentric gadflies, and obdurate dipsomaniacs." But when he writes that "on a good day you can revel in three miles of verticality to the tundra below," the colors and smells and the feel of a cold wind against my cheek come alive and I remember why I climb.

Among these stories, "Lone Wolf" transcends climbing literature. His exploration of the troubled, brilliant, and doomed solo climber (and his own phonetic namesake) John Waterman, who spent 148 days alone on Mount Hunter, is a significant moment in climbing literature. As I read it, I had the rare experience of forgetting that I was turning the pages. Most writers might achieve such excellence once or twice in a lifetime; Jon has written himself a hard act to follow.

Denali and the Alaska Range have been to Jon what the Himalaya has been to me: a personal crucible, a place to escape to from time to time, sometimes a place we have barely escaped from. *In the Shadow of Denali* is not only fine literature but also good advice if you should feel the compulsion to stand above all else in North America.

—Greg Child
author of *Thin Air*

Preface

IN 1992, ELEVEN CLIMBERS DIED ON DENALI, AND THE disaster quickly became old news. In 1996, eight climbers died on Everest and two years later the event still holds the public in its thrall. During that disastrous year on Denali, several news magazines and television networks ran stories, and the wire service carried the news (because disaster sells), but until recently no books were published about the calamity; now most people have forgotten about that terrible two week period on North America's highest mountain.

In chapter 10 of this book, I briefly revisit this epic summer in which the tragic and the heroic intertwined. Mugs Stumps, one of the most accomplished alpinists in North America, was one of the eleven, along with several foreigners and experienced Americans, who perished in a storm. But it is important to remember that such stories are not only about loss. There were many—Renny Jackson, Jim Wickwire, Ron Johnson, Brian Okonek, Roger Robinson, Scott Gill, John Roskelley, Matt Culberson, and Daryll Miller, to name a few—who risked their own lives trying to save those caught on the mountain.

Most people conjecture that the mainstream interest in Everest in 1996 was generated by the prearranged media already in place on the mountain as well as the deaths of those amateur climbers with whom the non-climbing world can identify. Because of the Everest debacle, it is very likely that the next disaster on Denali will become widely known—and there will be other disasters on Denali, as surely as snow inundates the 14,300 camp. Today, mountaineering death-in-aggregate makes best-selling copy.

Now that human drama and disaster have been so well chronicled, wouldn't it be ideal if an experienced Everest hand wrote an objective analysis of accidents on that mountain? It is what I tried to do with Denali. In my first book, *Surviving Denali*, I identified the patterns of disaster and placed each of them into separate categories, in hope of minimizing accidents. Subsequent statistics show that I may have succeeded. In my second book, *High Alaska*, I wrote both an educational history and a comprehensive guidebook to help spread out the impact and get people off the crowded West Buttress. And here in my third book, I collected those stories, mostly from my own experiences, about the emotional force of death, in order that people could understand the mountain viscerally.

Because we live in a technological age, we are often insulated from our deeper emotions, such as understanding death or perceiving the earth as an animate form. But the time I spent on and around Denali were years in which I abandoned much of the modern world and perceived the mountain and its surrounding wilderness as a living, breathing entity. This sounds half-crazed, I know. But it may have been a necessary means for absorbing these intense experiences about death.

Perhaps my preoccupation on Denali with death curtailed normal romantic interactions. For ten years, I may have allowed myself to become intimate with a mountain. I make no apologies for this; it is more exposure than literary pretense affords, and I now feel fortunate to have lived a portion of my life as intensely as I did.

One reader, who had shared a friendship with one of the climbers detailed in the book, wrote: "Your writing, not just that chapter, but the book as a whole, gave his death a context that I did not have before. The quantity of deaths of friends that you have experienced sits heavy with me. It goes somehow beyond death as a part of our life cycle."

So I have not diluted my observations about death. This subject recurs in the book because much of my time on and around Denali elucidates life's fragility. I would be lying if I claimed to never have considered my own death on Denali. On every climb, climbers wonder if this is the time they will "get the chop." So why not write as plainly as I felt? Since 1932, climbers have indeed been dying and will continue to die on Denali.

Nor is the possibility of death confined to the mountain. More than in any other place I have lived, evidence of passing is omnipresent: suicides, drownings, animal kills, development destroying the wilderness, and a fall season more spectacular and blood red than anywhere on earth. In my time living with the mountain I have learned that committing oneself to an extreme landscape demands that you confront the inexorable cycle of death.

I am angry at the growing trend toward irresponsible climbing on Denali. This is partly (and somewhat unintentionally) perpetrated by the park service's samaritan instincts to help climbers. Ultimately, climbers need to take more control of their own safety. The essential and missing ingredient for many Denali climbers is self-sufficiency. In other words, climbers must develop the ability and willingness to self-rescue, let alone climb without any outside assistance (such as relying upon park service weather forecasts, aircraft support, helicopter rescues, other climbers, or the heated medical tent at 14,300 feet). Clearly the system is being abused. If climbers don't start taking care of themselves, the government could implement yet more regulations and become Big Brother on Denali—which would be the demise of climbing freedom.

In the five years since I last climbed the mountain, the National Park Service has reacted to the aforementioned 1992 disaster. There is now a standby Llama helicopter in Talkeetna, waiting to whisk off unprepared or unlucky victims. Denali National Park has implemented a mandatory sixty-day preregistration process and $150 administration fee for all climbers. According to the rangers, no climbers complain about this new program. However, many climbers, particularly Europeans, have come to believe that the administration fee is their rescue insurance. It is not unusual for climbers to radio for a chopper evacuation—similar to an inebriated customer at the corner bar calling the tipsy taxi. We're told that this administration fee has nothing to do with the annual expense of a standby helicopter, but one only need multiply Denali's annual visitation of climbers by $150 to see how the helicopter fee resembles the administration fee.

In reality, helicopters are not like taxis. Denali rangers receive hazard pay every time they fly because engine power is reduced at high altitude, in sheer winds, and in downdrafts, hindering the rangers' attempts to pick up or winch off victims from precarious perches—all without navigational beacons. Since the odds are that the next Denali disaster will involve rescuers aboard a helicopter, we can expect to see yet another change in Park Service rescue policy and further limits on the mountain.

As a former Denali ranger and climbing bum, I recommend that the Park Service get rid of the standby helicopter. Next, they should drop the administration fee and only charge those victims who absolutely need rescues (membership in the American Alpine Club comes with rescue insurance; and climbers in the Alps can purchase rescue insurance that covers helicopter and rescue callout charges). And in emulation of the successful grizzly bear and wolf reintroductions occurring in the Lower 48, I have heard serious climbers jest about introducing a family of polar bears to the West Buttress.

Ursus Maritimus would find no shortage of food in leftover caches, let alone in those mortal remains laying in crevasses.

Then, maybe, for the first time in fifty years, West Buttress climbers would have to start paying attention to their own survival. After all, climbers climbed mountains in order to artfully court danger rather than eliminate it.

Denali became a sort of cottage industry for me in the 1980s. I was a guide, a rescue ranger, and I wrote books about the place. I quit all but the latter job, and with no marketing, scant advertising, and no book-of-the-month-club sales, *Surviving Denali*, *High Alaska*, and *In the Shadow of Denali* have each outstripped the sales of my two (non-Denali) books published by large presses. The profits of this freelancing (my 1997 wages resemble that of the average welfare recipient) allow me, by the slimmest of margins, to keep paper in the printer and keep writing.

Although writing puts grits on the table, I also write because I love it. As Petrarch, the first modern mountain writer, said six hundred years ago, "Nothing weighs less than a pen, and nothing gives more pleasure."

Many non-writers suppose that freelancers spend their time in dreamy abandon, letting their fantasies percolate out of their creative halves, down to their fingers, out onto the keyboard, then off to the publishers. To dispel these myths, and as incentive for my continued productivity, I save the rejection letters spawned by my writing. These rejections have been fattening my filing cabinets for years.

In the Shadow of Denali garnered dozens of rejections. For instance, the Mountaineers Books Editorial Committee responded: "While a book on Denali is worth pursuing, I think Waterman faces a mountain of work to produce a proposal suitable for our needs." They were right, at least in that it was a mountain of work.

In 1991, one editor (who, ironically, was working at the same press responsible for the edition you now hold in your hands), refused to publish this manuscript because the book was "too mountaineering specific to appeal to a general audience." Bantam Doubleday Dell subsequently printed the book in 1994 and sold most of the first printing in a year. Nevertheless, large presses are only interested in bestsellers, so they forgot about the book and it eventually went "out of print." I'm doubly pleased that the Lyons Press has brought it back to life.

When I first visited Denali in the crowded summer of 1976, 500 other climbers beset the mountain. Today there are over 1,000 climbers each year: 1148 in 1997. The environmental impact—feces, trash, and overcrowding—is obvious. And now, like good developers everywhere, state and federal agencies are mumbling about "improving" the pristine south side of Denali.

In the 1980s and 1990s, climbers routinely began repeating and even soloing the mountain's difficult routes; the Golden Age of mountaineering on Denali is ancient history. In the last half-dozen years, climbers have continued to add new routes, but unlike the new routes of the previous decades, these are merely variations, many of which avoid the upper half of the mountain, as if the technical difficulties and virgin ground are all that interest the modern pioneer. Another trend is "bagging the summit"—as if it is another species to be checked off a bird list. Equally deplorable is that these climbers are generally oblivious to self-sufficiency, the surrounding wilderness, and the passage of our predecessors.

As the reminiscing graybeard, I lament the most recent 1997 addition to Denali literature: an entire guidebook dedicated to the mountain's easiest route, the West Buttress. According to park statistics, 976 of last year's 1148 climbers followed the broken trail, partied, and stuck close to the Park Service's heated rescue tent at the 14,300 camp on the West Buttress. Is this the new millennium's version of adventure?

Last week, a well-known alpinist mentioned his interest of repeating a difficult route on the South Face. When I referred him to the lovely and unclimbed pink granite walls on the eastern side of the mountain, he looked at me with surprise. It was as if it were impossible that there were still frontiers. Or maybe the modern alpinist simply refuses to consider carrying a heavy pack across twenty-five miles of wilderness. My advice to the Denali aspirant: Meet the mountain on its own terms and have a true wilderness experience. Go to the uncrowded West Rib, the Muldrow, the East Buttress, or use your imagination, walk in, and climb a new route. Better yet, don't go. Two years ago, when the urge to have a good Alaskan adventure hit me, I simply went to another mountain more difficult than Denali, with no administration fees, where no climber had visited for two years.

Recently someone asked if I would return to climb Denali; I could not dredge up a motivation. I still dream about the mountain, so in a sense I am still haunted by it. But I will not return to tag the summit or assist G. I. Joe up (a Barbie doll summited in 1997), let alone celebrate my fiftieth birthday on top. I will go back and walk around Denali and ford its ice-cold rivers and nap in the midnight sun and listen for the hum of the northern lights and gaze up with requisite awe pulsing in my arteries.

I have already written a great deal about Denali. And the mountain is clearly finished with me. Veteran Everest climbers have reportedly formed an Everest Anonymous group, whereby they vow never to return to the mountain again, or else face the penalty of paying the group $1,000. I have a simpler solution. I refer to the words that I wrote while stranded with frostbite inside a Denali snow cave on March 9, 1982. It was thirty degrees below zero outside. My partners and I had just climbed the Cassin Ridge. My thoughts are preserved as a scrawl on the inside of a granola box, and the ink has run in places, but it's still legible:

I don't think I've ever suffered so much in my life and I decided a week before the climb (on the glacier approach) that I would do everything I could to get up but afterward I would do something a little different with my life . . . Now I'm a little worried because I know about the flood of feelings; fine joyous moments & bliss & glow of after exertion and ego; those sensations that seem to envelop me after a big mt.; I'm afraid that I'll lose my resolve and just put all my energy into another big trip and become stupidly obsessed again— missing all those things other people have like a steady girlfriend, a place to live. (Also I'm concerned that I'll get killed if I keep doing trips like this one because there is no margin for error here at all.) I miss greenness and real food and telemarking and just being comfortable. . . .

Just one quick read is all I need to keep me out of the shadow.

—Jonathan Waterman

1

DEFINING OUR LIVES

Then Don cried, "Oh, my God." Twenty-seven
years later, I still feel a chill as I recall that
moment. He was looking a bit farther to the right.
We had been Lilliputians discovering Gulliver's
foot. The summit we had seen was only one of
McKinley's snowcapped satellites. There, where
Don gaped, was McKinley itself—three times as
high as Gulliver's foothill. It was impossible that a
mountain that far away could take up so much of
the sky; but there it was.

—DAVID ROBERTS

IN 1976, SEVEN FRIENDS AND I JOURNEYED TO ALASKA. IT WAS A
huge leap of faith for a mountaineer not yet old enough to
vote, and until our jet lumbered up into high altitude above
Boston's Logan International Airport, I had never climbed
above seven thousand feet. We were members of the Lexington, Massachusetts, Explorer Post, and as veterans of winter
backpacks up New Hampshire's four-thousand-foot mountains, we fledglings planned to "conquer" Denali.

Most people refer to the mountain as McKinley, despite
the Alaskan preference for the original native name. Although
many names existed among the various tribes and visiting
Russians, the Athapaskan natives who lived and hunted closest
to the mountain deemed it Denali—the High One. In 1896, a
self-assured Princeton graduate, William Dickey, renamed

the mountain after a summer of prospecting for gold, performing a crude survey of the mountain, and drawing a map of the area. Since Dickey had recently argued with two Democratic silver prospectors who championed both free silver and William Jennings Bryan for president, Dickey retaliated by naming the mountain after his preferred Republican presidential nominee, McKinley, who championed, of course, the gold standard.

President McKinley, a generous man with a bearing that cartoonists of the day often likened to Napoleon, would never visit the territory. Shortly after his second term began, he was assassinated. Giving America a legacy like the remarkable mountain of his name was lost. One could even argue that it would be better to name it "Wilson," after the president who signed the 1917 bill setting aside the national park there and protecting the mountain.

For a few years Dickey continued to take credit for "discovering McKinley," despite the ancient native legends about Denali, and its first sighting by a white man, Vitus Bering, 155 years earlier. In later years, Alaskan lobbyists repeatedly introduced a name-change bill. Congress eventually compromised in 1980 by renaming the protected land around the mountain Denali National Park and Preserve. To this day, Ohio congressmen continue to block the name-change bills and guard the honor of Ohio's famous son, their "martyred president."

The distances separating most Americans from their highest mountain fosters preconceptions utterly removed from reality. For instance, our scout contingent was so deluded as to believe that climbing a 20,320-foot mountain in the Bicentennial year of 1976 would pay tribute to our predecessors who fought in the Revolutionary War. Naturally, our final attack on the easiest route would take place about two hundred years after the Lexington minutemen fired on the British redcoats.

Even if a few of our young team didn't champion the idea, the citizens of our town generously gave us thousands of dollars.

There are some expeditions, with even grander bank accounts, who use sponsorship to climb Denali for Women and Everest for Peace, and to explore Antarctica for the Environment. But most climbers scoff that mountain adventures could represent health concerns, corporate America, women's liberation, or Earth Day. Certainly, in June 1976, our crew of eight blithe Explorer Scouts didn't fully understand that climbing for anyone but yourself is making a mockery of mountaineering. However, our adviser back at the Museum of Science, Brad Washburn, might have been one of the all-time exceptions: His sponsored climbs—which he shared with millions of people through his photographs, texts, lectures, and museum exhibits—at least advanced art and science.

Washburn was too busy making laser-detailed maps and taking artfully vivid mountain photographs to go climbing anymore. When our team of boys had shuffled into his office above the Charles River, he graciously pulled out his photographs and map. "Look out for these hanging glaciers here," he said with his thumb pressed tight on a contour line at eight thousand feet, "and don't even *think* of camping on Windy Corner; we didn't name it *windy* for nothing."

But the advice that Washburn gave to our team (and thousands of other climbers) was the least of his gifts to me. Washburn became my earliest role model. Although his stature and contributions to science seemed remote to someone who rejected a college education, his passion and dedication to Denali was my unmistakable clarion call. To an impressionable youth, admiration assumes a form of imitation. I wanted to be like Brad Washburn.

At the time, our team, flushed from visiting with the grand old master, did not have any idea that climbing Denali with a large group was a mistake. Decisionmaking for eight people would prove arduous, and like most large teams, our group dynamics became a bigger challenge than actually climbing the mountain. Consequently, we naively blocked the voice of the wind, the crack of avalanches, and the mountain's many moods. Having all attended a Himalayan lecture by the famed British climber Chris Bonington, we could do nothing but admire the siege-style tactics of his army-sized team on Annapurna; we did not know that being a large and well-supplied team in Alaska served only to insulate us from real adventure.

In Talkeetna, a hundred miles north of Anchorage, when bush pilot Jim Sharp saw us unloading our stockpile of gear— occupying half of an Alaska Railroad baggage car—he wondered how it would all fit into his skiplane. We stared at forty days of food for a twenty-day climb; a twenty-five-pound wheel of Jarlsberg cheese; twelve hundred chocolate bars; a spare ice ax, spare crampons, spare rope, a spare sleeping bag, and a spare ensolite sleeping pad; a fifteen-pound first-aid kit; two radios; five decks of cards; twenty-two books; twelve ice screws; ten pickets; eight snow flukes; and, of course, an American flag. We figured that we would each be freighting two hundred pounds of gear. After loading and unloading Sharp's pickup truck six times, we became concerned. Moving such a load fifteen miles and ten thousand feet up the normal West Buttress Route was going to offer us all the joy of stone vassals bound for a pyramid.

Mark Hayes and I took the first flight in, strapped into the rear of Sharp's plane, sitting on a crunching box of cookies and a sharp duffel of ice axes. Our dashing pilot sported a handlebar mustache and a reputation for crashing more planes than any other Talkeetna bush pilot. He introduced us to Jeff Thomas, then invited him to sit up front in the only other real seat. Thomas had just been released from the hospital with blackened frostbite patches on his face and wanted to see if his partners were still alive on Mount Foraker. In place of shoes, Thomas wore ominous-looking bandages over his cold-injured feet.

Both Sharp and Thomas mentioned—too loudly, it seemed —that the Cessna 185 was dreadfully overloaded. We then bounced and gathered momentum down the potholed mud airstrip, which abruptly ended on a disintegrating mudbank above the Susitna River—a two-hundred-yard-wide brown torrent flushing whole trees, waving bushes, animal carcasses, ice chunks, and glacial silt toward the ocean at seven miles per hour. Suddenly Sharp shook his head and shouted, "Could be close, boys!" Although we knew our pilot had taxied down this runway countless times, Mark and I closed our eyes until we felt the plane lurch and shudder into sheltering blue sky. Sharp and Thomas snickered up front.

Sharp flew in via the traditional One-Shot Pass route, but after twenty minutes in the air, he started exclaiming to Thomas about how "tight" the pass was; a beer bottle clinked beneath the pilot's seat. Sharp pointed ahead frantically. "I just don't know," he said, "I just don't know." A mile ahead, One-Shot Pass appeared as a Volkswagen-sized notch between two formidable rock mountains. Sharp started yelling, "Oh, God, it's too late to turn back, we're going to have to go for it!" Mark and I exchanged uneasy glances just as Sharp shouted, "Hold on!" and he banked the plane up on one wing and held it there until we realized that the notch could take a 747.

Ten minutes later, as Sharp dove toward the glacier at seven thousand feet, he knew that talking us into being scared was unnecessary. First, he swerved so close to the serac-strewn north face of Mount Hunter that it took a concerted effort not to dishonor my clean knickers; then he buzzed over a row of twenty tents with mere feet to spare. By the time Sharp touched his skis down onto the snow and skidded up to a tent,

I was shaking. As soon as the plane stopped, I flung the door open before Sharp could change his mind and take us back up; I had to lever my body around Thomas and step next to his feet to jump out. When my big boots clomped against his frostbite bandages, he let out a howl that could be heard the length of the glacier. The sympathy I felt for Thomas was exceeded only by my relief to be out of Sharp's airplane.

Cliff Hudson was unloading his own caribou blood-spattered skiplane twenty yards away. Although a Cessna 185 can safely accommodate up to three climbers and their gear, we watched six bantam Japanese untangle themselves from within and jump down onto the glacier. All smiled and jabbered at Hudson, who jabbered back in his characteristic and equally garbled English as he passed out their gear.

Sharp elbowed Thomas and said, "Be some nip in the air this summer, eh?"

Despite Sharp's predictions, no Japanese fell off the mountain in 1976. That summer, twenty-one rescues of thirty-three climbers (mostly Americans) cost taxpayers $82,200—a figure not exceeded for another eleven years. Of all the nationalities at base camp—including Austrians, Germans, and French—the Japanese were the most gracious, inviting us over for ceremonial tea. Until they moved their tents, I couldn't understand why American climbers were always roasting Japanese climbers for "kamikaze" behavior. That afternoon, their reputation unfolded as they repitched their camp a half mile away, directly beneath the same precarious hanging glacier that Washburn had warned us about.

After the rest of our team arrived, ashen-faced from the flight in, Sharp begrudgingly made an additional flight to haul in our last several hundred pounds of gear. At first we had stared at the breathtaking north face of Mount Hunter, but now we stood with mouths agape beside a shoulder-high,

thirty-foot-long pile of boxes, wondering how we were going
to carry it all.

Suddenly, a lone climber came skiing into our camp. It was
the legendary Reinhold Messner, who had just completed a
new route on Denali. The Messiah of Mountaineering
amazed us; he had a small rucksack and a tiny bag of trash on
back of the red sled he was dragging. He was also generous to
a fault, giving us his leftover food that we didn't need, and his
sled, which made us realize that we needed seven more sleds,
in addition to a few porters.

I was awestruck and dim-tongued beside the well-known
author of *The Seventh Grade* and that brilliant treatise on
climbing ethics, *Murder of the Impossible*. His prose was as
direct and inspiring as the mountains he soloed. Although he
was a handsome fellow, next to big strapping boys who had
eaten meat and potatoes all their lives, he looked emaciated. I
wanted to fix our hollow-cheeked, anorexic hero a fattening
meal.

It struck me that Messner would now compose another
essay about the advantages of mountaineering light and lean.
Messner actually shook his head as he studied our mountain
of supplies. If you were really listening, hanging on his every
word like all good Scouts would have, you could hear him as
he walked away from camp, muttering *sotto voce*, "You Americans disgust me."

He was right: Our ethics were obscene. For the following
week, our green team marked the well-worn West Buttress
Route with caches of unneeded food and equipment—all to
be picked up on our way down. The meeting with the Messiah started a ripple of dissension among our group, and every
night we debated ethics and the concept of being fat, ugly
Americans.

At 8,000 feet we cached the snowshoes, spare stove, spare
ice ax, and spare crampons. At 8,500 feet, we bloated the

ravens with dozens of cookies. At 9,200 feet, we sacked the first-aid kit. And finally, at 10,000 feet, we presented the ungainly wheel of Jarlsberg to the Japanese, who acted quite pleased and refilled our cups with sake until we all crawled off to bed. We later heard that they rolled the cheese off Windy Corner and started a colossal avalanche.

Twenty-five years earlier, the first climbers on the West Buttress Route remarked, "This kind of climbing is about 90 percent trying to stay alive and warm, and 10 percent climbing." This team had camped at 12,900 feet, and a windstorm forced them to spend most of their time digging out their tents from Windy Corner—whose name was their creation. Their leader was Brad Washburn, who had advised us that shovels would be one of the most important pieces of gear we could carry.

While we were stormed in just below Windy Corner, digging out our tent with one of four ten-pound shovels, a solitary chickadee banged and fluttered against the tent walls. It chirped and wing-feathered the nylon with a rapid-fire desperation that made even the high-pitched wail of the wind seem trivial. I tried to bring the tiny bird in, to thaw the frost on its wings, but it flew off into the storm.

Athapaskan legends tell of the chickadee's *(K'its'ahultoona)* two-noted song as a lament for the passing of winter. It is believed that this song is an omen that the listener will soon cry over death.

In the morning I found the chickadee next to our latrine, curled into a coal-sized lump. Its underfeathers were softer than down against my cheek, and it smelled of sweet and distant roses. I held it to my skin as if body heat could make a difference while I dug with my other hand. When the hole was two feet deep, I set it in without looking and quickly smoothed the snow back over.

The bird upset me. I was shaken about the graceful shell of

feathers because its passing had alerted me to the fragility of life here, and if I was to spend any time on this coldhearted mountain, I would have to address the meaning of death. Maybe trying to understand death, I thought, would cast some definition on my own life.

At 14,300 feet we collapsed and gave our backs a three-day rest after two weeks of triple hauling and trailbreaking. Now that we were up high enough to transmit, we began flaunting our radios. Our leader, Bob Eaton, asked an Anchorage operator to dial our various moms and dads in Lexington. We made so many calls to our girlfriends that Eaton was forced to ban further transmissions.

Other climbers that summer radioed for helicopter rescues, to obtain weather forecasts, and to alert the media; radios provide mountaineers with the same swagger that gun-toting policemen practice. Although we did keep our friends and family informed, contact with the outside world depressed us. Mountaineering involves a necessary isolation, and, once broken, the lurid fantasies of showers, hot meals, and the opposite sex ravaged us as cleanly as a subarctic tempest.

Although Washburn was with us only in spirit, no one can climb the mountain without considering this remarkable man's achievements. Along with his five companions who pioneered this route in 1951, he left their radio at ten thousand feet and took a mere week to climb to the top; most modern climbers spend three weeks.

Washburn literally put the mountain on the map. Although he claims, "My Alaskan climbs were really just polar explorations with three dimensions," his lifelong efforts of cartography and photography were a deliberate campaign to share Denali. Consequently, there is no mountain in the world so singly associated with one person as Denali is with Brad Washburn.

His nickname of "Mr. McKinley" is, in fact, a geographic

understatement, because in addition to his exhaustive work there, he unveiled every major ice face and granite prow above the fifty-eighth parallel in northwestern North America. Directly or indirectly—by Washburn's own hand, through his omnipresent counsel, or because of his articles and photographs that encouraged climbers to attempt specific climbs—virtually every new route done within Alaska between 1931 and 1992, particularly on Denali, would be rubber-stamped or stomped upon by Washburn.

Washburn's beginnings had little to do with Alaska. As a precocious youth, this son of an Episcopalian minister attracted no small recognition. In 1926, at sixteen, he published his first book, a guide to the Presidential Range of New Hampshire. Washburn's prep-school education and Boston upbringing imply that he was a well-heeled blue blood supported by family purse strings. Washburn's mountain career, however, sprang from his machine-crisp mind and a perfectionist's inability to tolerate unsolved problems—Victorian-era maps, unexplored glaciers, "insurmountable" mountains, or lack of sponsorship.

Indeed, the ethic of those days (and of many of his colleagues today) was that climbers should not accept money for climbing, so Washburn will not admit to being America's first professional mountaineer. However, if he hadn't solicited sponsorship, Denali would have remained a light blue smudge on a government topo map.

Washburn had broken the ice long before the legendary American climbers of the 1960s, long before Yvon Chouinard forged ice axes, before Warren Harding sold wine ads for El Cap, or before Jim Whittaker mass-marketed Everest. In the late 1920s and 1930s, Washburn was the only American lecturing in prominent public halls about climbing. He arrived forty years before Bonington or Messner "invented" lucrative mountaineering lecture circuits and corpulent book contracts.

While Messner and Bonington remain virtuosos of mountaineering, Washburn had married his mountaineering with art and science, producing a career based on sharing information with others before setting foot on Denali. Although he elevated mountaineering sponsorship to a philanthropic art, no American climber has yet followed Washburn's lead.

His photography career started in 1923, when his mother gave him a camera. Mrs. Washburn later complained that his pictures were too small from that "vest pocket" camera, as well as lacking people. Mother's advice notwithstanding, the few climbers who appeared in his photos would become very lonely amid the tens of thousands of unpopulated Washburn mountain portraits to follow. When he compared notes with Ansel Adams many years later, Washburn was overjoyed to hear the master say that "there are only two people in every photograph, the photographer and the viewer."

After studying under the renowned Chamonix photographer George Tiarraz, Washburn made his first aerial photographic flight and became aware of the stunning advantages of photographing mountains from the air, a technique that would become the turning point for his work on Denali. Shortly thereafter, he got his pilot's license. He also studied the works of the Italian mountain photographer Vittorio Sella and learned that you can't make fine portraits without a large-format camera. His four-by-six-inch camera wasn't big enough—but anything bigger cost a lot of money. Washburn needed help.

He found it when he wrote his second book, *Among the Alps with Bradford*, for G. P. Putnam. The tiny book's royalties paid for most of his Harvard education and secured him a Model T Roadster for $520. Washburn wrote two more boys' books: *Bradford on Mt. Washington* and *Bradford on Mt. Fairweather*. He also wrote articles for journals and newspapers, then began lecturing on his alpine climbs—first with slides, then with film lectures. He appeared in such places as Symphony Hall in Boston, Carnegie Hall in New York, and the Academy of Music in Philadelphia. Most importantly, he lectured on his European climbs for the National Geographic Society at Constitution Hall in Washington, D.C., in 1930. This event resulted in a lifelong relationship with the society, which would sponsor Washburn on dozens of Alaskan mapping trips, epic explorations, and photographic assignments.

In the Alps, Washburn fine-tuned his winter camping and ticked off such first ascents as the north face of the Aiguille Verte. If Washburn had one great strength, it lay in his ability to analyze the difficulties of any obstacle, then acquire the necessary skills and technology to surmount them. He knew that climbing hard alpine routes and learning how to live comfortably on glaciers would empower him for his return to Alaska (he had attempted Mount Fairweather in 1929).

Despite his undergraduate degree in French history and a youthful fascination for all things Gallic, Alaska held his deepest desires. Alaska would become his Himalaya, his raison d'être, and, sixty years later, the environment of his magnum opus: *Mount McKinley* (coauthored with David Roberts).

Washburn returned to Harvard, gyrated 180 degrees from his undergraduate studies, and immersed himself in a graduate program of surveying and aerial photography. Grasping the brilliance behind Sella's photography (taken with a large-format camera), Washburn learned how to use an eight-by-ten-inch Fairchild camera.

With his scientific induction now under his belt, in 1935 he obtained backing from the National Geographic Society to map the St. Elias Range. Washburn, Bob Bates, and Ad Carter frequently looked to their grizzled dogdriver, Andy Taylor, for advice during their eighty-four-day winter grind through the St. Elias Range. "Don't get your balls in an uproar," Taylor the sourdough counseled his young Harvard upstarts during more than one blizzard. Certainly, a background of Boston parlors and French cafés would estrange most men from colorful-tongued salts of the earth such as Taylor. Yet Washburn retained a lifelong fascination and respect for the Denali sourdoughs, who "spent their lives out on the trail, chopping and digging, tough as bears."

While plowing through the St. Elias Range in 1935, Bates, Carter, and Washburn photographed, surveyed, and mapped the largest nonpolar ice fields in the world. The National Geographic Society awarded him its Franklin Burr Prize for discovering Mount Kennedy (he received the prize again thirty years later for mapping the mountain). Washburn's career was now off and running.

Washburn and his classmates—Bates, Carter, Terris Moore, and Charlie Houston—would brook no porters on their climbs, introduce America to lightweight, alpine-style climbing in the big mountains, and invent the Alaskan expedition based on Washburn's counsel. Although none of them was a rock gymnast, they created and shaped America's philosophy of alpinism. And Washburn jump-started them all.

He published his second article in the *National Geographic Magazine;* he lectured at the Royal Geographic Society in London; he harnessed himself above open airplane doors and cradled his Fairchild camera like a machine gun while overflying Denali in 1936 and 1949. Here, flying above the myriad of glaciers and shimmering ice faces, he felt his destiny call out to him. The National Geographic Society sponsored him to the tune of $1,000 during his first trip; Washburn returned $40 that he didn't spend.

In 1937, before Washburn acted on his obsession with Denali, bush pilot Bob Reeve left Washburn and Bates stranded in the Yukon. After splashing down on a soggy glacier with Reeve's plane-atop-skis (built from a stainless steel bar counter), they spent days digging it out and building a takeoff strip. Reeve wished them luck, said he wouldn't pick them up, and very nearly totaled while his plane broke off the sticky glacier and into the welcoming air.

Bates and Washburn then pulled off the stunning traverse of the unclimbed Mounts Lucania and Steele—climbs that honed Washburn's outdoor skills and showed him how far climbers could extend themselves on remote arctic mountains. This adventure would later make his three Denali climbs seem frolics. The duo staggered 125 miles out to civilization; naturally slender men, each lost twenty pounds gnawing on squirrels and mushrooms.

Washburn's subsequent article in *Life* about the landmark climb—pronounced *unclimbable* by that magazine in an earlier issue—caused the New England Museum of Natural History (later renamed the Boston Museum of Science) to offer him a job as director. The twenty-nine-year-old Washburn was elated, but he wrote plenty of exploration time into his contract. He also continued his photographic flights over Denali.

When he turned thirty he hired a secretary, Barbara Polk. At that point, the only mountain she had been to the top of was Mount Washington—in an automobile. She watched Washburn revamping a dusty, "three-dimensional dictionary under glass" into a world-class educational museum for young and old. She had graduated from Smith College, she was being wooed by an admiral, and she was nothing if not a shrewd observer of character. Although she didn't give a damn about mountains, and although she initially found him "quite stern," Barbara knew Brad had an avalanche of energy. He was an erudite companion, and she could tell he would share his life with her. A younger woman of today might well wish to pursue her own career interests, but opportunities were few and far between for a woman in 1940. Certainly, Polk saw a successful marriage offering much more than secretarial jobs.

He proposed, she accepted, and they honeymooned during their first ascent of Alaska's Mount Bertha.

Barbara Washburn is nonchalant, the soft counterpart to her husband's sharp-edged ambitions. "I wasn't interested in mountains. If he had been a sailor," she says, perhaps recalling her other suitor, "I would have gone sailing."

When asked how modern climbing couples might tackle the gulf of lengthy separations, Brad invokes the tone of a long-dead Andy Taylor. "Hell," he says, "take her with you!"

Some might call such a marriage old-fashioned. In the context of that generation, however, Washburn was the only husband among all his peers who took his wife with him on both climbing and business trips. He has done so for five decades.

"Besides," Barbara says, "if I stayed home, there were all these parties going on. . . ."

"Barbara," concludes Brad, "is the most important event of my life."

In 1947 Barbara became the first woman to climb Denali. During the descent, she led her husband down in a fierce wind, tediously sweeping out the filled-in and long-legged steps on the serrated Karstens Ridge, ever conscious of the Traleika Glacier yawning a mile below her feet. Finally, she turned and shouted back up to her husband, "Goddamn the son of a bitch who cut these steps!"

He replied, "I cut 'em."

She finalized, "Well, goddamn you, too! I've got three children at home!"

"Well," he answered, ever the scientist, "they're my children, too!"

Just below the knife-edged ridge, he and Barbara met another team of climbers. It was the first time on the mountain that two separate teams of climbers had met; after Washburn's widely publicized frontier-blazing, it became rare *not* to meet other climbers on Denali. At any rate, after having such a hot-blooded tête-à-tête with a spouse, most people wouldn't have carried on with the lighthearted antics Washburn then displayed. As the other climber approached, Washburn stuck out his hand and asked, "Dr. Livingstone, I presume?" The other man unimaginatively met Washburn's handshake and replied, "Morton Wood, Seattle."

After returning from that trip, Brad and Barbara were interviewed by a reporter who wanted to know why they climbed. Brad wrinkled his jutting forehead and aimed his sapphire eyes at the man as he explained that it was really all about sharing the experience with other people with the same goal. "I'd last maybe five minutes solo," he concluded. The reporter turned to Barbara, a striking and delicately featured counterpart to lantern-jawed Brad; she answered simply: "I like to be with my husband."

Fourteen years to the day after he had landed beneath Mount Lucania in 1937, Washburn was flown to the west side of Denali. Over the next four decades, more than six thousand climbers would follow. "It was a little like telling the pope that the rosary makes no sense," Washburn said, "when I advocated that climbers use the easier West Buttress Route instead of the long-established Muldrow Glacier." He recommended the route in the 1947 *American Alpine Journal*, and when another team prepared to tackle the climb in 1951, he asked if he could take his own advice and join them.

"It was very different from our climbs on Lucania or Hayes," he says. "We reconnoitered that thing so thoroughly, we knew we were going to get to the top. It was not *whether* we could do it, but *how* we did it."

Washburn's previous Muldrow Glacier climbs were mere exercises in logistics. In 1942, the military air-dropped his team more than two tons of supplies; in 1947 RKO Radio filmed the climb and spared no expenses. Yet in 1951, once he finished two weeks of surveying below the West Buttress,

Washburn flashed up the unclimbed route as if he were back in the Alps with a loaf of bread and a bottle of wine. His unencumbered week to the summit became his last true climbing expedition, but it bore all the finesse of his triumphs on Lucania and Steele. Within ten years, climbers would flock to his route.

In 1956 he published photographs and text in the *American Alpine Journal* that conclusively exploded Frederick Cook's bogus claim to have climbed Denali in 1906. Washburn and Ad Carter duplicated Cook's "summit photograph" from a hummock that is fifteen thousand feet below and ten miles from Denali. The mountaineering world—after having already seen Belmore Browne's 1910 photograph of Cook's supposed summit—now conclusively defrocked Cook. In 1960, after fifteen years of work, Washburn completed his Denali map—etched by his penchant for perfection—that would prove invaluable to the coming legions of climbers.

His aerial photographs of Alaskan mountains, long sought after by glaciologists, were now sought by climbers. He published numerous photo essays in the *American Alpine Journal, Mountain World,* and *Appalachia;* the accompanying texts encouraged readers to try great, unclimbed lines on various Alaskan peaks; dozens of these were subsequently climbed. Over the next four decades, his office at the Museum of Science was beset by climbers looking for advice. Washburn, who later turned to laser techniques and satellites for mapping the Grand Canyon, Mount Washington, and Mount Everest, always had the time to chat with climbers, whether it was Riccardo Cassin inquiring about the south face, or our young team on the West Buttress Route. His last words to us as we left his Museum of Science office were: "Look out for those altocumulus lenticularis, sons-of-a-bitch-a-cus clouds on the summit."

After recovering from pounding headaches at 14,300 feet,

our intrepid Explorer Scout team continued its progress up the mountain. Certainly, the climbers who call Washburn's route "a cattle plod" have been deceived by severe mountain sickness or a whiteout, because walking the ridgecrest from 16,000 to 17,000 feet is the penultimate mountaineering experience next to summiting. On a good day, you can revel in a three-mile drop to the tundra below—a greater drop than most Himalayan giants. Or you can look east and see Mount Sanford, more than 200 miles away. Or you can meet legendary international mountaineers stumbling down after having suffered up high.

When the salt-and-pepper-bearded Don Whillans first met our group at 16,500 feet, we wondered if the Briton's pack helped balance his tremendous beer belly. Several years earlier, Whillans had summited on Annapurna with Bonington's team. This year, he had just finished an alpine-style climb up the West Rib Route with two young partners—who were nowhere in sight. He talked about how much more splendid Denali was than the Himalaya, until he left me with some parting counsel: "Stay out of trouble, laddie." If intuition served me correctly, he was simply saying, "Don't die on the mountain."

An hour later, one of his young and strapping partners ran into us at 16,900 feet. He staggered up, burped, and let loose, in climbers' parlance, "a high-altitude Technicolor yawn." Afterward he gasped, wiped his mouth, and asked, "Have you seen Whillans?" It was only at the bottom of the mountain that the younger man caught up to the old and portly Whillans. They hopped on the first empty skiplane, and now that the summit had been dispensed with, their thoughts turned to swilling every available pint of beer in Talkeetna.

When their money ran dry, Whillans and his cronies began loading up their rental van. One of them spied a beer truck being unloaded in the alley of the Fairview Inn. Rather than merely purloin a six-pack, Whillans backed their van up and loaded in all thirty cases. They would have made a clean getaway, but a boy noticed that they couldn't fit their climbing gear into a van overloaded with beer. The state troopers escorted them directly to the airport—while Whillans stammered that, in England, beer in an alleyway was free for the taking—and the troopers told them never to return to Alaska.

Up at 17,000 feet, we had built a spacious igloo. Washburn had told us that you build igloos because they don't flap in the wind, and "because you have to go outside to find out what the weather is doing."

That year more than five hundred ice axes pricked Denali (as opposed to four hundred climbers in 1975, and less than a hundred in 1969). In 1976 there were often lines waiting to climb the steep headwall at 15,500 feet; the trail seldom needed breaking, and the ubiquitous human feces mining the snow—snow we melted for drinking water—caused us deep distress.

Even the undisputed king of guides, Ray Genet, was astounded when forty clients signed up for just one of his climbs in 1976. Weaving around the two dozen tents at 17,200 feet, stepping over tent lines, Genet came to admire our iglooplex. We boasted of how Washburn was the real architect; Genet grunted a friendly approval. Although it offered the soundest shelter on the mountain, after one night Hayes and I retreated. We preferred the flapping nylon over the claustrophobic, stove-fumigated, blue glow of an "Eskimo hotel."

Numbed by cold and headaches, our team decided to go for the top. It took our unwieldy group hours to fix hot drinks and get dressed. When we finally began groveling up Denali Pass, we could hear Genet's booming baritone below, leading his group in morning calisthenics. As a lenticular cloud hovered like a flying saucer above the summit, I wondered how aliens would interpret beings who practiced jumping jacks in twenty below, then forced themselves to the highest points of their geography for no appreciable gain.

All morning long I whispered the mantra of Goethe: "Whatever you can do, or dream you can, begin it. Genius has boldness, power, and magic in it."

At 18,200 feet I could no longer feel my toes, so Dave Buchanan let me warm my icy feet on his stomach. At 18,500 feet we stopped the group to do it again; Dave grimaced in shock as I slipped my feet under his sweaters. My head pounded like a jackhammer breaking pavement. And at 19,000 feet we could no longer see up or down. Dave and I turned back, while the rest of the group wandered up in vain for another two hours.

Denali had whipped us. It was not so much a defeat as it was a kind lesson. If it had been a good day, and we had heeded Washburn's advice to avoid the lenticular clouds, we might have found it in ourselves to stand on top. If we had traveled lighter, we might have had more energy for our summit day. And if we had been two people instead of eight, we would have had four times the fun and half the work.

Meanwhile, the Japanese waited patiently at 17,000 feet, six bodies politely entwined inside their two-person tent. When the storm clouds cleared and their sake ran dry, they reached the summit.

We camped at 14,300 feet, several hundred yards from the body of a climber who died from high-altitude pulmonary edema the day before. Genet had tried to save his client by carrying him back down the mountain, only to watch the young man gurgle and drown in his own fluids.

I walked over to pay my respects to the stranger's passing. The dead man was wrapped tightly in an American flag so that no one could see his death mask of surprise, the cyanotic lips flecked with frozen pink sputum and a face swollen with peripheral edema. A female companion stood weeping; the rest of the team celebrated up on the summit. Here, however, no one could speak. It was as if this pocket of the mountain had fallen to sea level: The air was heavy and listless and filled with the knowledge of what horror lay beneath the flag. Here on the frozen snows of Denali this twenty-one-year old had actually drowned.

We spend our lives trying to evade death and its myriad of black mysterious faces, but unless we kick and shout back and fulfill ourselves wholeheartedly during our precious short time, death will stalk us until our days turn to mere condemnation. I thought of my grandfather stiff in his open casket and, stinking in a river, a bloated body I had found as a sixteen-year-old, but this corpse on Denali seemed so terribly clean and correct that I regretted the helicopter couldn't leave the body where it belonged: where the cold can fill your lungs like a steely ocean and where death waits in shadowed crevasse tombs or up in a unearthly violet sky so filled with menace that climbers know they are merely visitors.

To ignore death's possibility is to deny the most primordial of all feelings. Many climbers experience the undeniable and powerful dreams of plunging endlessly through space, of blood rinsing your face with the smell of copper, of running but not moving in front of a monster avalanche, or any of a hundred deaths so textured and memorable that they give pause to even our best climbs.

One of our team members had refused to climb higher than 14,300 feet because he had seen himself dying in a dream. Although he was plagued with what he perceived as cowardice for months afterward, I admired him for being more in touch with his feelings, more willing to express his fears and his respect for the mountain than any of the rest of us.

We began our retreat. Walking down with enough gear to balk a sumo wrestler took us four days. At 12,000 feet, ravens circled above us like vultures, as if word had gotten out that we had more food than any other group. The ensuing pack-lightening food orgies caused us all to gain ten pounds each. We dragged ourselves the last few miles to the airstrip, dreading the most dangerous part of our expedition. Sharp droned up the Kahiltna Glacier in his battered 185, dropped into a strafing dive, and before we could run for cover, a six-pack of beer plummeted out of the sky and landed ten feet to our sides.

Five years later, I approached Denali more gracefully. My lightweight and unsponsored climbs elsewhere in the world had served as an appropriate apprenticeship. By all rights, climbing on an unclimbed peak in the Himalaya (Thelay Sagar) and a virgin ridge in the Yukon Territory (Mount Logan) should have compelled me to go anywhere but the most crowded 6,000-meter peak in the Americas. Initially it seemed a simple matter of settling the score from 1976; but after the climb, I had fallen prey to the same spell that Denali had cast over Washburn. Meanwhile, I trained by the widely respected Whillans's theory: curling multiple steins of beer and loading up on calories prior to the climb.

My partner from Thelay Sagar, John Thackray, was old enough to be my father, but when I phoned him with virtually no notice, he gamely agreed to meet me in Talkeetna. We had climbed together in New England, the Alps, the Himalaya, and Scotland.

Once in a Scottish pub called the Claichaig Inn, John suggested I order an unfamiliar-sounding drink to impress the mob of Scottish climbers. As the only American in town, I self-consciously elbowed up to the noisy bar, where the other curious climbers all clutched their beer. I then shouted out my order for a "half pint of shandy"—I did not know this was a concoction of lemonade and beer, widely considered a child's drink—and asked politely, "Do you have any cold ones?" Suddenly a hush fell over the bar: The bearded, tatter-demalion crowd members were all clutching pint-sized mugs of warm ale and staring at me. The bartender threw down his dishrag, smiled knowingly, and paused for effect before he spoke. "And would you like a white straw in it, too?" From across the pub, Thackray's titter started a cacophony of laughter.

On Denali, his erudite stories and ready laughter made up for any differences presented by his asthmatic disorder and the quarter-of-a-century gap between our ages. Meanwhile, Ranger Dave Buchanan lent us a three-pound tent, implored me to keep my toes warm, and suggested a radio—which we refused. A bush pilot (infamous for smoking dope and nearly crashing on the Anchorage tarmac after forgetting to retract his skis above the wheels) flew us onto the mountain in his peanut butter-scented aircraft. Although the pilot had prom-ised no aerial acrobatics, he couldn't resist a quick strafing run over the climbers at base camp.

After debarking, we were greeted by Sue Miskill. Her job was to brighten weary climbers down from the heights, pass them congratulatory beers, then summon their bush pilot on the radio. After she fixed us dinner, she gave me a small vial of cayenne pepper.

"Should I eat it, or what?" I asked.

"No," she said with a smile, "save it for the summit day, when it's really cold. Then sprinkle it on your feet."

I accepted graciously, thinking that Sue might know some-thing I didn't, and tucked it away in a pocket.

On the first day, John and I climbed together up the fifty-degree ice couloir into a storm. Unlike the climbers on the nearby West Buttress Route, we were secluded on the nine-thousand-foot west rib. The days fell into a delightful rhythm of step-kicking, cooking, climbing, singing, and reading. We climbed side by side, dispensing with belays, chatting about the texture of the ice, the shape of a passing cloud, and the distant green blur of trees on the horizon. When the snow-storms pressed hard on our shoulders, we feared our tent might collapse, but our stormbound days on half rations proved a gift of acclimatization to high altitude.

Our packs contained the bare necessities. We ate gas-producing freeze-dried food, employed aluminum foil for a pot lid, shared one toothbrush, dug out from storms with a light-weight plastic shovel, and wore gamy neoprene booties instead of wool socks. As further concession to light packs, I slept in a down jacket with a flimsy fiberfill sleeping bag. Graham Greene and Stephen Crane novels provided both cerebral sustenance and toilet paper. The only discord of our climb arose when John used up the pages of Crane faster than I could read them. We reveled in abstinence from the material world, our shivering, and our altitude headaches.

We also became dependent on one another in a fashion that we shall not repeat with other men in our normal lives. We cooked for one another, shamelessly warmed our fetid and wintry toes on each other's stomachs, and confessed secrets that we would otherwise share only with our wives. Being alone on a subzero and windswept mountainside for twelve days reduced life to its simplest yet finest moments. We often spoke of a mutual friend who had recently retreated from here after burning down a tent. If ours had burned down, we would have continued up and dug caves. Our time together on the west rib held a purity that we were afraid to let go of.

By the tenth night, we scratched out a tiny ledge between two boulders at eighteen thousand feet. The snow rose steeply above us in fantastic mushroomlike bulbs carved by the wind. One wrong step and one of these unstable platforms of snow would release beneath your feet and flush you three thousand feet down a chute that climbers had dubbed the

Orient Express. Two Koreans had died here two years ago; three Japanese women died in 1972. John and I tiptoed through here as if padding across a minefield.

We awoke at four the next morning to cloudless, thirty-below weather and immediately started the stove. While John brewed sweet English tea, I dumped the cayenne pepper into our neoprene socks. After an hour we were moving, shouting at one another to be careful in the strange collapsing snow.

We agreed to move at our own paces to keep warm. After several hours, time seemed to abandon me as I frontpointed up the headwall that led to my previous nineteen-thousand-foot high point. I could barely contain my excitement. My feet felt like wooden blocks, so I danced a jig until the circulation returned to my toes in the usual biting warmth. The cayenne pepper had not yet acted.

The summit was mine after a short stroll, and I knew how Washburn felt in 1951, climbing quickly and lightly with his close friend. Tears ran down their faces because it was their last visit to a place they loved more than any plot on earth; Washburn knew that his career obligations would never permit him to return. I remembered a comment murmured by one of the 1913 climbers: "It's like looking out the windows of Heaven." And suddenly my cheeks were wet, too.

The high altitude, the lack of climbers, the cloudless warmth, and the utter uselessness of our climb to anyone except John and me—all these pitched me into a blissful siesta, curled in a sunny hollow on the summit. A few miles away a skiplane circled and droned like an annoying mosquito, but I plunged into unconsciousness when I realized I was safe and secure, far from the clutches of any bush pilot.

I dreamed of staying on the mountain forever and holding court with my friends who visited in the summer while I roamed the high ridges with my lungs brimming over with frosted body fluids and my words dribbling out as unintelligible, bubbly breaths. The loneliness flowed into unbearable ache because even the stunning alabaster ripsawed skyline and pink orange clouds of a thousand shapes turned flat and ugly when I realized I was condemned to the mountain. I awoke in sheer terror.

Then I watched. I watched the green, beckoning tundra four miles below disappearing into a gentle curve of the earth, and I imagined the Bering Sea beyond like bluing infinity. I hung my legs out over the great abyss of the south face and contemplated the air rising and falling through the granite gorge of the Ruth Amphitheater. I knew then that our earth is really one big animal with me hanging on as a mere microcosmic flea. I could see it, I could almost feel it now, and I wanted to shout it to someone, but I was alone and John only a tiny figure wheezing along resolutely on the plateau below, so I gave myself to this new vision of the organism who lived and breathed and even tolerated us clambering on its back. When I looked out beyond the blinding white of the glaciers toward Talkeetna and the budding of life and rivers and greenery as far as I could see, it was almost too true and too terrible to behold. Seeing the entire earth as an animate being can make you understand just how important our relationship is to the planet, but when you are sitting alone shivering above everything else in North America, it can also make you feel very small indeed. The wind blew a wondrous warm breath over me. Heat waves shimmered above the jade horizon. The sun winked through a passing cumulus. I had found a happiness beyond all time and ambition and breathing. I ducked back into the hollow, closed my eyes, and let sleep take me away.

When John arrived and woke me an hour later, I stared at him for a long moment, shaking off a deep and hypoxic stupor, struggling to recognize the man who had become my close friend during two short expeditions. We embraced. I was dazed, shivering, incredulous; I didn't want to leave. He knew somehow, and he brought me back to earth with a joke as we traded the camera and lingered to steal photographs. Finally, we had both read the philosopher René Daumal, who wrote, "You cannot stay on the summit forever; you have to come down again."

More immediately, my feet were burning—the cayenne had finally kicked in. I had to get down. Quickly.

Although I intended to descend with John, I couldn't stand the fire licking first up to my arches, then below my ankles, so I ran pell-mell. At the fifty-five-degree headwall, my feet were throbbing, so I lunged down the ice and scarcely planted my ax. In the windslab area I jumped quicker than the unstable snow could pitch me down the Orient Express. I began cursing the potent spice of Base Camp Sue. After forty-five minutes of sprinting, I finally saw the tent heaving into sight. I plopped onto an ensolite pad, yanked off my boots, and thrust my bare, sweaty, reddened feet into a snowbank.

When John arrived, his face pinched in hot pain, he wordlessly yanked off his own cayenned socks and we laughed long and hard at one another. I threw our last freeze-dried dinner in a boiling pot of water, and John regaled me, in thick Scottish brogue, with stories of growing up in Glasgow. We talked forward and backward in time. The west rib had not pushed our limits, but it had worked in all the ways that a climb is supposed to. We became friends forever.

That summer I accepted pay from the National Park Service as a backcountry ranger in Colorado. A career seemed to beckon. During numerous mountain patrols, I learned to ride an animal feared by the other rangers—a spirited quarter horse named Chief. We got along famously, loping through meadows, shortcutting trails, bushwhacking, and venturing up mountains prohibited to horses.

I moved Chief to a corral outside my cabin. Each dawn his piercing whinny demanded brushing, oats, and hoof cleaning. Although I performed the expected search and rescues, picked up litter, and doused illegal campfires, my unchecked equestrian tactics (other rangers reported a half-uniformed ranger galloping "indiscreetly" without answering the radio) invoked the ire of my stodgy superiors. Furthermore, believing that education preceded enforcement, I refused to meet the expected quota of citations.

Even the most capricious summer could not suppress my dazzling memory of Denali; the confrontation of our fragile mortality and the subzero suffering were forgotten. On my last day of ranger work, I patted Chief good-bye and roughly stroked his neck the way no one else touched my muscular and spirited horse. When the district ranger sat me down and lectured that I was finished with the National Park Service ad infinitum, his admonishments went unheard; I was lost in Denali fantasy. I should have been through with the mountain, but it had captured me more thoroughly than a lover. As the boss prattled on about impieties with the uniform, recklessness on horseback, and irreverence to "the service," I was plotting my return to Denali.

Four years later, on Don Whillans's last evening, he shared several stories and a lot of ale with his mates at the local Yorkshire pub. He returned home, and while sleeping peacefully, his heart imploded inside his chest. Don had long counseled his friends: "The mountains will always be there. The trick is for you to be there as well."

My close friend John Thackray would make a few more trips to the big mountains, but none offered him the completeness of our two outings. In October 1987, in his early fifties, John and his partner fell from the top of a hundred-foot cliff.

John's friend hit the ground and died instantly, while a loop of rope snagged a cliffside bush and prevented John from grounding out. He pendulumed wildly toward a wall, and as he hit the rock there was a tremendous clanking of hardware and a frightful splintering of ribs—puncturing a lung, nicking his heart, and knocking him unconscious. When he awoke in the hospital with pericarditis, his wife demanded that he quit climbing. John fell into deep depression.

Many months later, he found the only cure. He told his wife that he was hiking, or bird-watching, even stargazing. Then he set it right with himself and his dead partner by skulking back to the far-flung crags and ice-shrouded mountains that define our lives.

I last saw Brad Washburn in Boston. It was the first weekend of December 1992, and we were both attending the annual meeting of the American Alpine Club. Unlike most social gatherings, where a stray climber is considered an olive shy of a full martini, at Alpine Club gatherings climbers actually celebrate one another's achievements. And unlike a benefit given by a baseball team, at Alpine Club meetings the amateur climbers can actually sit down and share stories with the Babe Ruths.

Brad was eighty-two years old; over the weekend he and Barbara cavorted in one another's arms as if they were newlyweds. I had also become a Denali expert, and over the past several years Brad would often call me, usually just after dawn, with questions about the mountain. When he sensed I had nothing more to contribute and his own agenda was completed, he would abruptly say "so long" and hang up the phone to get on with work.

This particular weekend a circle that had started twenty years earlier was now finishing its connective orbit. I shared a room with my high-school classmate and companion from the

Explorer Scouts, Ed Webster. Chris Bonington, whose lecture Ed and I had been inspired by two decades earlier, was on the Saturday evening program (the now gray-bearded Bonington advocated small autonomous climbs instead of siege tactics). And the Washburns would earn a standing ovation from more than four hundred dinner guests for their service to the climbing community.

On Saturday, before the evening's big events, Brad and Barbara were sitting together for lunch. Ever the social animal, Brad rushed out and grabbed my arm in the hall. "Come join us; it's terrible sitting without friends!"

The chairs scraped the floor. I caught my breath. I cleared my throat because dining with this accomplished couple always made me slightly nervous. Brad must have sensed this. So he broke the ice by joking about the title of his wife's supposed autobiography: *Fifty Years of Insanity*. He paused, and Barbara finished: *My Life and Marriage to Brad Washburn!* We all laughed.

I was curious about the next project. I wondered what would follow his satellite map of Mount Everest or his glorious coffee table book of Denali. What project could he possibly be on to now? I asked.

Brad must have anticipated the question. He glanced at Barbara for approval, then said, "We are preparing our graves."

He smiled over the awkward silence, but it was clear that he had worked hard and that their years dedicated to Denali and other mountains had made their lives incalculably rich and as full as any human beings could ever pass their days on earth. The time had finally come for Brad Washburn to relax.

2

DEATH WIND

Have you built your ship of death, O have you?
O build your ship of death, for you will need it.
—D. H. LAWRENCE

IN SEPTEMBER 1966, JOE WILCOX INITIATED AN EXPEDITION DES-
tined for ruin. He asked Brad Washburn if any team had
spent the night on Denali's storm-washed summit, or camped
on its north and south peaks simultaneously. "Please reply
soon," Wilcox wrote irreverently, "because the news media
are anxious to start releases."

With uncharacteristic sarcasm, Washburn replied, "Mc-
Kinley has not yet been climbed blindfolded or backward, nor
has any party of nine persons yet fallen into the same crevasse.
We hope that you may wish to rise to one of these compelling
challenges."

Washburn later told me, "This is the only time in forty
years of giving advice to McKinley climbers that I urged the
Park Service not to support a group."

Wilcox thought it unfair that Washburn had had his challenges on the mountain and wouldn't allow others the oppor-
tunity to stretch their limits. He countered with a series of
angry letters to Washburn, who was not only respected as a
mountaineer but also was the director of Boston's Museum of
Science, an author, and an adviser to the Park Service. Washburn duly filed Wilcox's letters away and avoided any further
confrontation. Many years later, Washburn wrote to one of

Wilcox's teammates, Howard Snyder, "If you get in a pissing contest with a skunk, you end up smelling like a skunk."

Wilcox wisely dropped the summit camping plans and the media angle, but still, no man or mountain was going to bend his dreams.

Meanwhile, the year before Wilcox and his seven teammates were planning their 1967 climb, the park superintendent refused permission to a Colorado team led by Howard Snyder. Snyder's threesome were more experienced than Wilcox's team, but the Coloradans fell below the Park Service's required four members—a rigid Park Service rule of that era. In a bureaucratic blunder that would eventually force the Park Service to discard most of their mountain climbing rules, they recommended that Snyder join forces with Wilcox in 1967; combining two weak teams of men mostly in their early twenties should make one strong and mature team, they reckoned. Thus the players were cast for North America's greatest expedition tragedy.

"Many things were to change in the summer of 1967," Snyder later wrote, "when the Joseph Wilcox Mount McKinley expedition challenged the mountain. The group witnessed nights when the hushed earth glowed under the fire of a midnight dawn, and days when death rode the wind."

More than seventy climbers have died on Denali since 1932. About half of these deaths occurred when climbers took long falls, but the second most common cause of death—claiming at least ten climbers—is storms; seven of these deaths were from Wilcox's expedition.

Denali is well known for its sudden storms; for other objective dangers, including subzero cold, crevasses, and avalanches; and for being the highest mountain on the continent, which explains both its popularity and its fatality rate. The mountain has long captured the imagination of Americans who have been raised to believe that "biggest is best." When veteran climbers succeed on smaller and more technically difficult Alaskan peaks such as Mount Huntington, Mount Hunter, or Mount Foraker, their ascents go unrecognized. Yet climbing Denali's easy routes draws praise and respect, and symbolizes the brass ring to a world that imagines that any route up Denali is the ultimate climb in North America.

The accident rate on the mountain also eclipses that of the more difficult, lesser-known peaks in the Alaska Range. Many of Denali's victims don't have the wherewithal to cope with sudden storms and objective dangers (which are just as prevalent on the other peaks). And many of "Big Mac's" suitors are inexperienced mountaineers prone to mistakes.

Denali does have two relatively easy routes for beginners. The Muldrow Glacier and the West Buttress Route are affectionately referred to by hard men as "walk-ups." Here, on these lower-angled glaciers, if the weather sours, climbers can dig snowcaves, or descend quickly—options that aren't available on more difficult routes.

Snyder and Wilcox wisely chose the Muldrow Glacier. Among Wilcox's eight climbers, three had strong mountaineering backgrounds, three others were moderately accomplished, and two were novices. Snyder's threesome—himself, Air Force cadet Paul Schlichter, and the pleasant-mannered Jerry Lewis—had logged a lot more time in the mountains than any of the other climbers.

Until the 1960s, only four climbers had died on Denali, among three different teams of veteran mountaineers. And by the late 1960s, the mountain had lost much of its mystique. Armchair climbers began arriving with Washburn's new map, air support, and radios. Weather reports and rescue helicopters were readily available; self-sufficiency was forgotten. Wilcox's team unknowingly marched into what would become a new epoch on the mountain; their expedition slammed shut the cautious Pioneer Era on Denali.

Snyder and Wilcox were two distinctly different personalities. Snyder was gregarious, an aficionado of classic literature, and a man who appreciated a good sense of humor. He was single, two years younger than Wilcox, and a geology/geography major at the University of Colorado. Snyder learned how to climb in the liberal and progressive Boulder climbing scene.

In *White Winds*, a book that Wilcox later wrote about the expedition, he described himself as "rather non-gregarious, with a strong straight-forward manner, sometimes lacking in tactful social amenities." He started college at Kansas State, then studied math and physics at four different universities until he married his first wife. Wilcox's decidedly serious and detached style as a conservative climbing instructor at Brigham Young University probably prevented close male liaisons.

Steve Taylor, whom Wilcox introduced to climbing, was Wilcox's lone acquaintance on his team; Taylor's friend Jerry Clark ended up recruiting the remainder of the team. Clark was a natural leader. He had taught geology at Purdue, instructed climbing, and in addition to difficult climbs around the country, he had adventured in Antarctica. At thirty-one he was the oldest member of the group and the least physically fit.

Many of Wilcox's team discovered mountaineering through the Boy Scouts and had served on volunteer mountain rescue teams—organizations that veteran climbers often avoid and defame as unseasoned, altruistic amateurs. Dennis Luchterhand was a relatively inexperienced climber and an ambitious geologist. Mark McLaughlin was a lighthearted guy who had served a suitable mountaineering apprenticeship in the Northwest, while John Russell was a serious young man with an avowed passion for climbing. Anshel Schiff, a beginning mountaineer and the second oldest member of the group, described himself as an introvert and eventually proved to have greater survival instincts than most of the group. Hank Janes was a rock climber who worked with disadvantaged kids. Steve Taylor, another beginning climber, was strongly influenced by the Mormon Church. And Walt Taylor (no relation to Steve) claimed that he used to climb mountains to tell people about it, test his courage, and get to the top. Two years before the expedition, Walt fell on his head while climbing and wrote: "[Now] I climb mountains to look at the climbers and the sky and the rock and snow and the flowers."

In June 1967, Wilcox's nine climbers and Snyder's threesome met in person for the first time beneath Mount Rainier for a training shakedown. The Colorado contingent arrived too late to join Wilcox's rescue practice, and the cold introduction and "hellos" of the two groups were far too formal for a team that would be spending the next month on Denali together.

Wilcox further fanned the fire by opening a piece of Snyder's mail and withholding it from him. Although Wilcox said it was expedition business from an Alaskan horse packer, Snyder was never shown the letter addressed to him. Snyder felt this was a deliberate slight against him, while Wilcox thought it only business as usual.

From Rainier they drove directly to Alaska. In the dust of the Wilcox team's van, one of the men scrawled with his finger, "Washburn is a do-badder and a no-gooder," referring to his facetious letter about falling into a crevasse, which provided a warped esprit de corps and seemed to salve the bruised egos of the Wilcox team. (Later, on the mountain, while debating which way to go around a dangerous avalanche area, Walt Taylor said, "Let's not give Brad too much of a chance.")

Initially the expedition was plagued by mishaps. On the Muldrow Glacier, Wilcox's tentmates had a close call with a stove flaring up; two thirds of the way up the mountain, the same crew burned down their tent. Conflicts and misunderstandings also hampered the twelve men, while the Colorado trio maintained their private alliance.

It was clear that Wilcox was not going to be voted most popular member. His brusque, Pattonesque manner, although unacceptable in mountaineering circles today, may have been a more common 1960s leadership profile.

After several weeks of hauling loads and breaking trail, the team camped at 17,900 feet. The next day, Wilcox decided to go to the summit with the Coloradans. It was surprising for Wilcox to leave his team in camp that day, but not remarkable, because his position as the aloof general had distanced him from his troops. It didn't matter with whom he climbed.

Wilcox, Snyder, Schlichter, and Lewis reached the summit uneventfully on July 15. They then descended to the 17,900-foot camp and spent a stormy day with the rest of the team, who prepared for their final climb. The next day, the four summiteers descended to 15,000 feet, accompanied by Schiff, who didn't want to go to the summit.

Clark, Russell, Luchterhand, McLaughlin, Janes, and Walt Taylor made a late start for the summit. Steve Taylor stayed in the tent, sick, at 17,900 feet. Although he should have descended with the other five, his enthusiasm about going for the summit had kept him at the high camp.

Later, Wilcox was criticized by Washburn and in the American Alpine Club's accident report for dividing his team, but Snyder and Wilcox seem to agree that if Wilcox had stayed at 17,900 feet, he would only have used their supplies and diminished their summit chances. Furthermore, this second summit climb was led by the popular Clark, whom everyone respected as a natural leader.

Although Wilcox's summit team had carried only emergency gear, such as spare socks and down parkas, this second team carried six sleeping bags. A sage climber of that era, Yvon Chouinard, wrote, "If you carry bivouac gear, you will bivouac."

The six men bivouacked below the summit, where altitude sickness and storms always hit hardest. The next morning, the six bedraggled climbers staggered to the top. On July 18, at 11:30 A.M., McLaughlin keyed the radio mike to talk to Ranger Gordon Haber 19,000 feet below, at Eielson Visitor Center: "Hey Gordy, you still sending postcards from the summit?"

Haber replied, "Ah, yeah, go ahead."

"I'd like to send one to my parents," McLaughlin said. "Have you got a pencil and paper there?"

"Go right ahead."

"Dear Mom and Dad," McLaughlin said. "Radio from the summit. A-okay. See you in a week or two. Love, Mark."

Haber asked what the view was like, and McLaughlin replied that because it was whited out, he could see only some sticks marking the trail, and his teammates. The radio transmission broke up while McLaughlin tried to broadcast his parents' address, but he said they would call again at 8:00 P.M.

Sometime later, as the men were descending from the summit and their high bivouac, they were hit by a sudden storm. They searched futilely for shelter on the featureless 19,500-foot plateau. As the weaker men succumbed to the white winds, the stronger ones tried to escape, bent into the gale, blown repeatedly off their feet until they could fight no more. The strongest mountaineers in the world could not have survived such a storm without shovels.

Shovels are essential to survival high on Denali. Dave Johnston, Ray Genet, and Art Davidson had survived a similar storm four months earlier during the first winter ascent because they dug in at 18,200 feet. Few, if any, of Wilcox's team had ever experienced such violent storms, and the only time they had built a snowcave was at 12,000 feet.

Down at 15,000 feet, Wilcox, Snyder, Schlichter, Lewis, and Schiff were trapped. They had heard nothing over the radio from the others as the storm worsened, thundering above them as a subarctic apocalypse. During a lull, they tried to climb to their companions' aid but were blown to their hands and knees a short distance from camp.

Being tentbound in a storm high on Denali can make even the kindest souls plot the murder of their companions. After several days of inactivity and staring at the walls, a tentmate's bad jokes, body odors, even his breathing can magnify into atrocities that no man can bear. For instance, flatulence from eating dried food is initially a source of amusement during the first week of a Denali outing. However, during a prolonged storm near the end of a long expedition, the loosing of gas becomes a veritable declaration of war. Combine this with the incessant flapping of nylon tent walls, and the accelerating anxiety for missing companions above, and you can picture the tortured occupants of the two tents at 15,000 feet.

As Wilcox and his companions clung to their shredding tents—without digging snowcaves—they could scarcely imagine how severe it must have been on the exposed upper reaches of the mountain. When their tent was blown asunder, Schiff and Wilcox were forced to jam into Snyder's tent. Here in this overcrowded tent the tension and fear and personality conflicts became a simmering time bomb. Lewis suffered frostbitten feet. Hope for the seven men above diminished. Although no one would ever confess to his actual misery, their incarceration here would be so indelibly imprinted that they would shoulder this hell forever.

The storm abated a week after it began. The five survivors crawled out of their cramped tent and limped down the mountain, with no idea of what had happened to the others. Wilcox would later write, "Every man who descended from Camp VI on July 23rd, abandoning the upper group, has a heavy burden of conscience and soul." Above them, it was too early to know that one frozen corpse appeared to be holding a deathlock on a missing pole from a tent shredded by the wind, and six other corpses were scattered to eternity.

One can only speculate how the storm killed the seven men above, because their bodies were never recovered. Eventually another climbing party found a decomposing body (probably Steve Taylor's) at 17,900 feet. And a passing bush pilot glimpsed two bodies at 19,000 feet.

Wilcox was the only one who walked out to get help. He was obliged by his responsibilities as the leader, concerned about the seven missing men, and spurred on by the thought that Lewis needed immediate medical attention for his frostbitten feet.

Wilcox swam two flooding rivers (while Snyder and the others waited for a helicopter) to save his companions, a self-less act of heroism. It was a miracle, or tremendous luck, given Wilcox's agnosticism, that he didn't drown in the gla-cier-fed McKinley River. "Kicking became swimming and once again my wind pants ripped down," he later wrote. "Fi-nally I could no longer struggle, and my body went limp. I was solitarily concentrating on the motions of swimming, but my limbs did not respond." He eventually washed up on the far shore.

Wilcox staggered out and found Ranger Wayne Merry at Wonder Lake. Merry, who later referred to Wilcox's expedi-tion as one of the best-organized expeditions he'd ever seen, began a futile battle with his superiors for a high altitude helicopter rescue. Before Wilcox left Alaska, Merry (accord-ing to Wilcox) warned him, ". . . a tragedy is always accom-panied by a great deal of criticism. As leader, much of that criticism will be directed toward you. There will be many questions that you will have to answer to others and to yourself. . . . If you begin blaming yourself for what has happened, you might end up on skid row or strung out on LSD." A few months later, Merry quit because of the sluggish response of the bureaucracy.

Wilcox got the media attention he'd initially sought, but came to avoid. He claims, with a suspiciously apocryphal tone, that a reporter from *Time* told him, "It may be a tragedy for you, but it's going to make one hell of a good story."

After the five men had all left Alaska, the mountaineering community came to find its scapegoat in Wilcox. Ask any Denali devotee why the tragedy happened and they will answer: because of Wilcox. Historically, when the smoke clears after such accidents, the armchair analysts always look toward the leader's inadequacies.

Washburn wrote to Wilcox, "I still feel as do all others who have studied this expedition, that serious tactical errors *were* made in the field—and I simply don't care to debate this matter further, as the facts speak clearly for themselves. The fact that an intense storm struck at precisely the wrong moment is irrelevant. . . . It was tragic bad luck, but the essential basis for this disaster was the distribution of sick, exhausted or inexperienced personnel with minimal supplies and extremely weak communications (or none at all) and support at or near the summit of a peak which is well known to be one of the world's worst weather spots."

One climber saw it differently. "Some would blame Joe [Wilcox] for the catastrophe, but I've studied the situation carefully . . . and I do not," wrote one Alaskan mountaineer, the late Vin Hoeman (buried two years later under an avalanche with six other climbers in the Himalaya). "Joe lived under a terrific responsibility for those lives that were lost, it has undoubtably affected his personality, but conditions on McKinley can far exceed what flesh can stand."

Even Washburn concedes that many other expeditions have made worse mistakes than Wilcox's team and gotten away with them. "For some reason, the Wilcox expedition paid for every one of their mistakes."

Washburn also refers to Wilcox as "a bull with a built-in china shop." And twenty years later, Wilcox would admit, "The controversy is in personalities." Here then is the key to what became the most tragic and bitterly contested controversy in Denali history. The critics would look to Wilcox for qualities above and beyond those of a mountaineering leader, but he is only an average man, prone to mercurial outbursts. As Wilcox began to feel cornered, he unknowingly did more to damage his reputation than Washburn, the accident reports, Snyder, or all of his critics combined.

The real conflict between Snyder and Wilcox escalated after the expedition. The first blow fell when Wilcox published a letter to the editor in the September 8, 1967, *Time*, responding to the magazine's story of the accident. "I was amazed that Bradford Washburn blamed 'serious tactical blunders' for the mountaineering disaster . . . [or] that the expedition made some mistakes that most mountaineers would routinely avoid and that these errors were largely responsible for the tragedy." Wilcox concluded that no one would ever know what had happened and that to suggest the accident could have been foreseen would discredit the victims and future expeditions. After reading the missive to *Time* many of the parents of the lost climbers wrote supportive letters to Wilcox.

Three months later, Wilcox mailed a letter to the parents and survivors: "I would like to extend my sincere thanks to those few of you who have helped out with the expedition debt. Unfortunately, the response has so far been rather small, leaving me with $900 unpaid expenses all in my name. This puts quite a bind on a graduate student's income, not to mention the adverse effects on my credit rating."

Wilcox wrote to Snyder that two of the families contributed, while one father sent a few dollars that didn't even take care of his son's original debt to the expedition. Oblivious to the crushing grief shouldered by the parents, Wilcox scribbled, "It doesn't appear that any of the other families will help out—they seemed obsessed with putting a memorial in the Park."

Howard Snyder became incensed. He felt that Wilcox was "hiding everything beneath a big, flat rock and someone needed to show the world what was underneath." Snyder asked Wilcox for the expedition log, Wilcox complied, and Snyder began writing a book. He accused the Wilcox team of burning stoves dry or throwing them out in the snow, leaving knotted ropes outside to freeze, kicking snowshoes to pieces, and generally abusing gear that their lives depended on. Like Washburn, he labeled the Wilcox team as inexperienced.

The major discrepancy between the two climbers involves Snyder's claim that the rangers had radioed them on July 13 about a huge storm that would move in by July 16. Everyone agrees that there was a storm on the sixteenth, the day after Wilcox and Snyder summited, and in the lull on the seventeenth, the second team started for the summit regardless of the warning four days earlier. Wilcox, however, vehemently denies receiving any weather forecast from the Park Service on July 13.

Snyder's most damning criticism is that Wilcox became a leader of a team he didn't know and had never climbed with, inferring that faulty leadership, combined with a violent storm, was the real cause of the tragedy.

Snyder's primary motive for the book, he claims, was to write a cautionary tale that would keep others out of trouble on Denali. He mailed *The Hall of the Mountain King* to Charles Scribner's Sons and claims that his editor published it without changing a word.

Arlene Blum reviewed the book in the 1974 *American Alpine Journal.* "Snyder is a bit too overanxious to prove his own blamelessness for the catastrophe," she wrote. "Consequently, we are treated to an abundance of quibbling details about both the extreme competence of the Colorado party, and the Wilcox group's lack thereof."

Nonetheless, the book became a classic for aspiring Denali climbers, despite Snyder's tone of self-absolution. In 1976, my seven friends and I read the book before our expedition, and it succeeded as a cautionary tale, for we all knew not to bivouac up high and to carry coal scoop shovels (as recommended in Snyder's appendices, because they had only one cracked and ineffective shovel). The book remains the most sobering piece of Denali literature that a team of neophyte climbers can profit from.

Snyder later told me, "I pulled many punches to take the heat off of Wilcox, and left out all the silly things he did and said, blaming any mistakes in leadership during the final catastrophe upon Wilcox's sickness."

But Wilcox denies being sick. When Wilcox first picked up *The Hall of the Mountain King,* he told me, "I thought it might be the sort of book which a person could put down and feel good about afterward." Yet Wilcox was devastated; another survivor, Schiff, couldn't read beyond the introduction and stood firmly by Wilcox. "If Howard believes what he wrote," Wilcox says, "he shouldn't have continued on the climb. Perhaps he was attempting to disassociate himself from the tragedy."

To clear the record, Wilcox began writing two books. One was *A Reader's Guide to* The Hall of the Mountain King, a one-hundred-page, self-published, page-by-page rebuttal of

Snyder's book. At the same time he began researching his five-hundred-page magnum opus about the expedition. His obsession to publish to refute Snyder would consume him for the next eight years.

Snyder calls *A Reader's Guide* "a comic book." He felt that Wilcox's method of extracting, then disagreeing with small details such as times and dates and various disputable observations made Wilcox "look so bad it was funny." Indeed, the discrepancies between the two men's points of view are so divergent as to make the reader believe they were on two separate expeditions.

Wilcox finally published *White Winds* fourteen years after the expedition. He hung his story on the infrastructure of Snyder's book—which allowed Wilcox to refute systematically everything written by his nemesis. Wilcox claims that he had offers from regular publishers, but since he felt an obligation to the survivors, the parents, and the mountaineering world to set it all straight—implying he wanted no editorial interference—he subsidized its publication with a press that Snyder believes to be spurious, Hwong Publishing Company (formerly based out of Los Alamitos, California). Wilcox's theme is that a "white wind," stronger than any hurricane and "in a class by itself," was responsible for the seven men's deaths. It may have been the "most severe, high altitude windstorm in the entire history of mountaineering."

"Absolute bunk," says Snyder.

"Howard's theme is one of conflict between personalities," Wilcox says, "rather than between man and elements."

"To say the storm was 'in a class by itself' is absolutely nonsense," Washburn explained. "The storm that killed those climbers was a typical McKinley summer storm, a southwester. If [Wilcox's team] had known more about mountaineering, they'd have seen all the portents of the storm developing."

As for the accusations of "inexperienced," Wilcox provides climbing résumés of all his men, and with the exception of Steve Taylor and Schiff, the party—on paper, anyway—appears to have logged a fair amount of time and experience in the mountains. The crescendo of *White Winds* is a fat chapter of research data from three Alaskan weather stations. Wilcox does not note that the same storm swept avalanches over a more experienced party during their successful first ascent of Denali's difficult south face. Rather, he asserts that survival is harder near the summit, where his team died.

To his credit, Wilcox does mention the winter ascent in which Dave Johnston, Ray Genet, and Art Davidson survived a similar windstorm at Denali Pass (where the wind is stronger because of a funneling effect). However, Wilcox tells the reader that the 1967 summer storm was more dangerous than the winter storm, which is the major failing of his theory: Weather data do not account for the increased dangers on climbs such as that of the south face or the winter ascent. The south face climbers survived constant avalanches. Furthermore, in winter it was much colder, the climbers were more strung out, and the draining physiological effects of altitude were increased. Nor does Wilcox point out that the experienced winter climbers survived because they dug a snowcave.

Writing a rebuttal implies that an author is on the defensive; with Snyder's book snapping at his heels, Wilcox treed himself with *White Winds*. However, he does not directly defend himself against Washburn and Snyder's most biting accusation: that poor leadership caused the disaster. Wilcox includes the preexpedition correspondence among the members, endlessly rambling about hard-to-find snowshoes and other pieces of expedition paraphernalia. But shovels are mentioned only once, in a group equipment list, completely overlooking the necessity of this lifesaving tool. And even if

Snyder believed shovels to be important survival tools in retrospect, during the expedition he never contested their lack of shovels up high, probably because he had brought only one small and faulty aluminum shovel.

Just after *White Winds* was released in 1981, Snyder's version of the story was resurrected through a play, *Storm*. The play premiered at Brigham Young University, Wilcox's alma mater, and won one of the most prestigious awards in the American theater. The play opened with a ranger playing a harmonica, backlit by Snyder's McKinley slides flashing on a screen.

Team member Jerry Lewis and his wife attended. After the performance ended, she said, "Now I understand what Jerry went through." She thought it was a catharsis for her husband, who said, "There was a lot of truth in the play." According to Snyder, the play was successful because there was "so much emotion on the stage and a feeling of really being there, that the audience had chills."

Although the production went no deeper than Snyder's book and did not directly place blame on anyone, Wilcox sued everyone involved in producing the play for defamation of character and asked for $50,000 in damages. In 1988 the suit was settled out of court. No money was exchanged, but the names of the climbers and the mountain must be fictionalized in future productions, and everyone named in the suit must remain tight-lipped under the judge's nondisclosure provision.

Wilcox's latest move reinflamed Snyder, who wrote to Washburn, "[Wilcox] has used the victims of his expedition as a security blanket, saying, 'If you criticize my leadership or comment on my expedition you are attacking the memory of dead men.' I found out only this fall that he has tortured the parents of the victims for fourteen years with letters. . . . [He] has declared himself the protector of the memories of the lost men, and has used this posture to manipulate the parents for both moral and financial support. Wilcox is a man obsessed with only one goal in a shattered life: vindication." Wilcox lectured more than fifty times around the country to promote his side of the story, and later, his book. Beginning at the Colorado Outward Bound School in 1969, his wife played the flute as Wilcox finished his slide show, lingering over portraits of Clark, Russell, Luchterhand, McLaughlin, Janes, and the Taylors on the screen. According to one Outward Bound instructor, Paul Maychak, "It was the most disturbing lecture that the audience had ever sat through, and rather than asking questions when it ended, everyone slumped silent in their chairs." Fourteen years later, another slide-show coordinator at a Utah college commented that it was more embarrassing than sad to see Wilcox break into tears on the podium.

Explaining this to me, Wilcox quietly argues that you can present a factual representation of losing seven close friends, or you can give people a better awareness of the tragedy. "The idea was not to cause sadness," he says, "but to take the audience on the climb and let the tragedy provide that intense sense of loss."

In February 1988 I visited Howard Snyder in Canada. He bristled when I pushed the November 1968 Kansas State *Alumnian* across the table, with Wilcox's summit pose on the cover; the inside story was titled, "McKinley Conqueror Reports on Disaster." "My goodness, that's my photograph," Snyder said. His hands shook as he flipped the pages. Now, when he hears anything about Wilcox, Snyder said, "I become so pumped with adrenaline, I have to run my six-mile loop around the farms." "Hatred," he said, "is a corrosive poison."

Yet Snyder reminisced about the other members, both dead

and alive, with great warmth. "John Russell could call you a bastard, but he'd be the first to help you out if you got in trouble. And did you know Schlichter was decorated for his flying in Vietnam?

"Steve Taylor was a real nice kid but the most tragic of the ones who died because he was initially refused permission to climb due to his lack of experience." Snyder smiled as he talked about Lewis, mentioning that "you tend to become close to people when you go through things like that."

He even asked a few questions of his own, politely trying to establish what I think of the controversy, never believing he has the last word, yet confident about his story. Snyder was fit for a forty-two-year-old family man with a wife and three daughters. An avid outdoorsman, he gets out into the mountains several times a year. His wool shirt lapel held a delicately smithed ice ax and rope coil; his belt buckle featured a grizzly.

Howard Snyder is still haunted by the expedition. He dreams of all but one of the missing men walking back down to him and Wilcox at the bottom of the mountain. In a similar dream Snyder vividly sees only Russell and McLaughlin coming down, one of them falling down again and again. "And whenever I smell kerosene," he said, "BAM! I'm right back at Camp II during the tent fire."

Snyder still empathizes with his rival. Wilcox had instructed at the Colorado Outward Bound School, so I showed his 1969 evaluation to Snyder. His close-set eyes wandered down the page to: "There appeared to be limited genuine communication between Joe, the instructors and students. The relationship, apparently, was one of a skill teacher to students with little or no effort to reach out for the deeper, human interaction. . . ." Snyder burst into tears.

"Nothing's changed," Snyder said. "Poor ol' Joe." Snyder struggled for composure. "Sometimes my attitude is strictly one of pity, [but] contempt is my more usual image. You can say that Joe Wilcox is living through absolute hell, but when you're the target of this, it dulls the edge of sympathy. It's such a shame that this whole thing would lead to a lifetime of misery."

He claimed that until *White Winds* came out, he steadfastly defended Joe, but now when someone asks him a question about the man, he tells them to go ask Wilcox instead. Interpreting Snyder's contradictory feelings toward Wilcox is difficult indeed. Is Snyder playing political? Does he feel guilty for vilifying Wilcox? It is fair to say that if Snyder had not written *The Hall of the Mountain King*, he and Wilcox might have buried their differences, but their separate burdens of guilt and their disparate personalities would not have permitted any sort of friendship or communication.

There is a condensed Rudyard Kipling quote in the opening pages of Snyder's book, one that Wilcox objects to because a few words were changed and points of ellipses are missing. Wilcox believes that the twisted quote casts aspersions on the credibility of Snyder's book:

> IF YOU MEET WITH TRIUMPH AND DISASTER
> AND TREAT THOSE TWO IMPOSTORS JUST THE SAME;
> YOURS IS THE EARTH AND EVERYTHING THAT'S IN IT,
> AND—WHICH IS MORE—YOU'LL BE A MAN, MY SON!

Aside from being an opportunistic coming-of-age statement in the face of tragedy, the quote does not fit Howard Snyder. One could construe his life in rural Canada as fleeing from the main pulse of society, and while achieving small career successes, he does not emanate much joy or hold the earth and everything in it by any means.

Snyder would like to climb even higher mountains someday, if he can train properly. He also dreams of writing a book about his hiking experiences across Death Valley and in the

Grand Canyon. Until recently, he owned a small, successful down clothing company, but now he writes screenplays for small Canadian productions. When Snyder and I parted, four hours after we met, he expressed hopes for an amiable relationship with Wilcox.

When I met Wilcox in Seattle, just after Christmas, I was struck by what is not conveyed by the photo on the dust jacket of *White Winds:* His sensitive face held great pain. He sported a full brown beard, rather than the clean-shaven, handsome face from his expedition photographs.

Frayed towels hung in his bathroom, while the living room of his small home contained a naked-looking fir tree. The austere decor was broken by a watercolor of Denali, and despite his admiration for the detail of the work, it could only be ongoing torture.

He was forty-four years old, possessing the broad-shouldered vitality of his former football days: a man who doesn't overindulge but who no longer works out. However, he said, "When I was forty, I ran a two-hour-and-forty-minute marathon, which was as big an accomplishment as climbing Denali."

When asked if he would ever go back to climb the mountain, Wilcox shook his head no.

"The mountaineering community has more unresolved questions than I do about the tragedy," he said. "But I don't want people to believe I'm a victim. I don't think about it [the expedition] very much, particularly since I wrote my book. A month can go by and I forget there are mountaineering books in my basement. A hundred years from now, if someone looked back on the expedition, it would be viewed much more objectively."

Wilcox was oblivious to recent developments within climbing. He rambled, then dropped into an analytical monotone that was without warmth, almost devoid of emotion. He had not spoken with any of the surviving climbers for eight years. For the second time, Wilcox expressed devotion to his two daughters, who lived with his second wife in Denver. His third wife plied him with a chocolate doughnut, which sat untouched in front of him. He had only one story to tell, and my questions fell off him like water so that he could get back to his own agenda.

When queried about shovels and snowcaves, Wilcox replied, "The tents were recessed down two feet; this was standard procedure. At fifteen thousand feet we put walls around the tents, but if the weather got bad, we would've dug a snowcave. Dennis Luchterhand built a snowcave below Karstens Ridge because he was bored to tears, not because he thought we needed it.

"Even in Bradford Washburn's accounts, he stressed tents. What we didn't realize until afterward was that previous expeditions were never in bad windstorms. If I was going to climb the mountain again, I would build snowcaves all the way."

Wilcox insisted, "The tragedy was one of chance and I would match [the missing seven men's] decisions with my own." I asked about the résumé he'd sent to the Outward Bound School, which included his Denali expedition under "Major Rescues." I told him this seemed strange, since, unlike the other rescues he listed, none of the victims was rescued or recovered. "When you're young"—Wilcox looked me in the eye—"you do a lot of things you wouldn't do when you're older."

Wilcox was taking what he called "a sabbatical" from studying at the University of Washington, with the exception of an astronomy course. In the past he worked as a surveyor and a schoolteacher. Given his former drive, barring the tragedy, he may have lived out the American success story, with a big, prosperous family, a BMW in the garage, and a position of corporate achievement akin to happiness.

When asked what his next adventure will be, he replied, "I like to have a project, but priorities change, because when you're younger you're more willing to take chances. Presently I see a responsibility to my children. I enjoy raising my kids." When I left, he shook my hand warmly, anxiously. Even if he did make mistakes, one cannot help but feel the void in his soul, his need to clear the record. Wilcox looked at me with eyes the color of a robin's eggs and said, "I really hope we can find a constructive end to it all."

In the end, an objective retrospective may evade both Wilcox and Snyder. One of the survivors, Jerry Lewis, commented, "Out of the twelve persons on the climb there would be twelve different accounts."

The dead men all had choices, and it was their own experience and training that brought them to the summit that day—not Joe Wilcox. These men may have survived if they had been experienced in the art of snowcaving, if they had known how important shovels were, and if they had understood how dangerous it is to bivouac high on the mountain. They were a strong-minded democratic lot, and Wilcox was an autocrat, a titular leader who could organize men on paper but lacked the sort of natural leadership skills on the mountain—where the older and more respected Jerry Clark took over.

Seven young men chose to gamble up high and lost. Five others trembled and clung to tents that were shredded in the teeth of this unusual arctic storm and lived. Accusations flew in the face of two books that were read by thousands. Lectures were given across the country. And a play enjoyed acclaim despite its limited showing.

Until Wilcox stopped attending the yearly American Alpine Club meetings, people he was introduced to asked if he was *the* Joe Wilcox. The affable and unrelated Rick Wilcox (who guided clients up Denali in the 1980s) joked, with fair provocation, about changing his last name.

The disaster cannot be left on one person's shoulders, for this complex series of events is complicated by men's egos, the passage of time, and desperate loss. Even a quarter of a century later, playing Monday morning quarterback will produce no heroes or villains. If there is any justice yet to be dispensed for the 1967 Joseph Wilcox expedition to Denali, those people in the mountaineering community wont to produce scapegoats should try to bear the abyss of their own climbing companions' deaths.

3

LONE WOLF
(THE *OTHER* JOHN WATERMAN)

> I live not in myself, but I become
> Portion of that around me; and to me
> High mountains are a feeling, but the hum
> Of human cities torture.
>
> —LORD BYRON

ON APRIL FOOL'S DAY 1981, JOHN MALLON WATERMAN BEELINED through a maze of crevasses. He seemed unperturbed that one of these black holes might swallow him alive. His destination —the unclimbed east face of Denali—hung above, bristling with hanging glaciers and avalanche slopes. "Johnny" carried a small pack—and an episodic madness that crippled him in the city. Here in the shadow of Denali, however, with the commitment of a samurai, and a considerable climbing talent, he knew a profound sense of belonging. Within days, Johnny disappeared from the face of the earth.

No soloist committed himself to mountains like Johnny. Where Charlie Porter spent thirty-six hours climbing Denali's Cassin Ridge in 1976, or Reinhold Messner soloed the north face of Everest over three days in 1980, Johnny Waterman spent 145 days soloing the comparatively bantam Mount Hunter in 1978. And his route, the southeast spur, unlike most famous solos, had never been climbed. In one prolonged swoop, Johnny would also complete Hunter's first traverse and its first solo. Mountaineers still murmur of this stunt, with both derision and awe; he remains a primordial myth of Alaskan mountaineering. *Outside* magazine's Tenth Anniversary issue lauded his Mount Hunter solo in a decade's worth of "The Ten Greatest Feats." In the same issue, eight pages later, as if unsure how to catalog Waterman, *Outside* depicted him in "The Ten Strangest Feats" for disappearing on Denali.

I happened to be climbing on Denali at the same time the rangers were searching for Waterman. Climbers to whom I was introduced on the West Buttress Route would raise their eyebrows and celebrate my survival—until I spelled out that I was J-o-n, and the missing J-o-h-n had not been found, despite extensive aerial searches. After two weeks of overflights, the Park Service closed the "Lone Wolf" file that belonged to John Waterman. The news traveled quickly. A nationally syndicated column was released about Waterman's death. In the trailer that served as the Talkeetna post office, the postmaster stamped "return to sender" on any mail addressed to a Waterman with a first name beginning "Jo." She didn't know that two climbers with similar names were sharing the same "General Delivery, Talkeetna" address, so on the back of every Waterman envelope she carefully penciled in "lost and presumed dead." These letters were returned to a score of friends. Some mourned my passing; others took the trouble to call a Talkeetna bush pilot and unravel the mystery.

Although I never met Johnny, my sense of kinship to him and his father would grow until the whole star-crossed event seemed more destiny than coincidence. The odds of two climbers with the same name establishing their reputations in the Far North are unlikely indeed.

Until age twelve, Johnny's obsession had been the Civil War. His older and younger brothers, Bill and Jim, respectively, made friends easily, but middle-child Johnny kept to his soldiers, war books, and complicated battle games. He lived alone on the third floor of the family's huge Stamford, Connecticut, home.

After Johnny turned thirteen, his father took him and his brother Bill up multipitch rock climbs at the Shawangunks ("the Gunks") in New York. Johnny was hooked. The Civil War was forgotten. Climbing became his sole focus.

Boyd Everett, who engineered new routes on Denali and throughout Alaska, also took note of Johnny. Everett had seldom given Johnny's father, Guy, the time of day, but now he engaged him in long conversations about Johnny's potential, then drove him to New Hampshire for weekend climbs.

Johnny trained every day. He walked the two and a half miles to high school as fast as he could. In the afternoon he'd walk home, tag the front door, walk back to school, then head back home at a brisk pace. Each evening he did forty sets of ten push-ups.

In a letter to me, Guy recalled leading an overhanging Gunks climb called Bonnie's Roof, harder than anything he had ever done before. "It took me a bit to commit myself to the desperate moves," Guy wrote, "with Johnny calling up encouraging exhortations all the while. When I finally pulled myself over the last move of the sequence, it was to the accompaniment of a peal of excited squeaks and squeals: Johnny almost beside himself with pleasure that I had done it. Then when he came up and got his hands on the final holds, I suddenly saw his feet swinging way out from the cliff: in his sheer exuberance and high spirits he just kicked his feet off for the joy of it, before putting them back on the rock and completing the move."

When Johnny was a teenage prodigy in the Gunks, he reached a zenith of ecstasy, soon to fall forever beyond his grasp. On another overhanging barrier of the day, mastered by only a few of the local rock wizards, Johnny finally finessed over the crux. In his elation up above the overhang, he hopped lightly from one foot to the other on a small hold—but missed and fell off. Everyone, including Johnny, swinging on the rope in space, guffawed with laughter.

Another partner recalled that "the sheer power of his enthusiasm for my climbing could inspire me to climb like I'd never climbed before. It was a great gift. Climbing with Johnny was like being inside a grand piece of orchestral music in which all is harmony and there are no wrong notes."

One gifted young climber, Howie Davis, became a fast friend. Howie taught Johnny that surpassing the highest standards (called "5.10 plus" at that time) was easy if you perceived climbing as part gymnastics and part ballet—and then rehearsed it again and again, a notion that preceded the ensuing sport-climbing revolution by two decades. So in a day when teenagers were rare in the Gunks, fifteen-year-old Johnny led one of the area's most difficult climbs, Retribution. When Howie said gently, "Go, Johnny," he committed himself to the overhang. On other days the two could be seen bouncing down Carriage Road beneath the crag just after dawn, heading for their first climb—Howie doing front flips and cartwheels, Johnny matching him all the way.

Shortly thereafter, Johnny's friend became enmeshed in an unhappy love triangle with another climber's wife. One gray morning Howie climbed to the top of a route called Jackie and flung himself toward a giant boulder below. Although he missed the boulder, he was still thoroughly dead once he hit the ground. Howie's theatrical suicide left indelible marks on Johnny.

That winter of early 1969, Everett invited Johnny to his apartment and showed the gathering of young climbers pictures of unclimbed Alaskan routes. Everett undoubtedly sowed the seed of Mount Hunter's south ridge to both Johnny and a medical student, Dean Rau.

A few months later, Everett, Dave Seidman (who first tied a rope on Johnny), and five others were buried alive when an avalanche pulverized the foot of Dhaulagiri in Nepal. Johnny heard the news on a weekday afternoon; Guy rushed home from work to try to console his son, but Johnny fled the house and brooded alone for several hours.

To most young climbers eager to make their mark on the mountains of the world, and filled with the peculiarly adolescent belief in immortality, death seems a most improbable and unlikely outcome. But to the impressionable young Johnny, having three of his most influential friends die while climbing had a devastating impact. Furthermore, at sixteen, Johnny had no girlfriend and knew no social life or sport other than climbing.

Johnny met Chuck Loucks and Ed Nester at the Gunks. Both were old enough to be Johnny's father and soon took over where Everett had left off. Loucks was a carefree imp and Johnny embraced his puckish humor. Loucks taught Johnny how to make huge airy leaps from boulder to boulder at their favorite rock climbing area. And that summer, Nester brought Johnny on his first Alaskan climbing trip; Johnny became the third youngest person to climb Denali, summiting from fourteen thousand feet with Brad Snyder and Tom Frost.

Of course, Johnny had no idea that he would later become the most talked-about soloist in Alaskan climbing, generating more ink and legend than any other soloist. This summer of 1969, the Japanese mountaineer Naomi Uemura wrote to the Park Service, which tried to refuse him permission to solo Denali. Since soloing wasn't illegal, Uemura arrived in August of the following year. After a secluded nine-day climb up the West Buttress Route, he reached the summit on August 26.

Many other soloists would arrive over the years. By the end

of the crowded 1970s, dozens had soloed the West Buttress Route. Once the route began to get busy, a solo could be done without any trailbreaking or isolation. At worst, a soloist might have to spend nights alone in his or her tent. There are other, uncrowded routes where self-sufficiency is paramount to a soloist's survival. In 1976 Charlie Porter made a remarkable thirty-six-hour solo of the Cassin Ridge Route; in 1991, Mugs Stump fired up it in fifteen hours, wearing only a fanny pack. In 1977 Ruprecht Kammerlander soloed the west rib in a week; in 1990, a Russian climber steamed up the route in a long day. All four of these soloists were largely reticent and received little press about their accomplishments.

Women, too, have soloed the mountain. In 1982, after being helicoptered off of Mount St. Elias and thrown into jail for bypassing Canadian Customs, fifty-four-year-old Miri Ercolani of Italy started up Denali. She spent ten days on the West Buttress Route and claimed to reach the summit in mid-July. During a storm at ten thousand feet, she was trapped in a snowcave, and since she didn't remove her boots for five days, she suffered severely frostbitten feet.

Eight years later, Norma Jean Saunders asserted that her climb was the first woman's solo. Saunders fed the voracious Alaskan press with a posed cover photo on *Alaska* magazine, followed by a sixteen-page article titled, "First Woman to Solo Denali?" The garrulous Saunders then told *Climbing* magazine, "There's no documented account. She [Ercolani] was seen roped with other parties; she was never seen above fourteen thousand feet. She has not answered any letters from *Alaska* magazine, the rangers, or myself."

Later, in Florence, when I asked the venerable Ercolani about the controversy, she evoked Johnny Waterman's philosophy: "Some people do it for the publicity," she said with a wink. "I did it for myself."

* * *

That summer of 1969, when Johnny Waterman, Ed Nester, and Tom Frost descended Denali and flew back into Talkeetna, they met Dean Rau, who had just finished an unsuccessful attempt on the south ridge of Mount Hunter. Johnny was impressed nonetheless. Rau drove Johnny back to the lower forty-eight, and the two went climbing together, hatching plans for Hunter a year later.

That winter, Johnny ate, slept, and drank climbing. Guy, who had once led his son up routes, now followed him. He observed that Johnny was the fastest person he had ever climbed with. Guy characterized his son's climbing as "explosive energy and ferocious ecstasy on rock or ice—a masterfully competent but electric, volcanic, creative vitality. When he—or I—got a hard move, his joy was almost uncontainable. He was not grace, he was power," Guy wrote. "He was not beauty, he was energy. He was not control, he was uncontrolled joy. In spite of all the deadly fanaticism of some of today's Eurorock devotees, I have never met anyone to whom climbing (as opposed to gymnastic exercises or competitive triumphs) meant more."

Although divorce would shatter the family like rockfall hitting fine crystal, Johnny and Guy remained close. Guy claims their laughter-filled relationship transcended the normal father-son relationship, particularly when they went climbing together. However, when Duane Soper picked up Johnny en route to Hunter in the summer of 1970, Johnny and Guy said a "distant farewell" to one another. It seemed obvious to Soper that father and son were not getting along. At this point, no one really knew why; Johnny rarely confided in his companions. Guy was receiving the brunt of what most parents perceive as a tumultuous teenage rebellion.

Johnny, Soper, Rau, and Paul Harrison arrived beneath Hunter's south ridge in a blinding blizzard. Rau arbitrarily walked up a snowslope and started digging a cave; two days later an avalanche stopped within yards of their new home. For the next several weeks they flung themselves on the difficulties above, to no avail, because storms stymied the final bit of climbing. Although Johnny was only seventeen, he did most of the leading.

Ever since Johnny had fallen on climbing, his grades in school improved significantly; he didn't want homework to keep him away from climbing on weekends. But there were penalties to his single-mindedness: Johnny felt he never learned how to interact well with other people, particularly girls.

After graduating from high school, he climbed in England, Turkey, and the Alps. He wrote Guy about "the incredible barriers in my mind toward meeting people and relaxing, the barriers that only let down when I'm alone in my 'home' in the mountains. I could go on climbing only and try to forget about other things. It would solve itself, only it would have been a very short and hollow life. Not much of a solution."

For a brief period in 1971, he attended Western Washington University in Bellingham. The five-foot, three-inch Johnny loved hard winter climbing, but it was difficult for him to find companions. Potential partners felt alienated by Johnny's increasing temper tantrums and his no-turning-back attitude. (His obituary in the 1982 *American Alpine Journal* read, "He had always had trouble finding partners of equal ability and commitment, and the partners had to cope with his bright ideas that could turn a hard climb into [real suffering].")

On December 20, 1971, he arranged to climb in the Canadian Rockies with America's best Himalayan mountaineer. Johnny wrote to his dad, "he's supposed to be fast. Hope I can keep up." Then on Christmas Day, Johnny wrote again, "Well, another fiasco, I'm down in Spokane with ol' Superman. He wants to spend Christmas with his girlfriend (fine time to decide, fucking fine time)."

Although Johnny would never enter the mainstream of American climbing, his mountain vita established him as a fanatic. In Yosemite he led all the hard pitches on El Capitan's Nose. He made the first solo of the difficult V.M.C. Direct on Cannon Mountain in New Hampshire. He soloed the north face of the Grand Teton in Wyoming. He climbed new routes on the north face of Stanley and the east face of McDonald in Canada. He would travel to Russia and climb in an international exchange. And in 1972 he returned to Alaska to attempt the unclimbed east ridge of Mount Huntington with a resourceful group of mountaineers: Rocky Keeler, Neils Andersen, Roger Derryberry, and Frank Zahar.

In his book *Mountain of My Fear*, David Roberts wrote that Huntington's unclimbed east ridge could "put a party in a perpetual state of nervousness." Its "huge hanging glaciers, the most dangerous formations imaginable, sprawled obscenely down the ridge."

Johnny led the crux, a tenacious performance of steep climbing and tunneling into a troublesome cornice while hanging from one arm. When the team summited on July 5, Johnny, according to Zahar, was not resting on the laurels of their difficult climb. There on the final summit cornice, while the rest of the team reveled in a grand event of their lives, Johnny stared obsessively at Mount Hunter, several miles to the west. He considered his climb of the previous summer to be an abject failure. And he began to equate Hunter as an animate being determined to thwart his every effort.

Later that summer, in British Columbia, he completed the third ascent of Mount Robson's north face, with Warren Bleser. And while guiding for his friend Leif Patterson, he took Peter Metcalf up the same mountain. "If I had any problems," Metcalf said, "he was very forgiving. But once I was standing next to him, not watching what he was doing, when I heard this explosion of curses. John was waving his arms, screaming—I thought something horrendous had happened. After a one-minute outburst, he said, 'Oh, I just put a little rip in my windpants.' " Such tantrums began to mark all of his outings.

At nineteen he wrote his father: "As far as John the climber goes, I've already defined my lines. It's John the rest of the time that needs to be found now."

When Guy got divorced, his three sons—Jim, Bill, and Johnny—accepted it, secure in knowing that they held first place in their father's affections. But when Guy remarried in 1972, he felt that they never really forgave him: A stranger now occupied his attention. Furthermore, Guy and his new wife (formerly Laura Johnson) moved to the woods of Vermont, forsaking any modern conveniences such as electricity and the telephone. Guy's self-described "vow of poverty" may well have left Johnny and Bill feeling financially abandoned; Jim had always made his own way without any help from his dad. Johnny and Bill took up permanent residence in Alaska, as if they needed to get as far away as possible from their ruptured family.

Waterman is not a common name, so our parallel desires as climbers made our shared name all the more unusual; then Johnny's father taught me how to ice-climb. In the early 1970s, John Waterman had become an Alaskan legend, as large and phantasmagoric as Denali to a New England teenager like me. His name appeared in the journals, and if the local mountaineers didn't know him, they at least pretended to. Sometimes my presence made other climbers hush, as if Waterman had returned from Alaska—until they realized I was not "the" John Waterman.

Once, in a smoky cabin under Maine's biggest mountain,

Katahdin, Guy Waterman entertained me and two dozen other rapt mountaineers by the glow of the lantern. On the other side of the frosted-over windows, it was twenty-five below zero; Guy pantomimed his son outracing an avalanche on Alaska's Mount Huntington. Before I slunk off to my tent, Guy confided under the saffron lantern light that maybe "someday Johnny and 'the other Jon Waterman' could climb Denali together in the winter." I went away transfixed by the power of Guy's stories about his famous son. But I was also vexed that no matter what I did in the mountains, there was another climber greater than I who shared my name.

While Guy seemed the ultimate father for a young climber, my own father was not entirely supportive of my proclivity. So in the same manner in which Johnny spurned Guy after he remarried, I turned and fled from my own parents' divorce, taking solace in the mountains.

Guy's letters followed me everywhere. Whereas Guy and Laura were articulate and full of puns, if my parents wrote at all, their letters were staid and succinct. Moreover, Guy and I frequently got together for mountain outings; my own father played tennis. Guy soon became a mentor.

I knew that he and Laura had completed an early ascent of one of New England's hardest ice-climbing test pieces: the Black Dike. They had even traveled to Alaska and attempted a new route on Mount Hunter; the route was completed half a dozen years later by two of the finest alpinists in North America. But Guy's mountaineering and environmental activism were only glimmers of the talents he had formerly displayed in the city.

At their remote homestead, Guy and Laura built their cabin around a grand piano and several hundred volumes of classic literature; if a visitor pleaded, they might play duets on the piano. Laura was high-powered enough, with or without Guy, and before moving to the woods she had turned her back on a blossoming editorial career in New York City. They both seemed torn from the pages of Helen and Scott Nearing's book about self-sufficiency in the wilderness, *Living the Good Life*, with one crucial difference: They were my friends.

Guy's preservationist philosophy had a profound effect on everything I did in the mountains. As Guy and Laura became renowned as the "Consciousness of the White Mountains," I was secretly pleased when people mistook me for their son. The Watermans never criticized my own actions, but they frequently debated the entrepreneurial and environmentally degrading aspects of the mountain huts I worked in. Consequently I tried to implement change: leading nature walks, minimizing the use of disruptive helicopters, and educating hut users about conservation. Guy had greatly influenced me, and it was not stretching the truth to say that he became a surrogate father.

One day, in a fit of restlessness about our "dinky" four-thousand-foot-high New Hampshire mountains, Johnny's father and I jogged up and down the northern Presidentials until we had gained the equivalent of twenty thousand feet of elevation. I limped back down disappointed that we couldn't finish another nine thousand feet, which—in our minds, anyway—would have equaled Everest instead of Denali. Although our exertions struck other mountaineers as a contrived stunt, to me it was only business as usual with the Waterman family—of which I now seemed half a member.

The following summer I tried to climb Denali for real, but turned around in a storm at nineteen thousand feet, altitude sickness as thick as clouds in my head. I later found a photograph of Johnny from his first visit on Denali; he was wearing the same model and color of Kelty pack that I wore. Although I didn't meet Johnny (who had also experienced altitude sickness as a teenager on the West Buttress Route), his stomping grounds gave my life new clarification. Whereas I had previously experienced mostly adolescent apathy, Denali began to form both my subconscious and actual horizons for the next decade. As a restless middle child, I planned to live in Alaska. Just like Johnny.

That winter he caretook Leif Patterson's home in British Columbia and threw some wild parties. Johnny was constantly talking about girls, but his friends all knew "Johnny's dalliances" to be pure fantasy.

Rau described Johnny's "delayed puberty and a delayed interaction with women. Then all of a sudden there was an explosion." The letters to Johnny's father filled with sexual fantasy. Johnny, however, would never find a steady girlfriend.

In the summer of 1973, accompanying Rau, Don Black, and Dave Carman, Johnny came back to Alaska to settle the score with Hunter. Although Rau thought that his twenty-year-old friend was climbing as well as anyone in the country, he saw that Johnny had changed in the intervening years. "In 1970, you could reason with him, but now Johnny felt that you had to put the climb above everything else. I thought I was with a madman."

While waiting to fly to the mountain, Waterman's companions watched him slam the hardware rack on the floor as hard as he could, or rage at some passing frustration, swearing and screaming like Ahab. On the mountain Johnny often sang strange ditties to himself. Although he became the driving force behind the climb, he was also fast to a fault. At one point Johnny did a sloppy job of hammering in a snowpicket. When he started rappelling, the picket pulled out, and unbeknownst to him, Carman held the rope until Johnny reached the ledge.

"He was your consummate alpine climber on mixed

ground," said Carman. "He was very quick, not beautiful, and kind of scary because he was so obsessed."

The climb itself was disastrous, at least in Johnny's mind. After a week of climbing above the col in frequent storm, Black, Carman, and Waterman reached what appeared to be the summit. Both Carman and Black were scared to death of climbing on friable "Coca-Cola ice"; Carman had recurring nightmares about the climb after they got down.

Later, after flying out and examining photographs, standing alone out on the banks of the desolate Susitna River, Johnny studied the distant mountain; it suddenly became clear that they had turned back two hundred feet below the summit. Johnny was crushed.

Then he opened up a letter from Leif Patterson. Instead of the expected check, Johnny received a bill for some furniture he'd smashed while caretaking and being a party animal at the Patterson house. Furthermore, the news about his companions from Robson and Huntington reached him through the climbers' grapevine: Warren Bleser and Neils Andersen had died on the Matterhorn.

When bush pilot Don Sheldon told them how much they owed for his services, Johnny burst into tears. No one could speak. Sheldon finally muttered something about accepting credit.

"Johnny knew he was a misfit," says Black. "After a temper tantrum he'd sometimes say, 'I know how difficult I am to deal with.' But you didn't push it after that, because you didn't want to fire him up again."

"The conflict of making money and the higher spiritual beauties in life was tearing him up," said Carman. "Also, the lack of a girlfriend was real painful to him."

His partners posed for a photograph with Johnny, standing nearly a foot shorter than his companions, staring at the camera wearing a court-jester smile entirely inappropriate for his perceived failure on Hunter.

Johnny felt at home in Alaska, famous for its stifling black winters, high suicide rates, eccentric gadflies, and obdurate dipsomaniacs. He shared a cabin with his brother Bill, with whom he was always very close. Although Bill was also passionate about mountains, an accident hopping freight trains left him with one leg. In 1973 Bill wrote a cryptic letter to their father, mentioning a long trip and that he would be in touch when he returned. One friend thought he might have gone to Vietnam; another said South America. To this day, Guy likes to believe that Bill went farther north and became engulfed in the life of some Eskimo village. No body was ever recovered; moreover, no one knew where to begin looking. Bill simply vanished.

Over the coming years, much of Johnny's actions would be interpreted as mad behavior. "Johnny's gone snake eyes," Duane Soper told Dean Rau. Rau himself was confronted at a local fair by "a spaced-out-looking" ticket seller with shoulder-length hair, laughing maniacally and shouting, "Hey, you ratfucker!" Rau barely recognized his former partner. Indeed, Johnny's mother had been diagnosed as psychotic, and such imbalances have been shown to be genetically coded. But the death of Johnny's closest partners and climbing mentors would have slapped even the most well-adjusted climber to rock bottom.

After the deaths of Everett, Seidman, Davis, Bleser, Andersen, and (probably) his brother Bill, Rocky Keeler died in a bicycling accident. Then Leif Patterson died in an avalanche, and Chuck Loucks fell in the Tetons. Finally, even cautious Ed Nester died, rappelling in the Selkirks.

After Guy wrote to Johnny about Loucks, Johnny mailed his father a letter: "What can I say? Your letter said it all. Last person in the world I expected to live longer than. I was really broken up for twenty minutes, and have had recurrences, but the pain is now through. The thing forever removes all legitimacy from climbing to me, but will bring us closer together, I think. I've never been so touched, except maybe by my brother Bill."

One could only imagine how it felt to be cast in the shadow of a father who was as gifted as Guy. He had supported himself through college by playing jazz piano; he published climbing fiction, ragtime pieces, and statistical essays for *Baseball Digest* magazine. And he could recite five hours of *Paradise Lost* from memory. Before he left city life, he was known as a "bright young man" on Capitol Hill during Eisenhower's administration and had written speeches for three different presidents (before or after their terms), and senators such as George Bush's father, Prescott.

Johnny tried to shock and outrage people as a means of gaining attention; he even confided to his friend Lance Leslie that he was trying to win parental approval. But Johnny misread his father. Hearing Guy paint his son's accomplishments, even before the Hunter solo, is to know both great pride and unqualified love.

By the mid-1970s Johnny's reputation was sealed. He drank bottles of salad dressing like soda pop. He strummed on a battered guitar and sang out of key in an amphetamine flow-of-consciousness fashion. He described "airy, sweeping, and lofty" symphonies he would compose about his climbs.

To prepare for his *succès fou* of all climbs, on Mount Hunter, he trained by bathing in tubs filled with ice. When the Talkeetna Motel owner got suspicious and caught Johnny ferrying buckets of ice to his room, he was evicted. Undeterred, Johnny, clad in crampons and floppy mountaineering boots, took long training runs on the snowpacked highway.

Two years before Johnny's climb, Doug Scott and Dougal Haston had demonstrated the "alpine style" ethic, rapid and unencumbered up Denali's south face. Johnny's climb on Hunter almost deliberately defied the new ethic with a dozen packframes and metal boxes and enough spare clothing to outfit several climbers. Lance Leslie and partners, who bumped into Johnny after he was alone for seventeen weeks on Mount Hunter, had never seen a climber with "such a huge pile of shit." Leslie sensed that Johnny was scared, which explained the need to surround and insulate himself with as many possessions as possible.

Many modern climbers, imbued with the ethic of climbing fast and light, came to see his climb as a protracted siege, which was true in terms of the number of days he spent on the mountain. Spending five months on Mount Hunter belied his abilities as an extremely fast and efficient technical climber, particularly with gear placement and belay changeovers. These efficiencies, which had been instilled by his dad on small crags a dozen years earlier and subsequently sharpened during big-wall climbs, have left countless partners impressed to this day. On Hunter, Johnny simply wanted to be left alone, to take his time, and to contemplate the universe.

On Hunter, Johnny freely admitted to bouts of extraordinary loneliness and crying with frustration and rage. While dozens of remote cabin dwellers listened in on their citizens band radios, Johnny begged his pilot to air-drop medication for body lice. "It was some comfort to know at least I was not alone," he later wrote in the *American Alpine Journal*. "My morale was low at this point. I was forty-three days out and was obviously not going to reach the summit plateau with any reserve of food even on two-thirds rations." His bush pilot, Cliff Hudson, rescued him with a big food airdrop on the plateau, and Johnny continued toward the north summit.

Once when Hudson flew by, level with a section of the climb called the Perch, Johnny emulated his long-dead friends Howie Davis and Chuck Loucks and flipped into a handspring above the abyss. As the plane shrunk into the sky-line, Johnny keyed his radio mike: "Did you see that, Cliff?"

"I'd appreciate it if you wouldn't do that," Cliff replied.

The first time Johnny fell during the climb, he was caught by a shoulder strap attached to his securely driven ice hammer. "The slip made me nervous," he wrote, parodying many understated British climbing writers. "It could have been fatal."

Another time he collapsed a huge cornice and fell forty feet before he was "surprised" that his belay system caught him. Or, matching a miscalculation he'd made on the nearby south ridge five years earlier, a poorly placed anchor pulled while Johnny was rappelling; he miraculously fell upright into his steps below.

The account he published in the *American Alpine Journal* implies that Johnny found Hunter to be an animate force. In addition to referring to his climb as "a vendetta," he wrote how "the mountain and I finally met on our own terms." Furthermore, he named three different pinnacles on the ridge "Judges," as if his performance were being evaluated. Such personification of the inanimate is usually scoffed at by mountaineering literati, but in this case Johnny apparently believed it.

"More than his fellow humans, [the mountains] had become his companions," Ingrid Canfield wrote about Johnny in a chapter from *Skiing Down Everest and Other Crazy Adventures*. "And he invested them with the frailties and duplicities, the enticements and charms of real people, relating to them powerfully and responding only to them with his true essence."

In a conversation with Glenn Randall (who wrote a book about his epic repeat of the route, threaded with Johnny's adventures), Johnny said that something "far more precious would be lost if I lived through it than if I died. Living through it would mean that Nature wasn't as raw as everybody wanted it to believe it was. Living through it would mean that Mount Hunter wasn't the mountain that I thought it was."

Bowing to the mountain, Johnny fixed all thirty-six hundred feet of his rope down the north ridge before he went to Hunter's highest summit, believing it more respectful to the mountain to be killed before he put the summit beneath his boot soles. When he finally went to the north summit, he was surprised to make it alive. After descending his ropes, he could have crossed over to the crowded Kahiltna Glacier base camp and been lauded as a hero, but he stayed on the deserted Tokositna Glacier. Johnny spent several days alone—nursing his frostbitten fingers and pondering his newly altered perception of reality—until Hudson flew in to his salvation.

That summer I spent thirty-eight days thrashing up an unclimbed ridge on Mount Logan in the Yukon. My three teammates and I took turns confronting steep water ice, digging trenches up scary snowslopes, kicking off avalanches, and crabbing across rotten rock towers. When I was nearly done with the four-mile ridge, a multiton cornice collapsed beneath my ice ax and thundered off to the glacier several thousand feet below—I quit for the day.

More than once, I tried to imagine how it would feel to solo our route: Getting hurt or killed seemed the lesser danger. The more pressing concern was keeping your sanity in a landscape so utterly unforgiving and so barren of humanity that you would have to scream to hear yourself think—or pretend the mountain was alive and start talking to it. If going mad didn't kill you, and you survived collapsing cornices and tent-ripping storms, you would forever walk twisted among your peers, changed irreparably by a stark and surreal world beyond most people's earthly experience. Just coping with the civilized world again after sharing such intensities with my three partners was all I could handle.

That year's *American Alpine Journal* came out with articles about two different Watermans on Mount Logan and Mount Hunter. Now I wondered how Johnny felt about another Jon Waterman traipsing up unclimbed ridges. While Johnny faded amid the recluses of northern Alaska, I fled to the mountains of Colorado. Both of us failed to make any lasting niche in society—we were too strung out by our experiences in those hauntingly beautiful mountains of the North.

Several years later, Randall, Peter Metcalf, and Peter Athens cut Johnny's time on the southeast spur of Hunter by more than a hundred days, but they suffered dearly and didn't summit. To date, the reputation of the climb has repulsed further attempts. Despite the extended siege, Johnny's accomplishment equaled Harding and Merry's El Capitan climb or Bates and Washburn's traverse of Lucania and Steele— both climbs were lionized in the mainstream media as well as in mountaineering circles. But beyond the microcosmic Alaskan media and several thousand admirers in the insular mountaineering community, Johnny's achievement gained him less renown than that of a barreler's descent of Niagara Falls.

"The tragedy was that he never got credit for his Hunter climb because he wasn't playing with a full deck," Dean Rau has said. "He should've gone all over the world lecturing."

Instead, Johnny borrowed $20 from Hudson and looked for work in Fairbanks. "To me that was really the ultimate in what was wrong with our society," Johnny said. "After this horrible climb—or, actually, this superb climb—my only societal reward was to be washing dishes at the very bottom of society."

The climb changed him irreparably. Lance Leslie said that before Hunter, "Waterman was odd, but little different than other climbers with his scruffy beard and down feathers clinging to his matted hair. But after Hunter he seemed almost dangerously psychotic."

In Fairbanks, Johnny ran a campaign for the presidency. Although no one took him seriously, he was deadpan about the whole affair. His platform was to feed starving people around the world, legalize drugs for schoolchildren, and promote free sex for everyone. Johnny began kissing acquaintances—male or female—whenever he met them in public. Even the normally unruffled Fairbanksians now wondered if Johnny had gone overboard.

In 1979 Johnny set out to try to climb the south face of Denali. Part of his plan was to gain enough notoriety so Nepalese officials would grant him permission to solo Everest in winter. Hudson flew Johnny into Denali with five hundred pounds of supplies. Johnny planned to climb a dangerous new route alongside (his late mentor's) Dave Seidman's Direct South Face Route. But December is the cruelest, windiest, and blackest period of the Alaskan night. Something in Johnny snapped.

On January 1, after contemplating the route for ten days, Johnny told his pilot, who had dropped off some more supplies, "Take me home; I don't want to die." Back in Talkeetna, he told a reporter, "The mountain defeated me, but he didn't eat me alive."

Two months later, the Talkeetna cabin he was staying in burned down, destroying all his notebooks. "That was the blow," Leslie commented, "which sent Johnny teetering toward the brink." Johnny told several onlookers that the notes he had accumulated over many years were the essence of himself; to lose them meant that he had burned up in the flames.

He convinced the Alaska Psychiatric Institute in Anchorage to admit him. After two weeks he walked out under his own recognizance. Later he told Randall that he was suffering from his Mount Hunter psychosis—fearful of being cold and hungry or lacking shelter.

After he got out he again laid plans to solo Denali. However, with a now-characteristic inability to act on his biggest project, he hung out in Fairbanks for nearly two years, enjoying a cult status and popularity that the community had never awarded a mountaineer. Many Fairbanksians knew him; most tolerated his behavior.

He charged about the Fairbanks campus of the University of Alaska with a flowing black cape and a silver star glued between his glasses. His Mount Hunter slide shows also became the talk of Alaska. At the lectern he would pull off his shirt, talk about the ache of profound loneliness, and then further shock the crowd by confessing to his secret expedition lover, "Rosie." He beamed shamelessly, holding up his right hand.

Finally, in February of 1981, he began walking from the ocean at Anchorage, tracing the frozen and desolate Susitna River, which carved a sixty-mile-long, mile-wide swath from Talkeetna to Cook Inlet. He staggered under a pack almost matching his own gnomelike frame. Ten days later, shortly after midnight, he banged on the door of the Talkeetna Motel and asked for a cup of coffee. Lance Leslie's wife, Lori, let him in. He was thoroughly soaked after breaking through the river ice. He came into the kitchen, and after a few minutes of rambling banter, picked up a carving knife, began various stabbing motions, and asked Lori how to hold a knife if you wanted to murder someone. It was weird, Lori thought, but it was all show.

Afterward he continued marching up the Chulitna, Tokositna, and Ruth rivers, thirty-five miles of forsaken moose and wolf habitat, emerging at the Ruth Glacier. This convoluted highway of ice is difficult walking, so Johnny stopped at two thousand feet. Denali rose as a great blinding citadel, within ten miles of walking and a vertical mile of climbing.

Johnny was yet unable to face the demons of his soul, and blaming the aborted attempt on a faulty stove, he returned to Talkeetna and procrastinated. When he finally summoned the courage to leave, he returned Cliff Hudson's hand-sized citizens band radio—a gesture that symbolized turning his back on all further communications with the world. Johnny repeated his farewell to Hudson from before Hunter: "I won't be seeing you again."

At six thousand feet on the Ruth Glacier, Johnny met some climbers from Fairbanks, who commented that he looked more run-down and tired than usual. He dallied for weeks up on the glacier, unable to commit himself. Finally, on April Fool's Day, he said good-bye to his friends, and *sans* sleeping bag, cut across the labyrinth of crevasses toward one of Denali's last unsolved routes—a place that the most accomplished mountaineer of the world, Reinhold Messner, rejected as too dangerous.

It would not be difficult to die on Denali while alone on such a route. Even if a climber was playing it safe, the margin between sanity and breakdown would be hard to define in such a chilling and sterile amphitheater, renowned for its fantastic avalanches. There would be temptations to befriend crevasses and hanging glaciers, and during the subarctic night, the only presence to talk to would be the mountain itself.

Two weeks later, everyone presumed Johnny was dead. Some climbers found a box of supplies at six thousand feet on the Ruth Glacier, marked in Johnny's handwriting, "the Last Kiss." A helicopter overflew his route, but with the exception of an old stomped-out tent site at seven thousand feet, there was no trace of his passage.

There are a few Fairbanksians who maintain that Johnny fooled the world and pulled a disappearing act, changing his identity. *Rock and Ice* magazine satirically wrote that he was living in Arizona, anonymously and illegally soloing desert spires on Navajo land; my own letter to the editor protesting the irreverence was answered by another climber's letter insisting that Johnny was a sexual deviant and a madman. Meanwhile, my unknowing high-school chums assumed I was dead and celebrated with a "Jon Waterman Memorial Golf Classic."

Shortly after Johnny's death, Guy wrote to me, "What is really too bad is that you and Johnny never knew each other, or that you could not have climbed together."

Cliff Hudson gave me a suitcase of Johnny's notes and poetry. That winter I kept it with me in my Alaskan cabin, and, falling to the depths of my own depression amid the winter's darkness, I clutched my alter ego's belongings as if they were my own. I also spent many hours that black winter critiquing Guy's proffered book manuscript, dedicated "To Johnny for whom these forests and these crags were a beginning." But the final time I tried to make sense of Johnny's illegible scrawl on random sheets of paper, I shut the case and never opened it again. I didn't have the heart to send the stormy scribblings to Guy, so when I left the cabin and fled Alaska for good, I abandoned the notes—which found their way to Fairbanks and were sold in the annual John Waterman Memorial Auction.

Six years after Johnny's disappearance, a woman who had lived with Bill and Johnny Waterman in Alaska telephoned me in Colorado, where I had found a job as an editor. She thought that maybe Johnny had survived and written the book *Surviving Denali,* which I had authored. She broke into tears as soon as I answered, because mine was not the high-pitched and reedy voice she had been praying to hear again.

When Guy received more of his son's effects, there were hundreds of pages of writing, mostly indecipherable and overwritten fantasy. One short story of Johnny's, however—remarkably controlled and underwritten—concerned his father's reaction to a telegram describing Johnny's death.

Guy is still trying to accept his son's death. "I found a lot of things along the forty-nine years that preceded the spring of 1981," Guy wrote, "and I can be aware of them even in the midst of the lowest lows. Johnny didn't find enough such things before the spring of 1981." Now in his sixties, Guy still shares a life in the woods with Laura. He actively climbs, sometimes solo, but usually with Laura in the nearby White Mountains.

Guy felt that his son had learned how to survive on difficult climbs in the Alaska Range. He was bothered that some would use Johnny's last climb to illustrate the risks of soloing. On December 29, 1986, Guy wrote, " 'See,' say the conservatives, 'even a super climber was killed when he made the mistake of climbing alone. It always catches up with you, etc., etc.' I trust you know that Johnny knew what he was doing," continued Guy. "He did not want to come back."

On a hidden subridge in New Hampshire's White Mountains, Guy erected a small memorial that contains an old pair of Johnny's boots. Every April, on the anniversary of his son's disappearance, Guy and Laura bushwhack to this aerie. Surrounded by their favorite mountains, Guy remembers earlier times while staring at Cannon—scene of happy epics with Johnny and Laura. Guy then sings three ballads and three poems, including an old Scottish lament played at his father's memorial service:

> Then here let him rest in the lap of Scaur Donald,
> The wind for his watcher, the mist for his shroud,
> Where the green and the gray moss will weave their wild
>   tartan
> A covering meet for a chieftain so proud.

For free as an eagle, these rocks were his eyrie,
And free as an eagle his spirit shall soar
O'er the crags and the corries that erst knew the
footfall. . . .

I once asked Guy if his son had fooled everyone and simply disappeared instead of dying on Denali. Guy answered: "I wouldn't want to say a 100 percent no, but I really don't think so. In the end, the mountains were the only place Johnny could feel at home, so that's where he went to stay for good." Concerning his son Bill, Guy says, "I never entirely extinguish the possibility of his return."

During a recent visit—no longer a dedicated mountaineer and trying to escape the grim weight of life for a while—I lost the path to the Watermans' rural property. I thought about Johnny a lot that day. I thought that few people indeed can afford to commit themselves irrevocably to their dreams, and I admired him deeply for that. Like Icarus, Johnny had cut off all moorings to his loved ones and flew into the alluring white heat of the sun.

I didn't find Guy until twilight, tending his garden a hundred yards off, under the light of a lantern. When I shouted "Hello!" he ran toward me clutching the lantern, with ecstasy and surprise shining with childlike joy on his face. When his saffron light finally fell on my face, he was plainly crestfallen, even though it had been years since he had seen me.

The next morning, Guy paused in front of a woodpile. He looked into my eyes; he tried a smile. Then he apologized about the way he had greeted me the night before. He explained that once in a while he will greet an unidentified visitor out in the dark and think for just a scant moment that maybe, just maybe, one of his sons has finally come home.

4

PAYING FOR THE SUMMIT

And still, men who by guts and skill had mastered
the farthest wilderness, they must have had a way of
standing and a look in their eyes. While they
scanned the faces of white men, their glance took in
the movement of river and willow, of background
and distance. While they talked as men talk nearing
home and meeting someone newly come from
there, their minds watched a scroll of forever-
changing images. What they had done, what they
had seen, heard, felt, feared—the places, the sounds,
the colors, the cold, the darkness, the emptiness, the
bleakness, the beauty. Till they died this stream of
memory would set them apart, if imperceptibly to
anyone but themselves, from everyone else.

—Bernard DeVoto

EACH YEAR A THOUSAND CLIMBERS ENGAGE DENALI. MORE THAN
three hundred of them are guided, and in years when the
weather is kind, more than half these clients reach the summit, steered, towed, cajoled, protected, and insured by an
amiable tribe of mountain guides.

Even the earliest climbers on Denali tried to hire guides. In
1903 a Canadian horsepacker warned the American journalist
Robert Dunn about his journey to Denali: "You don't want
no Swiss guides. They're handy high up on rocks and ice, but

lose themselves in the woods. Six weeks across Alasky swamps? They'd die or quit you the first day."

Dunn, Frederick Cook, three roustabouts, and fifteen horses beat through more than three hundred miles of brush and muskeg, "under the curse of mosquitoes and bull-dog flies," without guides. If an experienced climber or guide had accompanied them, they might have reached the summit instead of their ten-thousand-foot high point on the Northwest Buttress.

Before Hudson Stuck, archdeacon of the Yukon, first climbed Denali ten years later, he had hired guides on Mount Rainier and in the Canadian Rockies. Stuck did not go against the fold, and he knew that the continent's highest peak demanded the services of a guide. In 1913, Stuck underwrote all the expenses and gave everything but money to the legendary "Seventy-Mile Kid," Harry Karstens, to scout Denali, break trail, then chop hundreds of steps. Finally, Karstens and Walter Harper led the archdeacon to the top. When Stuck could plod no higher, he promptly fainted.

On America's highest alp, climbers weren't paid to take anyone to the summit until another several hundred climbers and forty-seven years had passed. But in the Canadian Rockies and the European Alps, guiding had always been linked to climbing.

European guiding originated when well-to-do sportsmen, often English, hired local farmers to pack their lunches, haul the ladders, and attend to all of the other mundane details of mountaineering. Guides seldom climbed on their own, but, for a price, mountain peasants were eager to pack loads, scout routes, chop steps, and break trail—tasks considered gauche by their clients.

Before World War II, America had few climbers, and mountains such as Denali were considered utterly remote. In the accessible mountain ranges of the world, guiding was rela-

tively straightforward. But on Denali, it couldn't begin until
Washburn and the skiplane "opened up" an easy route in
1951. Walking in sixty miles was not an option for clients.

Guiding began on Denali in 1960. Rainier guides and veteran climbers Lou Whittaker, Jim Whittaker, and Pete
Schoening escorted John Day to the summit. Day had convinced the three northwestern mountaineers to climb Denali
in a "speed ascent," which took them three days from 10,000
feet. While descending from Denali Pass, someone slipped,
fell, and pulled the whole team downward: Day broke his leg,
and Schoening—whose famous reactions with an ice ax had
saved five men from falling off K2 in 1953—was knocked
unconscious.

Fifty people mobilized to evacuate Schoening and Day.
The highest airplane landing up to that time had been made
at 14,300 feet. Another pilot stripped down his helicopter,
including the battery, then plucked off Day, Schoening, and
another climber, stricken with altitude illness. Rescue head-
lines blazoned in newspapers across the country.

Rainier Guide Service later made a few more tentative
forays, but most guides lacked the audacity to make such a
formidable mountain a business goal. Traditionally, a guiding
career involved a long climbing apprenticeship on many
mountains, and in the 1960s American guides were conservative and somewhat in awe of the suffering that even an ordinary ascent of Denali demanded.

So it stood to reason that the first full-time guide on Denali
was a European who had never followed American guiding
traditions and who had never climbed any significant mountain until he summited on Denali in the winter of 1967. Afterward, the expatriate Swiss Ray Genet and his companions
shuffled into the hospital with frostbitten toes. While Dave
Johnston and Art Davidson took months to recover, Genet
healed his frostbite in three short weeks by marathon dancing

in the nightclubs of Anchorage. That summer, he resumed his house painting business, all the while plotting his return to Denali.

By 1968—given Genet's European mountain roots, his entrepreneurial *savoir faire*, and his fame from the first winter climb—Denali became ripe for the picking. In his swashbuckling wisdom, Genet knew that his business would never flourish under the straitlaced image of most American guide companies, so he cultivated his bushy black beard, his outrageous orange climbing suit, and his trademark bandanna wrapped "pirate style" over his forehead. The Pirate's credo—"To the summit"—exhorted clients never to settle for anything less; Genet often brayed that clients would summit if he had to drag them there. His bombastic style made him undisputed king of the mountain for more than a decade.

He escorted huge groups, who left an indelible imprint of feces, trash, and overcrowding. He was also fond of saying that he was in the business of selling "ego trips to climbers."

Until he died, the Pirate lived by the sword. In 1972 one client fell and broke a leg. The next year three of his indisposed clients were helicoptered out from 14,300 feet on two different occasions. In 1976 the Pirate jumped out of a helicopter near the summit to save a young woman's life. It was not uncommon for him to shoulder his victims as if they were bundles of firewood. Had he lived to board the 1980s, rattling his ice ax like a saber, Hollywood would surely have courted him for movie rights.

In a time when American climbers disdained sponsorship, Genet's woolly face decorated countless Tang advertisements. Certainly the Pirate reached his own 20,320-foot apogee with much more frequency than the astronauts Tang usually sponsored.

When I first met him, in 1976, the burly *Bergführer* was

carrying a sick man down from 17,000 feet. Hours later, the twenty-four-year-old client died of pulmonary edema.

I also watched Genet retrieve a pack that an unguided stranger accidentally dropped from 16,200 feet and fell 1,000 feet; Genet ran down, then selflessly jogged this considerable distance back up the fixed ropes to return the pack to its stunned owner.

Three days later, on July 5, more than eighty people waited to stand atop the urine-stained summit that is no larger than an ordinary bathroom. Then Genet summited.

He would later boast that he went to the top of Denali forty-three times (actually twenty-four); once, on an un-crowded day, he claims that he and a companion became the first to mate on the roof of North America; in 1991 one of his sons, Taras (twelve), became the youngest climber to summit.

On that July 5 day of the crowded Bicentennial year, he only whipped out his radiotelephone to place phone calls to three separate women; first he yelled at the caller already on the party line to hang up. Dozens of remote cabin dwellers and mountaineers heard the Pirate's distinctive baritone booming over the airwaves. His opening salutation to these women, "Hi, honey, it's Ray, I'm on the summit of McKin-ley!" was answered three times with various degrees of incre-dulity. After praising each woman as his highest object of affection, he signed off: "I love you, baby!"

His client who had died of pulmonary edema preyed heav-ily on Genet's mind because even hauling the man down on his back had come to naught. That afternoon a helicopter flew into the 14,300-foot basin and picked up the stiffened client, wrapped in an American flag.

I saw Genet two days later. He was cursing out Frances Randall, caretaker of the Kahiltna base camp airstrip. Randall insisted that some frostbitten Mexicans had priority over Ge-net, who would have to wait his turn for a flight out. The quarrelsome Genet was unrepentant, arguing that it was *his* mountain. Sitting on their packs, the three Mexicans stole glimpses at Genet as if he were Pancho Villa reincarnated. When the long-awaited skiplane finally skidded onto the glacier, he jumped on board alone—even though there was room for the injured climbers. With his usual bluster he commanded the pilot not to spare any horses on the way back to Talkeetna, where his women would be queuing up at the airstrip. The black-toed Mexicans said nothing.

Most women back in Talkeetna reviled him because he'd walk up unannounced and pinch their rear ends. One climber recalled having to jump off the street because Genet would have run him over. When this pedestrian tried to stand up to Genet, he merely pushed him aside and shouted, "Stay out of my way!" Conversely, up on the mountain, after barking out orders to his guides, cooks, and clients all day long, Genet would come crawling into his tent at night and softly ask his tentmate if he would mind fixing Genet some warm milk and honey from the expedition supplies.

Genet really believed it was his mountain. When Gary Bocarde, Michael Covington, Rainier Guide Service, and others began arriving with regular clients during the mid-1970s, the Pirate bluffed that the Park Service had given him the only guiding permit for the mountain. Some guides even believed him.

Bocarde once told a reporter, "His attitude [toward clients] was, 'I'll get you up there, no matter what.' That kind of attitude can be dangerous."

Bocarde recently said, "He clearly handled 'em like animals, dragging 'em along with the rope. And if there was a woman in the group, he was always tied into her."

One of Genet's former chief guides, Brian Okonek, said, "It's amazing that he didn't have more accidents and fatalities, given his style; I don't know if it was his dynamic leadership or good luck, but he was *out there*. Genet did know how to get the most out of a person. He didn't do any pretrip screening for people, and he took people who didn't have any right being on the mountain, but he knew when to quit pushing them. Eventually, though, things fell apart because he wasn't real organized; he had too many clients and too few guides. Also, the community equipment was in terrible shape, the first-aid kit was nonexistent, and you didn't know how many people were coming until the clients showed up."

In 1979 sled-dog racers Joe Redington and Susan Butcher were hauled to the summit by Genet. Redington, who was otherwise impressed by his guide, conceded to reporter Bill Sherwonit, "I saw him work on some people that never would have made it there. Some of them he kind of abused a little bit."

When asked about the caches and refuse abandoned on the mountain, Genet said, "It used to be called caching and now it's called trashing. It's not a major problem." Nonetheless, Genet spawned a system of caches and trash dumps that environmentally aware climbers found loathsome. From 1971 to 1976, members of the Denali Arctic Environmental Project hauled more than a thousand pounds of refuse down the mountain. Its leader, Gary Grimm, carefully pointed his finger at Genet and blamed much of the trash on commercial guides "who seem to be more interested in profits than in environmental quality."

During his last few years of guiding, the indefatigable Pirate had grown so weary that he hired assistants. Climbers such as Jim Hale (eventually fired by Genet because he turned clients away from the summit in dangerous avalanche conditions) helped the clients up the mountain for ten days. Then Genet flew in, sprinted 7,000 feet up, and towed as many as forty-two clients, cooks, and assistants in one long, undulating summit mambo line. After topping out, Genet sprinted back down without dealing with any clients.

At the end of the guiding season in 1979, Genet told Okonek that guiding was getting old, that he'd had a long, hard summer and he wanted someone to help him. He didn't mention the upcoming Everest trip, but Okonek would never forget Genet's paternal advice: "There's a lot of people out there who can care for you, but mountains are dangerous and unforgiving. You gotta take care of yourself."

A month later Genet impulsively thrashed to the top of Everest after battling a gastrointestinal illness. On the summit he carefully left his last cache: a handwritten note.

While descending with the leader's wife, Hannelore Schmatz, Genet's supplementary oxygen ran out. Sherpa Sungdare insisted that they continue down, but Genet, in typical contentious form, refused. At 27,800 feet, Schmatz and Genet began the highest and longest sleep performed by any man and woman. He was forty-eight years old.

Sungdare ran down to the 26,000-foot South Col. He grabbed an oxygen bottle and hustled back up that very night to try to save his clients—just as Genet would have on Denali. But when Sungdare arrived, neither Genet nor Schmatz needed any more oxygen. Sungdare descended, utterly despondent. (Sungdare would lose nine toes to frostbite, climb Everest four more times, then commit suicide in 1989.)

Michael Covington escorted Genet's hysterical companion, Kathy Sullivan, and their son out of the Everest base camp. That winter, two Poles uncovered Genet's last cache on the summit. It read: "For a good time call Pat Rucker 274-8402 Anchorage, Alaska USA."

In 1980 Denali National Park officials finally began controlling guide companies. Seven exclusive permits were issued. Over the years, guides were asked to bring down their trash, defecate into plastic bags, and lead no more than fourteen members at once. For the most part, guides cleaned up their act. Although foreign "bandit" guides continue to plague the seven "concessionaires," the mountain is definitely cleaner and perhaps a bit safer than in the halcyon days of Genet.

Okonek, now one of the concessionaires, says, "Guiding has come a long way since Genet died. Now guides have more training; we know a lot more about altitude, screening clients, and things that were developed over years by trial and error."

The myth of the Pirate still lives. Genet Expeditions was a sought-after service that retained its credo, "To the summit," despite frequent reprimands from the Park Service for unsafe guiding. Finally, in 1992, the Denali National Park superintendent revoked Genet's guiding permit.

In the spring of 1981 I signed on under Michael Covington as a Fantasy Ridge Mountain Guide on Denali. My boss wore an electrified Afro, a euphoric grin, and a Nepalese Z-stone necklace. Michael insisted that he loved guiding; he'd sooner rot, he said, than work nine to five. Two years earlier he had leapfrogged a nine-hundred-foot rope up the Cassin Ridge with several clients climbing the ropes behind him. He claimed he had created a new technique—while Brad Washburn had fine-tuned *expedition style* on the West Buttress Route and Doug Scott had climbed the south face *alpine style*, Michael introduced *capsule style* to Denali.

Despite Michael's noxious "Slim Sherman" cigar smoke, the director of Fantasy Ridge Alpinism became my role model. After hiring me, he provided plane fare and a $700 monthly wage. Even though seasoned Denali guides made twice (now four times) as much, most climbers didn't grouse about free climbing trips. Furthermore, the salary included room and board—a tent plus all the freeze-dried food you could eat.

After climbing the west rib with John Thackray for fun, I arrived back at the base camp. Here I fell into repose and waited for my job, guiding eighteen circuitous glacial miles (three miles by raven wings) to Denali's summit. I assured Michael that reclimbing the mountain with clients would be, in climberspeak, "a real cruise."

While I was sprawling over a half-inch-thick ensolite pad—insulating me from the several-hundred-foot-thick glacier—a Niagaran avalanche flooded the mile-and-a-half-high face of Mount Hunter—two ridges away from Denali. After suppressing the instinctive urge to run, I turned back to my unflinching cribbage opponent, one of scores of nameless mountain guides who slink about Talkeetna's saloons and Denali's glaciers. The avalanche spindrift cloud passed over us like the radioactive fallout from a nuclear bomb; I tried to look as composed as my nearby associate.

Guide mercenaries can be identified by white "raccoon" eye rings where sunglasses have blocked the beginnings of skin cancer elsewhere on their faces. They share a cologne of urine and sweat mixed into their synthetic clothing, chicly labeled Petzl, Berghaus, or Helly Hansen—versus the Columbia, L. L. Bean, and R.E.I. labels sported by their clients. Some of these guides are unassuming and soft-spoken. Most of them curse, chew, spit, smoke, fart, brag, blow harmonicas, sing off key, flaunt their egos, and conduct themselves in a manner that would lead to their excommunication from church, their mortification in public, or their eviction from apartments.

I was not surprised when my fellow guide Steve Gall sauntered out of the skiplane wearing a bandanna pirate-style around his forehead. He was blowing smoke rings from a Slim Sherman wedged between his fingers.

As the seven clients jumped (and fell) out of the skiplane, I began to envision our group dynamics. Even a neophyte

Denali guide like myself could sense that there were insurmountable obstacles ahead. Our congenitally uncoordinated Baptist minister, Phil, told us that we didn't have to worry because God would see us safely up the mountain. Phil had been directly appointed by his own Chief Guide in the Sky to climb the mountain so that he could return home and better direct his misguided flock, sinners all, from the Baptist backwaters of southern Georgia. In Denali guide parlance, our minister appeared to be only one of "a school of tuna."

Our biggest catches were the Texans Ernest and Evelyn Chandler, living out the great American Dream by climbing its greatest peak. Ernest was forty pounds overweight with a heart condition, while his pale, slender wife would easily kite away if the wind blew more than fifty miles per hour. In this business, however, the consummate Denali businessman knows that as long as his clients' money is green, anyone can pay for the summit. I made several inquiries about our lame-looking clients, aged nineteen to sixty-three. *Tuna.*

My colleague Steve seemed strangely resigned about his new charges. Moreover, he was so unfazed and dedicated to the mission at large that he must have known something I didn't. Our troubles began only a mile up the Kahiltna Glacier, seventeen miles from the summit. The Chandlers, with the exception of their nineteen-year-old son Walt, could not drag their sleds; Steve took Evelyn's, while I took Ernest's. Another mile farther, Steve lashed Evelyn's pack on top of his. And a hundred yards from camp, Ernest collapsed.

He clutched his chest as his pulse raced like the traffic on Interstate 20. When he calmed down an hour later, he allowed that he would have been fine if he had taken his heart medicine. While slumped in his sleeping bag, he summoned his most authoritative basso and announced that he would be continuing up the mountain in the morning. I agreed with anything he said in order to comfort him, then continued plying him with tea as an excuse to monitor his speedy pulse and erratic breathing. At 7:00 A.M., after quietly radioing Doug Geeting for an evacuation, I bulldozed the protesting Ernest into the skiplane before his wife could interfere. I told Geeting not to bring Ernest back to the mountain under any circumstances, even though he had paid the $1,200 guide fee.

That afternoon, while Steve shuttled loads with the others, I escorted Evelyn back to the landing strip so she could rejoin Ernest in Talkeetna. After I lifted Evelyn aboard the plane, I asked the bush pilot, Don Lee, if he'd given my note to a friend, Chris Kerrebrock, who was attempting the Wickersham Wall on the other side of the mountain. Don's face dropped. "You didn't hear?" he asked.

"No."

Don walked me to the side of the airstrip. "Chris died in a crevasse fall."

I thanked Don for telling me, walked over the hill and out of sight from the climbers at base camp, then screamed as loudly as I could. "Why him?" I yelled, and suddenly climbing Denali seemed so frivolous and self-indulgent that I seriously considered commandeering the next plane to Talkeetna.

Certainly, no climber is immune to the death of a friend. It can happen to anyone at any time, but when it does, the surprise is inconceivable. The sense of loss darkens the dazzling light of the mountain; it sours the sweetest camaraderie; it turns all reverence to disdain. I felt (as the late Lionel Terray had titled his climbing memoirs) that I had become a Conquistador of the Useless.

It would be difficult to resume climbing now, even with a friend, let alone five paying clients who had never been on a big mountain before. "I'm spent," I thought. Escorting charges up the West Buttress Route was going to take everything I had. I convinced myself that since Chris had been a guide, too, he would've stayed with his clients in a similar situation, so I began skiing the five miles back up the glacier.

When I came to the first easily crossed crevasse and stared down into its onyx throat, I was so stricken that I sat down and imagined what it would be like to be wedged in fifty feet down like Chris had been, virtually unhurt after his companion tried every trick in the book to free him. Chris knew he was finished, so he asked Jim Wickwire to relay messages of love to friends and family. Chris thanked Jim for his help, made him promise not to solo up the glacier until help came (so Jim wouldn't also fall in a crevasse), then summoned his courage as he waited for the lying warmth of hypothermia to take him away.

The crevasse beyond my skitips seemed to plunge like an infinite elevator shaft, or it might have been twenty feet deep, but I cursed it until my throat grew hoarse. Then I held my breath. As I glided over the narrow crack, I imagined free-falling into black space—like Theodore Koven, Allen Carpé, Jacques Batkin, Johnny Mallon Waterman, and Chris Kerrebrock had all done on Denali—my heart pounding in arrhythmic terror.

Meanwhile, Steve dealt with our sanctimonious client Phil, who tripped over his snowshoes, dragged like bottom fish on the end of the rope, and spilled a pot of water in the tent. When I finally returned to the eight-thousand-foot camp in a blue funk, I heard a tirade: "Phil," Steve shouted, "you're nothing but a low-life, worm-eating, shit-licking son of a whore!"

There was nothing to do but laugh; I was back in the fray. I had to concentrate on the clients' needs now.

Our Baptist minister did not take kindly to Steve's rebukes. After a few days, following every new assault of profanity, Phil gently chided, "Stevey, I *jus doan* think *y'all* can talk to a human *bean'* this way."

Over the coming weeks, the other clients—Jack, Fran, Bruce, and young Walt—found solace in Steve's latest invectives against Phil. They would titter at every new "maggot" or "dickhead" or "pussyface" as if Steve were lampooning the Ayatollah. It became apparent that Steve was trying to relieve everyone of the frustration of Phil. Diurnally, Phil would spin judgmental Bible lessons to anyone within earshot; nocturnally, he would bellow out a cacophony of guttural snoring beside his tentmates.

When forced to share a tent with me one night, he implored, "Jonny, *y'all* really need to spend some time with this Good Book here." He knew that I was mourning Chris; Phil wanted to help. He would lift the Bible and touch my shoulder when he talked, but I let him sermonize unhindered, because a good guide is supposed to listen—despite Phil's drooping, drooling lower lip and basset-hound face. Despite his righteous and windy lectures. And despite his lone, spastic guffawing after jokes that we couldn't understand.

After the first week, Steve and I agreed that we could not take Phil to the summit because he would endanger the team if he "ran out of gas" the way he did while carrying loads. So Steve and I alternated baby-sitting Phil and keeping him on a tight rope.

Statistically speaking, Phil was fairly safe. During the 1980s, of 2,284 clients who attempted the summit, only 1 died; of 5,247 nonguided climbers, 33 died (5 in crevasses). Most Denali guides will concede that every team of clients is stacked with a "walking time bomb" like Phil. Usually "the Phils" retreat or get evacuated after the first few days. The fact that they rarely die, fall in crevasses, break legs, get frostbitten toes, scald fingers, torch hairdos, asphyxiate tentmates, or are strangled by their guides has a lot to do with the incessant vigilance of those guides. Phil, however, was convinced it had more to do with miracles.

While shuttling loads to 14,300 feet, I warned Phil to step over the obvious crevasse; I was particularly concerned about crevasses lately. By this time most of the climbers on the mountain had heard that four rangers took an entire day, chopping ice and rigging pulleys, to remove Chris's corpse from the crevasse.

Phil paused at the edge of a sixteen-inch by two-hundred-foot slot of blue space, squinted his eyes as if to make a calculation, then stepped directly into the hole. In the ten seconds it took me to sprint back to him, he slipped into the slot like a greased pig into a hay shredder, kicking away and widening the crevasse walls as he stretched the rope leading to a teammate and fell to his hips, then up to his chest. When I arrived at the lip, he was undermining his last vestige of support; I grabbed his chest harness and wrestled him back onto the glacier. Phil flopped on the snow with sweat streaming down his face, lips funneling for air, carabiners jangling on his harness. When he finally spoke, he thanked God for his salvation; I was not mentioned.

That night Steve and I pitched our own tent fifty yards away and out of earshot of Phil. The others gave Phil a gag order: All sermons except emergency prayers were forbidden. We had already put knives, matches, stoves, and cooking off-limits to Phil.

Phil had pushed us all to the brink. I had reached that point, inevitable for even the most patient and compassionate of Denali guides (which I was not), when even nine-to-five work seemed inviting. Steve was reconsidering being a roughneck, where he had worked long hours at no small risk to his health on the barren oil fields of Wyoming.

Even Covington, whom we had seen puffing cigar smoke and pitching his tent on the Kahiltna Glacier, would experience burnout. He had been red-eyed and ready to explode because one client, a former narcotics agent, threatened to bust him for smoking a joint. Three years later, after Michael brought clients partway up "the Cassin"—a sought-after ridge that ends on the summit ridge after three miles of undulating granite and ice—he turned to his charges and said, "We're going down." He later confided that he was "fried" and in such a state that he couldn't take responsibility for clients. Ever the gentle businessman, Michael refunded their money, just as he did for Ernest and Evelyn Chandler.

Clearly, burnout is a disease of guides rather than clients. It is not unusual to see the regulars returning to Talkeetna wasted, even if no one died on the mountain. You can find these guides with sunken eyes at the ranger station, nursing beers and blackened digits at the Fairview Inn, stuffing fistfuls of pizza into their mouths at the deli, or aboard the next inbound plane shouting inanities to their clients when asked questions as simple as the time of day.

The reasons for burnout are clear. When push comes to shove on Denali, the conscientious guide, like the captain aboard a sinking ship, will overlook his own needs to attend to those of his charges. Consequently, guides become thin, dehydrated, or frostbitten while they're haranguing their clients to eat, drink, or dress properly. Or they become exhausted because they can't trust anyone else to cook meals, break trail, or grope through a whiteout. And if a rescue breaks somewhere on the mountain, it is the guide who evacuates a stranger all night, then turns around to tow his clients another thousand feet up the mountain.

Furthermore, the caliber of clients on Denali is not equal to that of guided teams on difficult and lesser-known peaks such as Mount Huntington, Mount Foraker, or Mount Hunter. The clients who are drawn to Denali tend to be executives or white-collar workers who equate "biggest with the best."

As Okonek says, "They don't love mountains like guides do; they don't make it part of their life. Nor do they really have the desire to climb; they just want to *have* climbed and then move on to something else."

There are three other well-known climbers, all in their forties, who have cumulatively worked the mountain longer than any other triumvirate of Denali guides. Collectively, these three men (all passing into and out of Talkeetna each summer) have logged nine marriages—due, no doubt, to their sporadic income, the stress of their prolonged absences from home, and their inability to leave the pressures of work up on the mountain.

With a few exceptions, even the most acclaimed Denali guides stop challenging themselves on their personal climbs. Going on a fun mountaineering trip, without clients, is so easy to associate with the burnout work of mountain guiding that many guides stop climbing altogether. Mountain guides share that dilemma of tennis pros, football coaches, and ski instructors, who seldom compete or even play at their former levels of glory because they're too harried making a living from their expertise. The end result is the exclusive separation of these pros from their salary-paying clients.

One renowned Denali climber and former climbing guide, David Roberts, wrote, "Guiding was being teacher, dorm mother, drinking buddy, cook, and janitor rolled into one relentless package. You set up an ironic gap between yourself and the students, taunting them with private jokes shared with coleaders. You kidded about 'repairing to the nearest pub' at the first drop of rain, but you began to hope that nobody would show up so you could cancel a trip. You stopped explaining the rules and simply dictated them."

At 17,200 feet, on the eve of our departure for the summit, I told Phil please to shut up. After pulling his ice-cold and rancid bare feet off my stomach, I swore an oath not to ruin my vision of Denali by guiding it ever again.

We left at 6:00 A.M. The prescience of great disaster seemed to hover closer than the lenticular clouds over nearby Mount Foraker. Despite Phil's presence, I prayed for mercy.

Every trip has its saviors. Jack, Fran, Bruce, and Walt had put up with Phil for seventeen days without complaint. Hopefully, Phil would become too weak to ruin our summit day; then Steve or I would take him back down so his long-suffering teammates could reach the summit in peace. But at 19,000 feet, Phil, despite his sluglike pace, could not be persuaded to turn back. And Walt felt too sick to continue.

Steve volunteered to pull Phil and the others to the summit. Before I turned around to escort Walt down, I pulled the emergency Dexedrine out of my first-aid kit and handed it to Steve.

"What's this?" he asked.

"Speed," I replied, "in case Phil runs out of gas."

Three interminable hours later, Steve finished yanking Phil the final ten yards, blessing him with the usual round of heated verbs and graphic nouns. Phil collapsed onto the snow without his traditional reply, and unlike Archdeacon Stuck sixty-eight years earlier, he could not even utter the *Te Deum*. Steve reveled in the exuberance of Jack, Bruce, and Fran, and they all forgot about Phil as the continent fell beneath their cramponed feet. As Phil lay unconscious, they had much to celebrate, not the least of which being that Jack was sixty-three years old.

When it came time to leave, Phil couldn't move; Steve was shocked. He asked Phil to stand up, but Steve's desperate and gentle prodding bounced off deaf ears. Steve pulled out the Dexedrine with shaking fingers, pried open Phil's lips, and helped him wash it down with a slug of water that was mostly ice cubes. Now Steve lit into him anew, unleashing a litany of original verbiage more brackish than anything he had ever heard on the Wyoming oil fields. As if responding to a dream,

Phil rose to this fresh layer of indecency, as if the devil himself were speaking, and forced himself to his feet, morally outraged and croaking, "*Y'all* can't talk to a human *bean'* this way."

Steve figured that if he could just keep Phil moving, the Dexedrine might jolt his adrenal glands into action. During the first hour, Phil toppled a dozen times. Steve let him rest briefly, pumped him to his feet with more verbal heresy, and wondered if Phil would force them to bivouac in thirty-below zero, which could doom them all. The other three lurched down in distressed funks, alternately turning to yell such provocative suggestions as "You're a loser, Phil!" toward their martyr.

A half mile below the summit, at the 19,650-foot Archdeacon's Tower, Steve realized that Phil was still moving, that both the drug and the blasphemic insults had taken effect. The minister became a veritable jukebox of complaints, which offset some of the barrage from his companions and turned his face blue. They arrived back in camp eighteen hours after leaving, and I spent the rest of the morning monitoring Phil. Although everyone else snoozed in blissful exhaustion, Phil was wired for sound. He couldn't shut up.

The next day Steve had bloodshot murder in his eyes. Since it was my turn to deal with Phil, I insisted that Steve take the day off; if Phil didn't somehow kill himself, Steve would gladly do the job. Guiding novices down the most interesting 3,000 feet of the West Buttress Ridge and Headwall is never relaxing, but with Phil tottering every step of the way, our passage became one of the most angst-ridden trials since Whymper's ill-fated Matterhorn descent of 1865—when one climber slipped and pulled his ropemates to their deaths.

At 14,300 feet Steve had napped and spent the day kibitzing with other climbers. Since he seemed relaxed again, I offered him the rope with everyone but our minister; the foursome trotted down to the 11,000-foot camp while I chaperoned Phil. Five hundred feet down, I strapped Phil's pack onto my own. At Windy Corner, Phil stepped into the same crevasse from a week earlier.

Phil asked for frequent rest stops. After he caught his breath he issued that patronizing smile and boasted of the glory of his Chief Guide, who had lifted him onto and back down from the summit. In that syrupy drawl Phil schemed of the magnificence of his homecoming. Wiping the drool from his lip, he predicted how all the troubled teenagers in his parish would come to him for advice, *"Ah'll* say that *Ah,* too, have *experu-minted* with drugs." I couldn't forget that Phil had exhausted his tentmates for three weeks with his stentorian snoring and his presumptive preaching. By now I pondered violating the First Commandment.

I had long concluded that getting to the top of Denali was not worth an iota of blackened tissue, let alone giving up one's life. Phil was probably similar to hundreds of other clients who had been dragged to our highest piece of geography. His physical unpreparedness and naïveté about his own survival, let alone the safety of his companions, had spoiled the trip for most of the clients, whom I now appreciated greatly for their efforts. His lack of respect had also defiled the mountain.

Phil's experience seemed an off-kilter joke to the memory of a safe climber such as Chris Kerrebrock, who suffered a cruel, slow, and unjust death. If the God of Phil's prayers did exist, Chris would not have been made to wait for three hours to die inside an open ice coffin, looking up at three vertical miles of cocked avalanche slopes.

When Phil demanded his fiftieth rest stop of the day, I took action. "To the base camp" became my credo; I performed just as relentlessly as Genet and Covington and Bocarde and Okonek and Gall had performed in their own long and distinguished guiding careers, but in reverse. In front of thirteen stunned clients from a Rainier Mountaineering group, and forty yards from Steve's tent, I began dragging Phil with the rope, belly down in the snow. Most of the camp watched in silence; Fran and Bruce and Jack and Walt applauded vigorously.

The only voice that could be heard under the otherwise placid sunset clouds was a nasally distinctive but snow-muffled Georgia-twanged judgment. "Jonny, Jonny," Phil whimpered, "*y'all* can't treat a human *bean'* this way!" When I reached the tents, bathed in peach alpenglow, I untied from the minister as if unhooking an inedible bottom fish.

Steve passed me a cup of steaming tea, a smoking cigar, and a smile pregnant with congratulations; he would chaperon another dozen groups up Denali. I never guided the mountain again.

5

WINTER OF OUR DISCONTENT

On McKinley in winter our struggles also brought
us closer to each other and to ourselves. . . . In my
mind the full moon is still rising over the Kahiltna
and that silent world of glaciers, ice and rock. The
stars are still burning in the black sky we looked up
to from the summit. I can see the northern lights
swirling out beyond the mountain and the sun
breaking cold and golden over an icy ridge. . . . As
my own life began to slip away, I was struck with
an overwhelming sense of how wonderful it is to be
alive.

—ART DAVIDSON,
Minus 148 Degrees

TO PREPARE FOR CLIMBING DENALI IN WINTER, I DREAMED WITH MY
eyes wide open. These sensual dreams of choreographed body
movement—flashing ice axes and legs stemming rock chim-
neys and mitted hands stroking fluted snow—took place amid
a stark, frozen wilderness that I craved more than any place
on earth.

As a teenager growing up in Lexington, Massachusetts, I
was drawn to winter. My friend Ed Webster and I found rib-
bons of frozen water around town on which to perfect our
craft: prancing up frozen water on crampon-clawed boots and
placing our ice tools as gently as finish carpenters or swinging
as brutally as lumberjacks—whatever the variable ice condi-

tions required. In the mornings, I ran to high school on my toes to build calf muscles, shunning a jacket and clutching snowballs until my numbed hands turned as white as porcelain faucet handles, dripping with snow melt.

Once Ed and I, both sixteen, hiked up New Hampshire's Mount Washington in a January gale. Frost clung to our eyelashes just as the rime feathered the spruce boughs; we felt we belonged here. We laughed at the sign that read, "Many have died here from exposure. Turn back now if the weather is bad."

Black, house-sized boulders shrunk beneath the soaring blue bulges of ice in Huntingtons Ravine. We pulled our hoods tighter and left the Goldline in Ed's pack because it was too cold to rope up that day. Ed pretended he was on Everest (where he would lose most of his fingers to frostbite sixteen years later), while I fantasized of Denali.

Ed started up first. I whacked in my ax, and the two of us moved spastically up the gully, gripping our axes tighter when the wind threatened to pluck us off. Suddenly my ax popped out of the ice, and Ed's eyes widened as I slid just out of his reach. While I was trying to self-arrest, my pick caught and dislocated my shoulder as I continued sliding down the ice, clawing desperately while seconds stretched into breathless clarity. The boulder field grew larger as my crampon caught on the ice and my tibia bent, split, and came apart with a dull snap that erupted into an eyeful of fireworks. I cartwheeled to a stop.

Ed climbed down. We splinted my broken leg to an ax and bound my shoulder with webbing. We denounced an outside rescue because climbers are supposed to extricate themselves from their own messes. Ed grabbed me by my good arm and dropped me over a boulder; then I'd hobble to the next boulder and we'd repeat the process. He felt bad that he was

Denali as a ghostly presence above the Tokositna River.

Herb Atwater (left) with the author (center) and Scott Gill.

Denali guide Steve Gall.

Mugs Stump at the Moonflower Buttress.

Jeff Rhoades (foreground), Kelly Rhoades, and Dave Wood battling around Windy Corner.

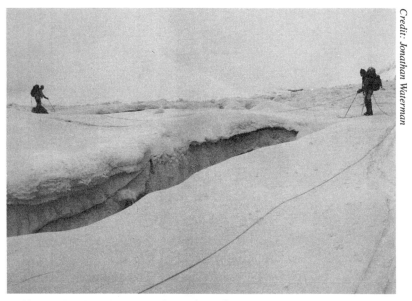

Jeff and Kelly Rhoades circumventing a crevasse.

The author leading up
the Japanese Couloir
on the Cassin Ridge.

Credit: Roger Mear

Credit: Jonathan Waterman

The author at 17,000
feet on Cassin Ridge in
winter.

Denali's West Buttress above the clouds.

Coming back from
Denali toward the
landing strip.

Denali's twin peaks seen from the north side.

Digging a snow cave
during the winter
ascent.

Descending Karsten's Ridge.

The High One.

unscathed while I was almost totaled, but mostly we kept on with the work.

The pain seesawed back and forth as the ball of my humerus grated outside the shoulder socket. Ed sympathetically pulled out some first aid from his pack: a joint given to us by the stoners at the ice climbers' cabin. We lit up with great trouble in the wind, then took turns filling our lungs with acrid warm smoke. Relief was ours, or so we thought marijuana was a painkiller, until I became aware of the pain as a new spine-tingling and continuous electric ache. Ed tried to hide his giggling.

When we heard people approaching, he stopped dragging me and propped me against a tree. When they appeared, Ed prattled on about the wind while I contrived a smile. After the unsuspecting snowshoers walked away, Ed continued his assignment as my crutch. Eventually we caught a ride back down the mountain in a Snow-Cat and hitched a ride home in an unheated van. As I lay in bed convalescing, all my fantasies of Alaskan peaks were dashed.

It took three years, a summer attempt of Denali, and a job as a winter caretaker on Mount Washington to regain my waking dreams of climbing Denali, or perhaps the Yukon Territory's Mount Logan, in winter. Moreover, my partnership with a restless Rhodes scholar, Will Sayre, changed my approach toward mountains forever.

While I was employed by the conservative Appalachian Mountain Club (AMC) in Tuckermans Ravine—halfway up New Hampshire's Mount Washington—Will showed me how to expand my mountaineering horizons. We often climbed during subarctic storms when other climbers stayed inside. Will continually challenged the Forest Service snow rangers, who chased him out of the ravines, fined him, and wrote nasty letters about Will setting a bad example by climbing under dangerous avalanche conditions. The opposition merely incited Will. While I quietly ducked the avalanche closure ropes and avoided the rangers if it seemed safe enough to climb, Will openly sought out the rangers and challenged their authority. I often acted as mediator between my newfound friend and his rapidly growing list of adversaries.

We believed that there were no limitations to our climbing as long as we trained hard. Together we determined to climb all six of the ice gullies in Huntingtons Ravine, twice in a day, a rumor that made the rangers squirm anew with discomfort. That winter of 1977, America's most talented climber, Henry Barber, stirred up the local climbing community by racing up all six of the gullies in five hours. We knew that Henry seldom trained. Our training was partly about building muscle fiber and expanding our lungs, but it was mostly about stretching our imaginations.

One twenty-degree day in January, we climbed Yale and Pinnacle gullies naked, wearing only boots and crampons and gloves, tilting our rear ends back so the ice chunks dislodged from our axes wouldn't hit our genitalia. On another stormy day we sprinted up all six gullies, which bewildered the climbers "stormed in" and playing cards in the ice climbers' cabin. In February I crossed all nine peaks of the Presidential Range in a day of jogging above the tree line, but when I hitched home in the subzero dusk, numb-tongued with giddy exhaustion, the first driver who pulled over was my boss. "Don't ever do that again, or you'll be out of a job. Furthermore, I'm concerned that Will Sayre is going to get you two killed."

The insular community of AMC employees at the Pinkham Notch Lodge spurned Will because he was perceived as a reckless sybarite, spending his nights with a lover at the lodge and taking free meals instead of manning his post up at the drafty ice climbers' cabin. Moreover, the educational system that spawned Will made him challenge other people's intellects. He was not above playing devil's advocate and ridiculing his peers, who perceived him as "playing with their heads."

The crew of neophyte mountaineers also idolized the snow rangers, and when Will arrogantly challenged the rangers' expertise, his rating fell immeasurably. Undoubtably his six-foot, four-inch, broad-shouldered frame—with a wide head, expressive face, and outsized teeth—simply intimidated people. If he wasn't a teetotaler, perhaps he could've shared a good drunk at one of the many parties and become accepted as a "regular guy." Instead, Will ostracized himself until he was no longer welcome in the lodge for showers, food, or even sleeping with his girlfriend. I liked Will because of our similar climbing strengths and mountaineering interests. But even if he had not been a climber, I felt an affinity to underdogs who had been kicked out of the house. Defending him, feeding him, and accepting the brunt of his demeaning quips became my winter's métier.

At that point in my life the only place and activity that really mattered was climbing mountains anyway. The others didn't climb with me. Will did. Eventually his companionship alone made me overlook our differences.

One February dawn, "Reinhold and Peter" (Will and I addressed one another as members of a famous European climbing team) set out from the lodge after devouring two disarming stacks of pancakes—eating was one more competitive event for us. When we got to the ice an hour later, we began a vertical ropeless jogging technique that had taken us all winter to master. Breathing like locomotives, we progressed by a repetitive series of four kicks and two ax jabs, vaulting ourselves ten feet higher with each kick-jab-breathing revolution. Our movements were not graceful or flowing, but no climber could say we lacked in passion or confidence.

Halfway up the twelve-hundred-foot Yale Gully, we passed a guide belaying his client; twenty-five minutes later, we had

run down to the bottom of the ravine and scrambled back up
Yale Gully, catching the guide and client, who were now three
quarters of the way up their day's climb. In five hours we
finished climbing all six of the gullies twice, and we raced one
another down to the lodge. Most of the armchair mountaineers at Pinkham Notch presumed our morning's activities to
be more of Will's tall tales, but we didn't care because we had
done it for ourselves. The synergy developing between us
seemed more precious than the thin air we craved on the
highest peaks of the North. Eventually, the guide—a renowned ice climber—affirmed what we had done. It seemed
like nothing could stop us.

In the summer of 1977, we bought a used Volkswagen and
tore out the backseat to fold our six-foot-plus torsos and
crates of climbing gear into the tiny "bug." The AMC unknowingly donated a case of chocolate bars that became per-
meated with white gas vapors; our poverty forced us to eat the
entire gross of chocolate. So we drove across the country
singing folk songs in wretched harmony, burping up gaseous-
smelling chocolate, and swapping the secrets of our life with
climbs in Colorado and California.

That winter Will enrolled in the University of Vermont
Medical School, while I worked in a climbing shop. We reveled in the lack of heat during long drives to ice climbing
areas and pronounced our shivering as perfect training for our
ultimate winter climb. I had been on Denali only once, in
summer, and even though we did not reach the summit, I felt
lucky to get off without blackening any toes or fingers. Court-
ing Denali or Logan in winter seemed the most dreadful and
alluring of all fantasies.

One weekend, on a steep cliff bristling with ice in northern
Vermont, the ice boomed and settled on Lake Willoughby
below as we climbed. Friends watched from a heated car. Will
and I switched leads up a three-hundred-foot wall of ice called

Glass Menagerie. The difficult climb took us less than an hour because I broke my hand overdriving my ax and wanted to be done with the pain as quickly as possible. While our friends below were impressed at how fast we were moving, they couldn't hear the insults Will and I traded with one another—insults instigated by Will to "stoke our competitive engines." Nonetheless, our speed together was addictive.

When I moved out West, we continued to scheme through the mails of our upcoming climb. I went on other climbing expeditions, and although Will did not come, for years I deluded myself into thinking that we were close friends. I didn't yet know the meaning of friendship.

Climbing in storms and pushing your limits were not always the predetermined arts that Will and I initially supposed. One quietly sensitive and determined young climber—a friend from my hometown—emulated our brash techniques. During a violent and blustery winter day in Huntingtons Ravine, Dave Shoemaker had climbed most of Pinnacle Gully. Then the wind stole him and his partner and slammed them back down to the bottom of the ravine, fifteen hundred feet below. When I heard the news of their deaths, I felt both wrecked and responsible.

Sitting with Don and Julian Shoemaker in their home, I tried to shed light on the tragic and wasteful loss of their only son. "It's what made him happy," I said. "Dave would have climbed for the rest of his life, and he died in a place that held great meaning for him." Dave's sister stared at me with curious and dilated pupils while her parents clasped one another's hands tightly on the couch, speechless and smiling, as if I could impart just the fiber that their son had been made of.

I visited my newfound friends several times and once stayed over at their summer cottage. I published an obituary suggesting that Dave still frequented Huntingtons Ravine; Don found the courage to hike up there, past the ominous warning sign, where he could finally and fully grieve for his son.

We stopped talking of Dave, but I sent them letters from distant ranges and described mountains just as their son knew them: alluring and more magnificent than any woman I'd met, geographies of hope that filled me with peace. When I described my goal of climbing an Alaskan peak in winter to them, they immediately nodded assent and supported me without question. Although I never saw them again, for a brief two years I had tried to show them who their son really was.

Will and I knew that the finest mountain route in North America had long been a psychological watershed for alpinists. During the 1961 first ascent, Riccardo Cassin and his companions paid dearly. All of the team were frostbitten on the nine-thousand-foot-high Roman nose of granite that unyokes Denali's south face. On the summit they prayed for their deliverance and left a statuette of the Virgin Mary. Riccardo, veteran of numerous epics in the Andes and the Himalaya, returned to Italy with numbed fingertips and close calls burned into his long-term memory.

Six years later, several members of an expedition paid an even steeper toll for the first winter ascent of Denali: One died, and the three who made the top were frostbitten. Art Davidson wrote a book, *Minus 148 Degrees*, titled after the extremes of temperature during their 1967 ordeal. I often defended the team's decision to continue climbing after their companion's death. Certainly the book had been the headiest drug I ever absorbed as a sixteen-year-old. But after meeting the winter climbers, I thought it strange that they never climbed together again. It appeared that climbing the mountain in winter—aside from the obvious risks to fingers and toes—could also jeopardize the integrity of a partnership.

From 1971 to 1982, another dozen teams vied for the second winter ascent of Denali; no one even tried Mount Logan. These expedition-style teams stocked camps, dug in during storms, weathered high winds, and grappled with their sanity. Some lost toes; others saw God. Four Swedes bickered and split up. The soloist Johnny Mallon Waterman committed himself to an asylum. No one reached the summit.

We had a few advantages over the 1967 climb. Technology had improved climbing equipment, while changing philosophies allowed us to attempt the technically difficult Cassin Ridge alpine style, with no fixed camps or tedious load relays.

Will applied two tactics to climbing from his track and basketball years at Yale: competition and confidence. Whether at the bottom of a climb or the top of the key, Will shifted into high aerobic gear until the summit was in the bag or the ball was in the net.

In the summer of 1980, Will fell 100 feet into a hidden crevasse below the Cassin and pulled his ropemate to the brink before he stopped. Will climbed out unhurt. They retreated, although Will wanted to finish the route alone. In 1981 I, too, jumped crevasses and listened to avalanches pulverize the glacier during my first stab at the Cassin. My partner and I timorously settled for the easier west rib.

That same year, when I asked the Englishman Roger Mear to join Will and me on Mount Logan, 19,524 feet, I mentioned that the game was not only to climb it but also to get up without blackening fingers or friendships. Roger immediately agreed to go with us.

Roger called undue physical exertion "mindless graft." Nonetheless, following the tradition of the early British explorers, he flung himself on the least-traveled passages of the world. When asked about his "necky" winter climb up the north face of the Eiger, also known as the *nord wand*, he replied with typical understatement: "Right, 'twas a good climb, a wonderful place, you know?"

Roger was irreverent and mischievous. He would ridicule us as we strained at pull-ups or endured ten-mile runs. Will the Ivy Leaguer was initially piqued by Roger the queen's jester: rolling joints, pretending to lose car keys, or sleeping late. But after their uncertain initiation, they soon became an act, wholly complementing one another—and excluding me.

A month before our climb, in January of 1982, I tore ligaments in my ankle but deluded myself by casting it with a stiff double boot. Then the Canadian park authorities denied us permission to climb Logan in winter: "they didn't want to rescue us," they said; we quickly switched to Alaska's Denali. I had nightmares of falling through clouds and cartwheeling over ice cliffs with a flopping ankle. Or the wind would wrench me away from the mountain as the air exploded from my lungs and I wafted into the thin air flatter than paper. I wondered, but never asked, about Roger and Will's dreams. For consolation I returned to my visualizations, and dreaming with my eyes wide open, I saw us step-kicking and ax-punching in rhythm up the summit ridge, higher than all of the continent, higher than birds fly, higher than rain or grass or any being of North America.

For years, Will and I had argued the merits of our plans with anyone who would listen. We said that the southern ridge maximized our exposure to the sun. We told mothers, friends, and lovers—skeptics all—that we would be sheltered from the north winds that buffet the mountain in winter. With the prescience of air-conditioner salesmen badgering Eskimos, we bragged that February and March have the longest days of the dark winter, and we flaunted equipment designs that should keep us warm at sixty below. Most people, including climbers, thought us cracked.

Among ourselves, we reveled in Will's irreverent confi-

dence, Roger's hard-core alpinism, and my willingness to suffer. We were quite willing to push one another to the ends of
the earth and agreed to brook no weaknesses. Consequently,
when I contracted bronchitis just before leaving, there was no
turning back.

On February 17, 1982, we flew onto the Kahiltna Glacier
as Will muttered about white beaches in the Caribbean. As we
vaulted out of our skiplane, another team barreled into a second plane, so grim-faced after their failed winter ascent that
they stared straight ahead, refusing to acknowledge our ebul-
lient waves.

The wind poured a thirty-below-zero chill through my zippers and into my crotch like liquid ice. Since Will and Roger
pretended not to notice my coughing, I pretended that the
spasms were mere sneezes. True to form, Will strutted around
without a hat, remarking on how warm it was; Roger discovered a *Penthouse* stashed in his haulbag by some rude joker.

We set up a tent and promptly snapped a pole. The cold
would continue to break stoves and lanterns and zippers and
boots and cameras. Even removing a mitten to tie a knot
could cost you your fingers. Because cockiness was the only
way to disguise the layers of terror in our hearts, we never
discussed the cold, which shadowed us like an omniscient being.

Denali's winter mood was completely unlike the more be-
nign and sun-kissed summer pastels. Even the sunset was violent: The orange light was plucked right off the mountain as
it pulsed into abrupt nightfall. Unlike the perpetually lit summer climbing season, the sixteen-hour winter nights meant
that camp chores began and ended in the dark. That night the
Cassin Ridge stretched taut and arrow-straight beneath the
rounded summit bow, tinted violet by stars.

In the morning we put our heads down and trudged into
the relentless north wind, pulling loaded sleds ten miles

toward the Cassin. We made pitiful progress. I coughed and limped behind Will and Roger on the end of the rope, tilting back a bottle of cough syrup and chewing its frozen shards. Images of hot showers, warm beaches, and an ex-girlfriend plagued me like a toothache, while my ankle rode fat and unforgettable in its double-boot cast.

On the third morning our ten-foot-long snowcave tunnel filled in with windblown snow. Feeling a burgeoning morning urgency, I slipped out of my warm sleeping bag and struggled into my climbing suit, bracing myself for the inevitable hell outside. I wormed my way into the tunnel, shoveling and kicking back chunks of snow into our living quarters.

After twenty minutes of burrowing, I poked my head up into a ground blizzard. When I stood, the wind blew me to my knees. Leaning into the gale, I staggered away from the cave and futilely searched for a windbreak. In this nether winter world where fantasy merges with reality, I imagined a toilet flushing; I yanked off my mittens, unzipped my suit, and squatted until that loathsome wind blew me over and I was back in kindergarten: shamefaced, helpless, reduced to tears as I crawled back stinking into the cave. Unwilling to bear witness, Will and Roger promptly exited and performed jumping jacks in the wind while I boiled my underpants and suit, then dried them over the stove.

I had a recurring intuition that I was going to die during the climb. Worse than the specific nightmares of falling, I was now haunted by a diurnal dread that I had stepped away from the living. Discussing my premonition with Will and Roger would only earn their scorn, and they had made it clear that the climb demanded no less than three climbers. If I turned back, Will and Roger would probably be relieved, although our defeat would rest totally on my shoulders. Because I didn't have the courage to confess my fears, I grappled with the premonition constantly.

I wondered how it would be. A brutal but quick fall like Dave Shoemaker's? A painless nodding off from hypothermia? Or maybe I'd wait patiently to meet it while trapped in a crevasse like Chris Kerrebrock. If I could have laid down money, I would have bet that the summit would equal my last day, either in a storm, as in Wilcox's expedition, or with high-altitude illness.

I became the odd man out as Roger and Will became friends. The more they came to know and trust one another, the more I was excluded from decisionmaking, route-finding, and even the nightly philosophical debates in our snowcaves. When I had been strong, my relationship with Will flourished. Now, with a sprained ankle and bronchitis and my consternation about dying (my partners sensed this), Will openly castigated my weaknesses, yelling at me to pack faster, criticizing my route selection up an icefall, and berating me for dropping his water bottle into a crevasse. It now became a dangerous game because I was determined to show Will that I would not give up.

I had rarely risked everything for a dream. Knowing that our modern, soft world has removed us from much of the suffering and physical toil of our forebears, I wanted to harness those remnant genes and live by instinct and nerve endings. In the process, I wanted insight into this magnificent mountain, but I also wanted just once to exploit all my weaknesses, and by stripping myself bare to the mountain, discover of what pith my soul was made. So on the fifth day, I buried all my wimpy thoughts about dying and cut loose from the defeatist moorings of retreat.

One night, Will tried to define the wind. As it whipped and whistled out in the tunnel, he waxed Shakespearean—a subject he had devoted considerable study to as an undergraduate. With a sweeping gesture of his arms he announced that the wind was the breath of God. I never heard anything so false in my life.

As we left the snowcave, two ravens arrived and jumped down into the tunnel. They were looking for food. In Athapaskan stories, the "Great Raven" was the creator of the world. Even in modern times, Athapaskans make prayers to ravens, because as descendants of the Great Raven, Dotson'sa, the birds are purported to carry magic. Just seeing the birds was a good omen, and these ravens had flown a long sixty miles from the nearest forest to our snowcave.

On our fifth night we dug a palatial snowcave, with a customized "quick johnnie" chamber carved into the tunnel. Inside, Will disgustedly swatted at Roger's clouds of burning dope. Roger assured him he would stop once we began climbing.

My bronchitis dried up while optimism warmed us beneath the Cassin. Below the climb, on a wind-protected glacier called the Valley of Death, the sun lulled us into naps, sprawled over avalanche debris, until the cold shadow of Denali brought us awake, shivering. Ten thousand feet above, the wind sounded like storm-driven surf. Its waves crashed and broke over the summit, swirling giant banners of foaming snow over the southwestern face. Our route, however, lay still and taunting.

Early on February 27 we emerged from a snowhole beneath the Japanese Couloir. Roger couldn't get over the *Bergschrund*, so he stood on his pack, reached over the gap, and mantled up. We hoisted the packs, chinned ourselves over, and spurred by the fear of changing weather, we pumped our legs as fast as we could. Our calves ached under the huge packs.

It was impossible to avoid knocking plates of ice onto each other. When someone in the lead screamed "Ice!" the unhelmeted followers tried to duck beneath their packs. Four hundred feet up, Roger took a hit in the face and swore violently; his dark blood speckled the opaque ice like graffiti.

We swung our axes and kicked our feet repeatedly into the cold belly of the mountain. We were jumpy, nervous, yelling at each other to hurry. My left ankle felt good while frontpointing, but at each flat-footed twist, electrical jolts shot up my leg. I put each jolt into a little green box in my head and quantified the jolt's strength and its prickly texture and its exact relationship to my ankle, and in so doing I drifted far away from my automated climbing movements to a place inside my mind where I hid like a child. Roger and Will both remarked on my "self-absorption," and when they caught my eyes going dreamy and unfocused with the pain, they'd shout at me to climb faster.

We finished the twelve-hundred-foot gully fumbling with our headlamps. The night hung above as if it were the mid-Atlantic becalmed: vast and black and mirror-still. We tied ourselves into pitons and made our beds on a narrow rock shelf, swinging and clomping our feet over the void with great delight. Getting off the avalanche-fired glacier and coming to grips with the climbing felt so nice that we temporarily forgot the business above.

The stove's flames licked at a pot full of ice. Two hours later we slurped down freeze-dried swill, and when Will and Roger hurled my homebaked fruitcake into the void, I feigned indifference. We slept fitfully, wiggling toes and adjusting hoods, ogling the full moon as if it offered the heat of a lover.

Several hours before dawn we started melting ice for tea. Getting out of warm sleeping bags and pulling on frozen boots made us shut our eyes, clench our stomachs, and flutter our breath. Packing up was awkward with mittens, so we would take them off, make an adjustment, then rewarm our fingers in our armpits; our feet felt blocky and sore and distant.

Will and Roger raced without a rope to the east, axes squeaking in the Styrofoam-like snow; I caught up to them as they reached a rock cliff. As Roger led a hundred-foot cliff-band with down-sloping holds, Will and I looked away, cringing as we thought of Roger's seventy-pound pack. His crampons raked the rock like fingernails screeching on a blackboard. After a dutiful curse he was up.

We followed him onto a long ridge that sliced the sky and, to my delight, made the wind hum in subjugation. *À cheval* along this corniced arête, we kicked steps into the snow and ice for hours, weaving around cornices, oblivious to the space beneath. We laughed and taunted one another; I sang at belays. The mountain gave us what we had come for, and as we straddled it and held it and gently kicked it, I loved it more than I have ever loved a mountain before or since.

On such days you can see every snow crystal sparkle; at times I even thought I heard music. Some might say that we had too many endorphins rushing around in our heads or that we were surfing a tsunami and staring down at our own reef of mortality, but those people will never hug sun-warmed granite in subzero cold, gnaw icicles from their mustaches, or hazard that a mountain and its wind have become a living, breathing entity.

Our competitiveness, however, only grew, and the tension surged like a hot current along our climbing rope. If we didn't climb the Cassin quickly, we would have to answer to weather conditions beyond any of our experiences. So, fervently kicking around a cornice, then running across a knife edge, I pulled Roger off his feet behind me; snatches of blasphemy attached to my name blew past me in a fiery breeze. I now felt strong again, ready to match my partners step for step.

That night's campsite was the only flatness of the route. Instead of pitching our tiny tent, we jumped into a crevasse and chopped out a snowcave. Later, bathed in eerie ultraviolet glow, Will and Roger gagged on freeze-dried chili and dumped it into the crevasse's bowels. I forced mine down, hoarding every calorie.

As we slept, the wind gusted and swirled and shook at the cave entrance like a wolf worrying a caribou's flank. By morning our sleeping bags were frosted with snow.

There, at 13,500 feet, the climb became our only focus. We were married, chained, and bonded to Denali because a lesser dedication would have been dangerous luxury. Once we climbed higher, retreating during a winter storm, or even just surviving a storm, seemed unthinkable. We had to get up.

That day the climbing was superb, although strenuous. After stringing moves together across ice-plastered rock, I'd shout, "Boy, that'd be great with light packs!" Roger and Will replied with glowering anxiety on their faces, as if enjoying ourselves wasn't permitted. We clambered over tawny granite and gray ice, pinching rock with one hand, swinging an ax with the other. We rested on ledges, calves burning, chests heaving.

Because we couldn't afford to rest and acclimatize properly, we all had minor altitude illness. It was a question of getting pummeled by a storm, weakening to the cold, and being kited off by the wind versus dealing with headaches, weakness, and loss of appetite. We took the latter course, and if the cold had only tickled before, now we could feel its talons prickling our skin. Fear and dehydration now constipated me.

At the end of our third day of climbing, two weeks into our trip, we chopped a tent ledge into steep ice. Since it was too crowded for three, I built a separate platform with snow blocks and clipped into an ice screw. Then I lit the stove, put on a pot of ice, and hid inside my bag. Gusts of wind blew out the stove, or the pot needed more ice, so I would emerge from my embryonic cocoon, shivering and hating the cold.

My fingers turned wooden, and the blood crept back all too slowly as I winced and thrust my icy fingers into my crotch.

When the northern lights first appeared, I dropped the lighter in astonishment. A single ghostly strobe swept the horizon. Then the entire sky filled with tracers. I yelled, nearly knocking off the stove, while Roger opened the tent. Outer space was raining translucent bands of jade and saffron, stealing time and the cold away from us, reeling us beyond the bounds of our banal earth. Dinner somehow got cooked but had no taste; I no longer felt the cold.

The Koyukon or Athapaskan name for northern lights, *yoyakkoyh*, means "pulsing lights in the sky." Legends tell of an ancient man, *Yoyakkoyh Dinaa* (Northern Lights Man), who broke his bow while caribou hunting and later burned up in a fire. When the lights actually illuminate the land, as it did this night on the Cassin, it means that the Northern Lights Man is shooting his arrows into the heavens.

Sleep was elusive, so I gave a running commentary of the colors to Will and Roger, burrowed inside their sleeping-bag wombs while, raving like a lunatic, I studied the flaming heavens.

I knew then that the wind is not God's breath, but Lucifer's; it is the northern lights that are the aura of the Creator. Every man-made monument—from Buddhist temples to cathedral frescoes to paintings stored in the Louvre—will remain forever artifices, forever cast into the shadow of this night and its aurora.

Although Roger and Will kept rolling onto one another inside the tilted tent, their grumbling—like the distant neon glow of Anchorage—was overshadowed by the sublime specter that blazed above and around us. I felt lifted and freed from earthly cares, while my anxiety about the climb was replaced by exhilaration and spiritual awe. Finally, the world was born anew as the northern lights dimmed into dawn.

The days began to blur into one another. We grunted up rock pitches, leaning heads and knees wearily on the ice, always guessing how much farther. I kept looking over my shoulder, wondering when the Great Fly Swatter in the sky would squash us like the insignificant insects we were. When Roger dislodged a boulder from a long chimney, he screamed "Rock!" and I shrank under my pack. The forty-pound missile crashed a foot away and bounced fifty feet down, then crashed again and gathered more rocks, pounding down until I could no longer see them. Ozone filled my nostrils. I imagined falling with the rocks as if I had become the clipped bird of my nightmares, down past the blinking blue eyes of tottering seracs, feeling the air burst from my lungs as I cartwheeled through wreaths of cloud and bounced off slabs of pebbled granite and slammed into the maws of the crevassed glacier below, finally free.

The falling rock had come and gone in the blink of an eye, but when events move quickly and adrenaline surges through your vessels all day, you stop becoming afraid, as if you are experiencing everything from outside your body. The close call with the rock became a mere fleeting distraction. Roger shouted "Sorry!" and we cheerfully continued up the chimney together.

As the climbing became easier, we grew weaker from the altitude. The thermometer read forty below at 16,500 feet, so Roger hid our "negativity indicator" in the bottom of his pack. That night, Will dispensed sleeping pills—I did not realize that they are respiratory depressants that can predispose climbers to high-altitude pulmonary edema. The Valium allowed me to sleep soundly that night. At this point, I felt strong and healthy, with the exception of a minor headache and my anxiety about spitting in the face of the coldest winter on earth.

We wore every piece of clothing we had, and the wind still

came right through our customized suits. I didn't envy Roger, who was harassed by a headache and nausea that evening, taking his turn outside the tent like a dog.

Morning fell loud and clear, but I was stuporous and still groggy from the pill. We packed the rope away and I began step-kicking up a long couloir. Will and Roger followed on my heels, grousing about the distance between my hard-won steps. So I cursed back at them—our tacit mode of climbing communication. Near the couloir's top, I felt dizzy and let them pass.

Stomach acid clung to the back of my throat. After a brief rest, panting over my ice ax, I raced upward with a pulse drumming in my head. Lost in an otherworldly spell, I stepped on a patch of windslab snow, which broke away beneath my sore ankle and started me sliding. The world flashed around me: Distant icefalls and endless peaks and cobalt sky whirled with flying saucer clouds. I jammed in my ax pick and clawed to a stop. Through the fog of my pom-pom head and my now-throbbing ankle, I forced myself to concentrate, then climb. I caught up to them at eighteen thousand feet only because they had stopped. We chopped out a platform, then set up the tent, continually looking over our shoulders at the sky.

Now everything changed. I felt ever conscious of my earlier premonition of death. I performed the only option left: Hidden inside my sleeping bag, I assumed a praying position and whispered, "Please, please, please give us one more good day." In the grip of forces beyond my control, righteousness and prayer had come to my agnostic lips as if I had been born thumping the Bible. Such alchemy is frequently denied afterward, but during the heat of action it can shrink a climber's skin with all the swiftness of a frigid baptism. No one could deny that Denali rose higher and whiter than any church on earth.

We slept deeply, and it dawned miraculously clear.

Up, up we went while the tempo of the drumbeat increased in my head. My feet turned leaden. I could not find a rhythm, let alone go more than one step at a time. Will and Roger yelled for me to hurry up, but I could barely move, so after cursing like brigands, they pulled gear out of my pack to lighten my load. Still, I stumbled back and forth, woozy with Denali's thin air, a derelict destined for the gutter.

Finally, after a paltry thousand feet, they stopped and chopped a platform. When I arrived, their anger hung indelibly, like the calm before a great storm, because they could have gone on to the summit. Bivouacs this high on the mountain are foolhardy, maybe even deadly, because bad weather or high winds would trap us. But short of being dragged, I could not go on.

We piled into the tent. I was too weak to talk. My world spun and dipped and hovered as I held my head and tried to find my breath. Will plied me with tea while Roger looked out the door and analyzed the sky; they took turns looking out the tent, as if something were coming to get us. I'll never forget their wide eyes, the creases on their foreheads, the tension that shook the tent like the wind. Even sick, I knew how worried and scared and tiny we were.

I had destroyed our speedy climbing formula, so I closed my eyes and let sickness spin me away from the bitter realities into unconsciousness. That night the tent became a frozen coffin. We tossed and turned and rolled onto each other throughout the long, long night.

Just before the dawn I dreamed of drowning. I came alive thrashing and lunging for my sleeping-bag zipper, desperate for air. I sat up and realized that fluid had infiltrated my lungs: I had pulmonary edema, and I could steal only panting breaths.

It was here. I wondered if Chris and Dave had seen it so

clearly. Death is so omnipotent that it wins merely by reducing you so low and removing all of your hope and making you so scared that you simply give up and lay back and let it take you. Will's eyes betrayed his fear as though he, too, had identified the beast beating at the door. That day if there was a discussion about leaving me I knew that Roger would never hear of it.

While the stove roared, Will diagnosed my problem as a return of bronchitis and changed his socks. His two big toes were black with frostbite, but when Roger peered closer, Will yanked the socks back on. "Oh," he said, "it's nothing."

Stuffing my sleeping bag seemed to take hours. After breakfast, Will and Roger departed the tent as if leaving a funeral home and began pulling down the tent as I zipped the door shut. I steepled my hands together and prayed for good weather and the strength to survive the coming ordeal; there were no ravens foolish enough to come this high and hear me out.

Will heard me. He knew. "You say something, Jon?"

"No," I said, my breath bubbling. "Nothing."

There was only one option now: Praying wouldn't change anything; I would have to find my own resolve to survive the coming ordeal. Backing down our steep and complex route was never discussed because going up and over was the easiest way down. I followed their steps, oblivious to the sea of clouds I would see later in the photographs, oblivious to the passage of time, and acutely aware of the irrefutable heaviness of gravity that repeatedly sent me sprawling to the snow.

After several hours Will and Roger topped out on the Cassin Ridge, dropped their packs, and strolled the anticlimactic fifty yards to the summit. Roger photographed Will holding up his ice ax and they scurried back to their packs. They were not amused to see me crawling down below.

Will jogged down and relieved me of my pack. Twenty

minutes later, I finished crawling to the ridge two hundred feet below the summit. I looked briefly upward, but on this day my success would be measured in survival, not a summit. I could manage only two steps before collapsing over my ax and fighting for the privilege of breathing. The wind was mild but the cold was vivid and, despite wearing three sets of layered mittens, we couldn't touch our metal-topped axes. Somehow it registered that my toes had frozen.

We plungestepped down, and after a dozen strides I was completely winded. Even the descent of Denali's easy route was going to be tough. Roger and Will were too cold to wait, so I urged them onward. After several minutes I caught my breath, although sitting down in the hundred-below-zero windchill didn't improve my mood. I shivered violently.

I had to pace myself. Breathe twice for each step, then rest for ten breaths. Again, again, and again. I forced myself into the rhythm, eyes locked on my feet. It became a revolution not unlike our technique for speedy ice climbing, but I wondered how I could move with such diminished lung capacity. I flaunted the other option continuously, and each time I considered how easy it would be to lie down and let it take me, I berated myself for even considering it. When I gave up on cursing at myself, I deliberately twisted my ankle in my boot and felt the electricity wash over me in a salty wave that lent new definition to our short gift of time on earth with all its requisite pain and abbreviated glory and undefined love. I cried with the pain I inflicted on myself.

My partners watched and waited as long as they could in the cold. They shouted at me in shrill voices, alternately mad and caring, and after Will dispensed a tablet of Dexedrine to me, they left me behind. I swallowed the speed knowing full well it would be mere candy next to the natural adrenaline already being produced by my own body.

At Denali Pass I lay down for a long time, terrified I would even consider giving in to the demon squatting so heavily on my chest. It was a faceless, nameless presence, and just to spite the single greatest temptation I have ever been offered in my life, I contemptuously spat out a frothy green bile from my lungs and forced myself to my feet again. I tripped and tottered alone down the steep traverse known as the Autobahn, notorious for the many German climbers who fell, sped out of control, and wrecked themselves a thousand feet below.

Just before dark, I caught up to Will and Roger at seventeen thousand feet. Roger was curled outside the tent, so I crawled in with Will, thinking they might keep the temptation away if I couldn't. The tent walls shuddered with this awful presence, and inside I didn't bare my skin for more than a few seconds. Even exhausted, I could still enact my preprogrammed warming functions: Brush off snow; remove Gore-Tex suit, mittens, boots; get in bag; dry feet; warm toes with hands. I turned on my headlamp. "Wait a minute," I thought. "White toes! Frostbite?" I massaged my swollen bluish ankle and toes until I fell into a sleep racked by coughing.

Strong winds blew in daylight and clouds as we fixed cocoa in the tent. As Will dressed me ever so condescendingly, he looked me in the eyes and told me I would die if I didn't get down; then he shoved me out into the wind and I stumbled downward as they yanked apart the tent.

The sky darkened. Taking only three or four steps at a time was disheartening, but I thought I might get down. Will easily caught up and passed me while Roger stayed with me, cajoling and coaxing me downward. At 16,200 feet I Batmanned madly down the old fixed ropes, stopping constantly to catch my breath, not sure how much longer I could continue. I tried to downclimb the *Bergschrund* neatly, but in my sickened torpor I fell and landed on my back next to Will. He laughed. I'll never forget his laughter and the emptiness of our fallen friendship.

In the past, our partnership had rarely suffered because we had always been strong together. For seven years I had envisioned Will and me laughing and hurting and starving and lusting after ice-blasted mountains that no one else gave a rat's ass for. Although we would later be hounded by the media and receive letters and phone calls of congratulation, as I recoiled below the *Bergschrund* I knew our expedition possessed terrible compassionless proportions. Ours was a breakdown of humanity.

I lay gasping on my back. Maybe we were both delirious, or perhaps Will was trying to scare me into moving, but after I suggested calling a helicopter, Will suggested to Roger that they leave me. No sooner had the words left our mouths than the clouds swirled apart and we saw climbers below. The seriousness, the madness, and the isolation all disappeared as we smiled for the first time in a week.

As we stumbled down, some Brits walked uphill with congratulations and hot tea. I stared at them, speechless, exhausted, elated. They pumped our hands and we looked up at the mountain wondering if we were dreaming. Someone helped me untie from the rope. "We're alive," I said to no one in particular. Later, in their snowcave, we warmed up and the mountain disappeared. While their nurse massaged my toes, one Brit confessed that when they had first seen us they thought we were crazed because our expressions had been those of asylum escapees. The weather would not permit the Brits to reach the summit.

In the morning Will was angry, no longer willing to wait for me. His blackened toes mandated immediate descent. Fortunately, I had now recovered in the thicker air, so we roped up and raced one another down the low-angled slopes.

We reached our seventy-eight-hundred-foot cache that afternoon and dug out some food. Will apologized to me (at Roger's behest) and said his frostbite was his own fault; he had already diagnosed my own frostbite as minor. Will was denying his own actions, and I wondered how we could ever set things straight. The words froze in my mouth, so we acknowledged without speaking that this climb had wrecked our friendship.

Will announced a bout of competitive eating, and since we looked for any distraction to conceal our disappointment with one another, we glutted ourselves with canned ham and pineapples. Then Will reminded us of his toes, so with distended stomachs we packed up and trudged toward base camp in the gathering dusk.

Darkness hit quickly, and we became puppets jerking along to the pull of Will on the rope in front. Unlike Will, Roger and I had no snowshoes and often broke through the crust, floundering in deep snow. Mincing strides seemed to give us a few more yards without smashing through the crust. Sometimes we crawled, which was slow, but it prevented us from wallowing. On the final "Heartbreak Hill," Will untied from the rope and snowshoed ahead to dig out our landing-strip snowcave and fix hot drinks. Roger collapsed several times, and I went back to cajole and coax him onward. Over and over again, he murmured the name of Sir Robert Scott, who had died crawling back from the South Pole in 1912.

Recovering in the snowcave, I couldn't believe we had climbed the Cassin in winter. Roger came alive, too, so we dug out a Walkman and listened to Judy Collins while sipping steaming cocoa. The music stirred me deeply. When I realized the extent of our sensory deprivation, how much we had suffered, how far the cold and the dark and the altitude had twisted us, I ducked into my sleeping bag and let the briny tears wash my face.

When I came out, Roger was grinning contagiously, holding his breath. Smoke filled the cave and Will was coughing, trying to wave the cloud away. Will said the climb hadn't really been difficult and he had never felt extended; I half-believed him. Roger's lungs were close to bursting and his eyes were narrow slits. He offered me the joint, but I waved it off, because I could scarcely control my emotions.

By our second day of waiting, our various irritations with one another and our tardy bush pilot would no longer permit normal conversation. The cave turned into a soot-blackened repository for all of our frostbitten misery. We ached to leave this frozen hell and endlessly fantasized about the pleasures we would own once we escaped.

Unbeknownst to us, our pilot flew in three Spanish climbers on our third afternoon of waiting. Although he saw our ice axes and crampons lining the cave entrance, we could not hear his shouts, so he flew back out.

At dawn I hobbled out into the subarctic gloom and discovered the Spanish tent. At this point I no longer knew what was real, so I shuffled over, yanked off my mittens, then rubbed the tent fabric between my fingers. The Spaniards woke up, unzipped their door, and jumped back when they saw the stark and childish terror on my face.

From then on the only subject Will and Roger and I talked about with any mutual accord was our pilot's rationale in leaving us stranded in subzero anguish. Although Roger had been the only uninjured one among us, on the fifth day of waiting he fell into a crevasse and destroyed his knee cartilage so badly he could not stand. Thereafter, three derelicts grunted monosyllabically at one another, limping out of the cave only for matters of the toilet. Food rationing began. Will began "obsessing," explaining to us that he was attempting telepathically to impart guilt in the mind of our missing bush pilot.

Fortunately, the Spaniards swore they would not begin climbing Mount Hunter until we were successfully evacuated. On the eighth day, after our *compadres* dug the word *OUT* in forty-foot-high letters, a passing bush pilot came to our rescue.

The depressive ennui that followed our unsuccessful high adventure totaled me. Out in Talkeetna Will emphasized to the reporters that I didn't go the last ridge to the summit, and I knew Will well enough to see that he was really saying that the weak or the sick didn't belong at his side.

Next to climbing Denali in winter, everything—relationships, work, exercise—seemed worthless. It took me months to readapt to normal living. While I recovered from my frostbite (nearly losing an infected toe) and inertia in Colorado, a friend lent me a room and a car, which I promptly crashed into the garage. Because I had squandered all on Denali, I had neither a cent nor a job.

Other climbers heard of our "success" and invited me on the big Himalayan trips I had always dreamed of. I told them that Denali had defeated me; I told them that I had quit climbing and I told them that summits had lost all meaning.

My inability to quit the climb, even with the red flags of injury and sickness waving in my face, can be written off to competition and the brashness of youth. But I am still haunted by the betrayal of a friend, by a cold with claws, and by a wind so corrupt I could smell its breath as it knocked me onto the glacier with my pants fouled with shit. I did not lose my innocence in 1964 when I saw my grandfather's corpse, nor with my first lover in 1973. I lost my innocence on the Cassin Ridge in the winter of 1982.

In the ensuing years my back stiffened as I heard about the third winter ascent of Denali. In February 1983, after Charlie Sassara and Robert Frank had reached the summit, they began descending fifty-degree ice. Both were unroped and exhausted from their accomplishment. Suddenly Frank, who was twenty feet above Sassara, yelled "Falling!" Frank knocked Sassara off. While Sassara managed to brake to a stop with his ax a hundred feet lower, Frank cartwheeled thousands of feet, spraying flecks of bone and skin and blood as he smashed his way down the west rib. Sassara picked up a two-inch chunk of his partner's flesh and descended to camp, stunned. No one ever found Frank's body.

In February 1984, the Japanese soloist Naomi Uemura disappeared after trudging down alone from the storm-washed summit on his birthday. That April I helped twenty Japanese search for Uemura's body, but we never found it.

In the winter of 1988 Vern Tejas soloed the west buttress. Tejas, who had been inspired by Uemura, not only showed the world that the mountain could be soloed in winter, but he also climbed it during a stormy February, *sans* frostbite or serious mishap. The following winter, Dave Staeli walked in to solo the Cassin. He took one look and wisely proceeded up the west rib.

Meanwhile, three Japanese alpinists, who had climbed several Himalayan giants in summer and winter, were blown off the west buttress and killed. Staeli abjectly snuck up to the summit a day later. Although the Japanese autopsies read "hypothermia," anyone who has withstood the breath of Denali in winter knows that the wind murdered them.

During these climbs, I envied the climbers not a whit; I worried about them a lot. I occasionally run into these winter survivors of Denali—Art Davidson and Dave Johnston and Charlie Sassara and Vern Tejas and Dave Staeli. But when we greet one another in Anchorage, we stop and look into each other's eyes and beam at one another with little talk. We know full well what we got away with.

Climbing changed for me because of the Cassin. Now I like to revel in the mountain's virility rather than my own. I like to say that in eleven trips, with friends and clients, I have only put the summit beneath my boot soles once, via the west rib in 1981—which feels more than fair. Certainly I have gone high on the mountain many times, but once always seemed to be plenty. Trampling the summit regularly seems part sacrilege, part conquest, and more to do with business than climbing.

I like to say that we climb because mountains are sacred places and climbing is a form of worship. We climb because the mountains are our church. Indeed, *It*—the Chief Guide, Raven, God, the Great Fly Swatter, or Buddha—can't be greater than flaming arrows shooting into the heavens at fifty below where the wind hums over a fin of ice and the light cuts right through to your soul. Most importantly, by bringing myself over the edge and back, I discovered the passion to live my days fully, a conviction that will sustain me like sweet water on the periodically barren plain of our short lives.

In 1983 Roger wrote an understated article for *Mountain* magazine that showed the power of the mountain while omitting our near collapse as human beings. Will also wrote a concise account of the climb, laced with a didactic evolution of Alaskan climbing, for the 1983 *American Alpine Journal.*

According to the long-held Victorian traditions of mountaineering and the "sacred bond of the rope," writers rarely divulge any disagreeable personality details from a climb. Nonetheless, while living in Colorado during the winter of 1982–83, I published in 1983 issues of *Climbing* and *Appalachia* a forthright, stream-of-consciousness rendering about our failings. Will, still in denial, subsequently initiated a letter-writing campaign to many of our mutual friends.

Will even tried to solicit Roger's support against me, but Roger refused to take sides or make any judgment about who was at fault. Nearly a year after the climb, Roger mailed a letter to me. "You have my respect," he wrote, "well earned for the guts and determination you came through with. . . . As for Will, I'm real sorry for the way it turned out and selfishness he showed—I thought I got on well with Will in the initial stages but my feelings now are of a lack of trust. In that I'm sure he'd not think twice of dumping anyone to save his own neck.

"So in all it was good to do the climb but the unity or lack of it leaves a hollow feeling. Please don't get the idea that I do not put myself to blame, I do. I'm sorry I didn't show more consideration to your plight. The trip was an expensive lesson."

After surgeons overhauled Roger's knee, he returned to Alaska in May 1983 and limped up an unclimbed, saber-edged ridge on the coveted Mount Deborah. Afterward, he was nearly arrested in the sleepy hamlet of Cantwell, two hours north of Talkeetna, for counting his own change out of the cash register. When he got to Talkeetna his smile lit my afternoon.

Several years later, still gimpy, Roger pulled a sled to the South Pole, retracing the footsteps of Scott. He refused to carry a radio, his support ship sank, and he went into six-figure debt. In 1991 he and a partner flashed up the Diamir Face on Nanga Parbat, one of the boldest, most idealistic, and unpublicized Himalayan climbs in years.

While Roger had moved on with his life, Will and I were still trying to come to grips with the winter climb. One weekend he and I arranged to meet on a hillside in Utah. He greeted me with the usual gibe from ten years earlier: "Still dating those fourteen-year-olds?" The conversation further faltered as Will accused me of slandering his name, and as we both tried to wrest apologies from one another, the din of Salt Lake City below grew louder and we stopped talking altogether.

Will went on to bag a new route on Annapurna IV in the Himalaya. He got married, splintered his leg as a result of a long fall in the Alps, and fathered a daughter. In 1989, just before the sap ran in northern Vermont, we met again. He was thirty-six, I was thirty-two. Encountering Will that day was extraordinary and unplanned. He lives in California and I live in Colorado. Our spontaneous rendezvous at the home of some mutual friends (Guy and Laura Waterman) could only be explained as one of the inescapable circles that connect climbers' lives. His arrival at the remote cabin was announced by four whitetail deer charging out of the clearing and into the protection of the forest. When he clomped onto the porch and came through the doorway, surprise painted both of our faces.

My skin prickled with terrible and textured remembrances: the acrid smell of falling rocks, Will's anger when I dropped his water bottle into a crevasse, and the mountain trembling as an avalanche crashed down beside us. At first I couldn't speak.

The timbre of Will's voice was as familiar as an old rock-and-roll tune from high school, and I was surprised to intuit his thoughts before he spoke. Undoubtedly I did the same for him as I finally opened my mouth and asked him about his career. I could scarcely imagine Will as a team player on a hospital staff. His stately, protruding eyebrows jitterbugged above an unlined face, and he had the same untended chocolate mop of curls. I said that he looked no different from before.

"What did you expect," he asked, "an old man?"

Still, the climb would not go away, and we were held apart as if Denali sat between us on the table. We exchanged stilted formalities for a long hour. Finally I asked him if he wanted to go for a walk. He pulled on his double boots.

We strolled side by side up the trail and sank into the snow rather than walk behind one another. Neither of us knew exactly how or where to begin, although our intended destination was clear.

As a preamble, I called it providential that we had met again. Without knowing my next words, I blurted out that I had been trying to forget what happened to us on Denali. I told him that nothing would make me happier than to go climbing or skiing together. In turn, Will told me that he recently soloed Yale Gully, stopping midway at a bulge where we had passed the guide and client twelve years earlier. Will said that he treasured these memories, and I instantly recognized the kinder and higher-pitched burr to his voice. I also knew that we both made mistakes—all of which can be forgotten. We laughed. Too soon and we were standing at the trailhead exchanging addresses.

The following winter, Will wrote to me (and a dozen others) about an ice climbing reunion at Lake Willoughby. "We have a return appointment with the Glass Menagerie. . . . I have been shooting films of climbs so we can watch ourselves on TV at night in the motel. On slower nights we can head south and find a Clint Eastwood movie to make our day. Perhaps even a brief return to Huntingtons Ravine is in order, although I hear that the ravines 'have the worst weather in America. Many have died there from exposure, even in summer. Turn back now if the weather is bad,' " he wrote, quoting from the familiar sign from our youth.

I didn't go. Only one climber met Will in Vermont. I half-heartedly invited Will to come backcountry skiing with me in Colorado, but nothing ever came of it.

A year later, at the American Alpine Club meeting in San Diego, we met again. I was surprised to see him because he used to declare that formal climber gatherings—with all their attendant glad-handing and self-congratulation—were a waste of time. But he let it slip that he had come to be with friends. I introduced him to several people and watched him insult a magazine editor about the dearth of "real literature" in

climbing magazines; then he neglected to congratulate a
climber for succeeding on the penultimate mountain, K2.

Sunday morning we matched one another's strides during a
long run along the beach. Will breathlessly derided the medical accomplishments of the keynote speaker, who was widely
considered the grandfather of high-altitude medicine and was
my generous friend. I had also presented a mountaineering
film, and Will roundly criticized it. Nothing had changed. A
mutual friend confided that city life and Will's family dilem-
mas dogged him relentlessly; while lashing out at everyone
around him, he held his own problems in so tightly that he
seemed ready to explode.

Through all of the lectures about other climbers and different mountains, we hung near one another and endured the
weekend. It felt as if we were still relying on one another, but
uncomfortably so, as if still jailed in that putrid, soot-smeared
cave during the winter of our discontent. Because of our competitiveness and our numbed toes and our mutual betrayals,
we know one another better than I know any other climber,
or any climber knows me. As those around us basked in their
own deeds on warmer and higher peaks, Denali preyed on
both of us.

Will wanted to do the right thing. Finally, when no one
could overhear, he said something in his tiny voice that made
me crave my old friendship with Will Sayre, despite all else.

"You know," he said, "we really pulled off a coup up there,
didn't we?"

6

TOURS OF DUTY

Something besides courage and determination is
needed to climb a mountain like this. Forgive me if
I call it intelligence.

—ROBERT DUNN, *Shameless
Diary of an Explorer*

BY A GRIEVOUS ERROR OF THE FEDERAL RECRUITMENT REGISTER,
and my own recondite need to pursue Denali, the National
Park Service rehired me in May 1982. My employment
thwarted the efforts of a few ranger bureaucrats in Colorado
determined to bar undisciplined climbers like myself from re-
joining their ranks.

For the next four years Denali National Park coerced me to
explore the untrammeled corners of Alaska. Traditionally, my
ranger cohorts and I opened each year with a week-long
training patrol. So in late March of 1983, four of us flew into
the Kichatna Spires, fifty miles from Denali, where we would
gaze up granite walls, carve telemark turns through champagne powder, and try to justify our $8.65 per hour existence.
Our mission was partly to learn about the "blank spaces" on
the map that climbers always asked about. And as rangers
employed by Denali National Park, our mountain "boondog-
gles" were considered on-the-job training.

Our ski circumnavigation of the Kichatnas would be an
enlightening yet simple seven-day adventure: skiing fifty miles
to a hunting lodge. No climbing or suffering, just ski touring.

151

Nine-to-five government work. Good money, fine companions, no epics . . . or so I thought.

From our post in the village of Talkeetna, another ranger, Scott Gill, and I flew in first. The Spires soon rose below us: Polished granite thrust from the glaciers, hundreds of summits rankled the clouds. We stared uncomprehending, dizzy for the privilege of such unlikely suspended grace. Our rookie pilot dropped the plane onto a sparkling snowfield and touched down with a bounce, his nostrils flaring, hands nervously fluttering the wheel back and forth. Sallow-faced, he craned his neck to detect lurking crevasses.

Recently, on a different flight, our fearful pilot had miscalculated while making a landing and flipped the plane upside down; out of courtesy, we avoided mentioning his painful *faux pas*, not wanting to get the poor fellow more gripped than he already was. I had begged my boss to let us fly with someone else, but he rejected this plea. "The Park Service," he said, "can't patronize just *good* pilots."

After unloading our gear, and with the exit of our reluctant aviator, we looked up the nearest hill. Scott underwent his usual transformation while standing in powder snow. While the plane strained up into the air, the pilot shuddering at the helm, Scott stepped into skis like Lawrence of Arabia mounting his camel. I followed his tracks up the hill.

As Scott and I ski-signatured the slope, our colleague Roger Robinson and our Park Service superior Bob Gerhard landed on the glacier. For four years, these people occupied as prominent a position in my life as family. Roger jumped out of the plane, gesturing wildly, muttering whatever popped into his mind, and turning his camera on the omnipresent Kichatnas as if to gun them down.

Robert Gerhard, Mountaineering East District ranger, was a portrait in self-effacement, ceaseless work, and complete and incessant loyalty to the U.S. Department of the Interior.

Nonetheless, he took good care of us; in return, we sometimes wore our uniforms.

The next day we entered telemarker's heaven, loosing our sleds down from the top of a pass and cutting hundreds of ski turns behind them, whooping with joy, weightless powder snow feathering our waists.

The snowstorm began that night. When we peeked out of the tent in the morning, huge, uncompromising flakes filled the air until our entire world took on a white opacity.

That third day we trudged though deepening drifts, our faces bent into the wind, our bodies submerged in the maelstrom. Days three and four were worse. The leader broke trail in an exhaustive, monotonous stride: Slide one ski out, weight it, sink up to the thigh; slide the other ski out, weight it, sink. We took turns plowing at the front, stopping regularly to dump ten extra pounds of snow that would accumulate on our sleds. We had barely covered two miles, so we began food rationing, worried about escaping these now not-so-casual mountains.

The next morning, as we each slurped down our half cup of hot cereal, avalanches thundered down the chestnut-colored granite towers and onto the ivory glaciers. We halfheartedly broke trail for an hour, questioning the odds of reaching the now thirty-miles-distant hunting lodge, where our pilot would pick us up. Wary of dangerous snow conditions, and temporarily accepting defeat, we stopped wading and set up the tent.

In any other situation, tentbound like this, my associates and I would have passed the time discussing the opposite sex, exchanging climbing lies, or plotting future mountain extravaganzas. But in the boss's presence, we respectfully talked about how we could do a better job, how we could communicate more effectively and avoid hours of idle gossip with climbers that kept us from working, and how we would fix up the ranger station—a derelict, moldering trailer perched un-nervingly close to the railroad tracks on the edge of Talkeetna. Naturally, we all fell asleep from sheer boredom. Even Bob.

On day seven Scott and I took to the slopes. The weather cleared and the Kichatnas rose above us, cloaked in veils of blue ice, or frosted with snow. We put in a track to the base of Mount Jeffers and took off our ski skins, then swooped bliss-fully through crystalline powder as if we had wings.

We all heard an airplane that day—or thought we did. Ev-ery time we stopped, we heard droning and buzzing—the god of the propeller, coming to relieve us from further trailbreak-ing. Many other bone-weary climbers, hunters, and trappers throughout Alaska have experienced the "phantom propeller phenomenon," but Bob had an explanation: radioactivity. "It's true," he said. "People claim the Kichatnas have extraor-dinary uranium deposits." We never argued with our boss.

Our pilot didn't look for us that day, let alone fly to the lodge on this appointed day of our pickup. Of course, the hand-held radio was useless unless the pilot flew directly overhead. Scott and I optimistically ate all of our lunch food, burning off incredible amounts of calories while skiing in the cold air. The weather soured, and since it looked as though our plans were being buried, inch by inch, we resumed sur-vival negotiations. We had to make our own way out, despite dangerous avalanche conditions.

In a blizzard on the eighth day the four of us set out for the distant lodge, resigned to the fact that if we didn't reach the lodge, we would not get picked up. We trudged, half-blinded, over a pass. As we tiptoed around giant crevasses, an ava-lanche poured off Nevermore Spire and thumped down onto the glacier, scouring the slope beside us. This filled Scott, the ski patrolman, with perverse glee. When the tent poles fell out of Roger's pack, Bob and I swore like brigands waiting for him to backtrack and play pick-up-sticks.

After threading among the crevasses, we found the Monolith Glacier in a complete whiteout. We coasted for miles over the featureless landscape, occasionally poking out at the snow with a ski pole to affirm we were actually moving. At times the pervading white became so disorienting that one of us would fall over like an imbalanced drunk.

Finally we stumbled off the moraine and along a river lined with thick alder and occasional stands of spruce. Dinner was six ounces of soup mixed with instant mashed potatoes. For after-dinner conversation, we blasphemed men who fly bush planes. "Where is our fucking pilot?" we wondered bitterly, knowing that we were overdue. With addled reasoning we theorized that his absence could be due to a long drunk, a new girlfriend, another upside-down landing somewhere, or maybe just the typical Alaskan rancor of the "Feds." Whatever the alibi, we were here and he wasn't.

In the warmth of the tent during our pitiful excuse for breakfast, Roger pulled up his shirt and displayed the ribs of one whose malnourished body was consuming itself. Bob had lost his desk worker's paunch and, in an effort to inspire us protégés, gave us a dissertation on Gandhi's epic fasts, which included drinking his own urine. I offered Scott the contents of my pee bottle, but he graciously declined.

That ninth day we were in bad shape. I couldn't stop skiing in the subzero cold for two minutes without my toes and fingers turning wooden. Scott bragged about how much food he would take on his next patrol up Denali. As we forged a trail toward the overcast Moose Pass, ghostly ptarmigan began flushing out of snowholes. These were sleek and unblemished creatures, but in our state of hunger, we saw only barbecued wings and breasts and legs squawking through the air.

Scott, Roger, and I dove at the startled prey, thrusting and batting with our ski poles.

Bob maintained his composure, however, saving his energy, preferring starvation over decimation of the wildlife he was sworn to protect. These birds we had always thought stupid and slow were now in their element, and with maddening ease they fluttered out of reach. After an hour we gave up, empty-handed, exhausted, and even hungrier.

We pressed onward. Soon Roger pointed at a spruce tree and joked, "Dinner, you guys!" Beyond his finger perched an Alaskan "thornbird"—a porcupine gnawing on a branch. Bob was disgusted that we would even joke about eating a pro-tected creature of the park and continued trailbreaking; Robinson dutifully followed. As they disappeared from sight, Gill and I exchanged knowing glances.

We did the deed mercifully, as quickly as possible. The snow fell in a lazy *danse macabre* as I knocked the critter out of the tree and Gill performed *piolet* porky.

The next step was to skin the fifteen-pound porcupine, carefully avoiding quilled revenge. Athapaskans accomplished this by throwing *dikahona* (stick-eater) into a fire and roasting the barbs off, but we had no time. By skinning it out from the smooth belly, we managed to keep our hands quill-less.

Scott and I knew that the National Park Service wouldn't discharge us over this wanton carnage (it would be easier to keep the paychecks flowing than process weeks of termination papers), especially under the circumstances. We debated an immediate cookout, or even a quick sushi-style porky, but, being thoughtful savages, we wanted to share our plunder.

Scott and I followed the others' trail to a half-buried hunt-ing shack. We hunched through a doorway into the dim inte-rior and without a word I proudly unveiled my plastic bag of meat and dangled it in front of Roger and Bob. Their eyes glared with momentary disapproval, but their stomachs churned with a rush of digestive juices and overruled whatever moral outrage they felt. Our pact was sealed.

We stoked the rusted-out woodstove and hung up sodden clothes, dazed by the luxury of a roof, salivating in anticipation of the coming feast. Bob cooked up the first course, carefully ladling out half a cup of spaghetti to his handpicked personnel; we inhaled our portions within a half minute. With stomachs revving, we watched our commander savor every bite and sustain his meal for nearly five minutes—the GS-9 teaching his underling GS-5s the meaning of discipline, leadership, and grace under fire.

We had now missed out on several days of regular meals; our pilot was two days overdue. On a hot desert island, it would have been different, but here, with temperatures below zero and all of our trailbreaking exertions, the craving for calories was well justified. We had metabolized much of our body fat; muscle tissue was vanishing from our arms and legs. Another few days of this and we even would begin to see the rationale behind cannibalism.

Porky's lilliputian legs and rib cage hit the pot water with a splash. We sprinkled in the last dregs of soup mix and brought it all up to pressure in the cooker. After boiling for a half hour, the concoction smelled so awful that another hour passed before we dared remove the lid again.

Athapaskans also ate porcupines, but only in the late summer, when "stick-eater" was fat and its taste compared to that of pork. Starving rangers might be the only people stupid or hungry enough to eat a lean porcupine so late in the winter. The cabin filled with a resinous stench, worse than a retriever bonefart, as Chef Bob pulled apart ribs and passed them around. Everyone snatched a leg. At first we chewed tentatively, briefly doubting its digestibility, but then we chomped wholeheartedly into what little fat remained, oblivious to the stringy texture and livery, spruce-sap taste. No one talked.

Bones snapped as we sucked the marrow. Someone wiped his chin, another burped, and our shrunken stomachs bloated as we threw the splintered bones into a pile the size of a shrunken porcupine.

We slept warm and somewhat satiated, our dreams filled with images of lascivious women, a certain bush pilot hog-tied at the Park Service firing range, and banquet tables bowed under with food—all swirling wildly in a Felliniesque bacchanal. At dawn, back in the clutches of reality, we bounced our last and already used teabag in boiling water as the sun rebounded into the sky.

Athapaskan lore says there is no retribution from the stick-eater's spirit for killing or eating it; nonetheless, we now felt a little bit sorry about our deed. If we had a better sense of geography, as the low-slung *dikahona* was reputed to, perhaps we would not have been forced to eat it. "The whole of Alaska," as one elder once told his son, "is just like something inside the palm of a porcupine's hand."

We took turns trailbreaking on the eleventh day, marching along silently, heads bowed to the grueling task. Through moose yards, meadows, a marsh, spruce forests. Pulling up a long hill, we reached the top of an open plateau and discovered that our toil would soon end. The snow became shallow and windpacked, and the lodge appeared only a mile away. We raced like horses to the barn, filled with trailhead fever and gluttony; newfound strength emerged from muscles sapped by hunger.

Our arrival at the lodge startled a young caretaker. He hadn't seen a soul for weeks and assailed us with a seamless barrage of chatter—clearly, he was suffering from the uniquely Alaskan disease of cabin fever. Bob managed to squeeze into this one-sided conversation long enough to ask if we could use the lodge radio to call our pilot in Talkeetna. As the caretaker led us into a spacious log building, one of us mentioned food, but the man just kept on talking. Bob set the prototypical ranger department example: smiling, nodding, listening raptly.

Meanwhile, Scott, Roger, and I may have been only seasonal employees, but we knew we had entered the food storehouse. We tried to keep our eyes away from shelves stacked with canned fruit, bags of Oreos, crackers, bread, meat, vegetables, beans, potatoes—the manna of our dreams.

While I was wondering how I might broach the food subject tactfully, Roger put off all decorum and dove right to the quick, interrupting the caretaker in midsentence: "Do you have any food we could"—Roger searched for the right word —"*borrow?*" The boss received this unprofessionalism with a scowl, but Scott and I felt only unbounded respect for Roger's forthrightness.

We followed the caretaker into the kitchen like wolves to a kill. He threw us a box of crackers and cookies and some cans of fruit. Bob tried to set the proper tone, daintily picking up a cracker and holding it, unbitten, in front of his mouth while listening politely to our host. Our ill-mannered trio assailed the box of crackers: gone in scant minutes. Scott tore into the cookies as I inhaled canned peaches with assembly-line efficiency. The contents of a can of sardines swam down our throats. Bob, contemplating the second bite of his cracker, was appalled but slid his chair back to give us room.

Even the lonely caretaker stopped babbling to watch the strange ranger gluttons at work: We finished off the appetizers without using the silverware, and, as we picked up crumbs from the table and checked the floor for spillage, the caretaker threw a loaf of bread with a half-cooked caribou sausage into the feeding area.

By this point Bob was so repulsed by our activities in the kitchen that he was forced to leave. He stuck his head in the doorway sometime later to announce that the plane had arrived. We seized the last piece of meat and offered our greasy hands to the caretaker, thanking him profusely. Seated in the plane, no one could begrudge the pilot. Even though he had not come to pick us up on the appointed day, we weren't at the lodge. I loosened my belt and smiled, thinking that maybe I was ready for a vacation.

The Park Service was never unkind. In return for nearly ten tours of duty, a patrol up Denali, and assorted rescue work, my employer granted just enough paid vacation for my colleagues and me to squeeze in yet another ski trip during days off. The only problem was in deciding where to go, for Alaska presents a bewildering repast of peaks.

Scott and I recruited another connoisseur of high mountains, Andy Lapkass. We loaded up my customized 1970 Dodge Dart (slick tires braced with snow studs, rust-ravaged, vomit-green paint job, a single headlight, and a screwdriver in place of the lost ignition key), then left immediately for the Wrangell Mountains, home of mostly dormant and eminently skiable volcanoes such as 16,237-foot Mount Sanford. This particular mountain has become sought after for ski descents because of its relative accessibility and 10,000 feet of skiing from summit to tundra.

We drove for five hours, dodging citizens out practicing the state's number one sport: drinking and driving. Being smart rangers, we avoided making contact.

Since we didn't know the bush pilot in Gulkana, we accepted him with no questions asked; we had no choice. He seemed to be a pleasant apprentice who probably had passed all his written tests and just needed several thousand more flight hours to become a safe pilot. First he flew in Andy and Scott. When he reappeared and pulled the Super Cub over to me, he unexpectedly gunned the prop to turn the plane. I dove to the ground and narrowly avoided decapitation.

I watched my main man closely during the flight, wondering about these amazing planes and the men who seemed equally amazed by flying them. Although the flying was no problem, landing the plane really worried me. I even began to miss the eccentric pilots of Talkeetna.

We landed hard on a gravel strip, bounced five feet, then plummeted and bounced again amid a flurry of small stones. When I opened my eyes, I saw Gill grinning, then sprinting away from the airstrip as the Super Cub drew closer.

We left the 3,000-foot-high airstrip and struck out across the tundra in the general direction of Mount Sanford. Although the mountain was hidden by the clouds, we knew that by walking south we were bound to run smack into it. Since my companions summarily left me in the dust, I substituted my savvy route-finding abilities for their brute strength and tried to beat them by walking along a stream bottom as they jogged across a circuitous-looking ridgetop. This alternate route left me floundering in mud and willows, spooked by a nearby grizzly, and cursing under the weight of my pack and wounded pride.

That night we camped on tundra above the Sheep Glacier. Sharing one tent with two other six-foot packhorses can be compromising indeed. Scott removed his eye-watering neoprene socks, pedicured himself, and dumped the nails into the cookhole; he then fell into a sleep racked by guttural snoring and farting. I had suffered similar hardships on dozens of patrols with Scott, who liked to point out that sensitive-nosed grizzlies almost always avoided our camp.

Certainly, the most seasoned outdoorspeople in Alaska would be lying if they said they had not pondered a bear mauling at night—when grizzlies like to roam. Scott, Bruce Adams, and I had once chartered a floatplane to the headwaters of the Talkeetna River. We inflated our raft, set the oars, and let the river pull us to the white-water rapids of "the canyon." Grizzlies were swimming the river and fishing the banks for the last fall run of silver salmon.

Our first night we camped on a small island. We sipped from a flask of bourbon, and the darkened wilderness around us became a great joyous respite from all the pressures and complexities of the "civilized" world sixty miles away. We knew there were wild animals, but we supposed that they feared us more than we feared them. This was our home, our earth in all its brisk autumn glory, with its barrier thickets of yellowing alder bushes lined with thorny devil's club, its roaring rivers, its glaciated mountain, and its unpredictable bears. Just as on our Sanford trip, we would not have traded that cold, pitch-black wilderness night for any city on the planet.

Before sleeping, we concurred, with slurred voices, that if a grizzly terrorized our camp we would fire three shots in the air to scare it away. If Mr. Bear chose to stay and maul us, we would use the remaining three bullets to commit *seppuku*, and then the hungry bear could eat us trespassers in peace. Bruce crawled into a sleeping bag under the stars, while Scott and I escaped the frost inside the tent and placed the handgun between us for quick access. We were loaded with our own hubris that night, unwilling to admit our darkest grizzly fears.

I dreamed of drooling grizzlies puncturing our raft and leaving us up the creek with paddles but no boat. At two in the morning I sat bolt upright: noises outside. I listened carefully and heard it again: a bear swimming the river. Then, as rounded stones clicked on the shore, I could almost picture the bear shaking water from its fur like a great shaggy dog. More clicking from the stones, and then behind the tent. I thought the bear was avoiding us and walking around to chew up our raft tied on the opposite shore.

Scott snored softly at my side, and rather than wake him needlessly, I quietly clutched the cold gun and slid out the open doorway of the tent. To reach the raft, I stepped over

Bruce, visible under the amethyst starlight as an oversized, frost-covered cocoon. Just as my foot came down beside his head he opened his eyes, assuming that I was a bear, but rather than make any noise and incite a mauling, he waited until my shadowed form moved toward the raft. Then Bruce screamed in an unearthly voice: "IT'S A BEAR! FIRE THE GUN! IT'S A BEAR!!"

Scott sat up in the tent, thumped the shoulder of my sleeping bag only to find it empty, then groveled fruitlessly for the gun. Within seconds he screamed back: "JON'S GONE! THE GUN'S GONE!"

I had now reached the raft, still intact, and finding no bear anywhere, I fell on the gunwale and began laughing. Our anxiety about grizzlies had reduced us to prowling sleepless in the middle of the night and crying out at unseen monsters in the dark.

After being roundly cursed out by my companions, I refused to give the gun to Bruce, who would shoot the next time he detected anything suspicious. Bruce joined us in the tent, and we pretended to sleep until Scott got up and circumnavigated the island at dawn. When he came back he summoned his deepest basso and announced, "Jon, I looked for your *bear.*" He paused, and joined Bruce's penetrating stare. "And there are no tracks anywhere."

Fortunately, that morning beneath Mount Sanford, once we climbed onto the barren glacier—*sans* forage—bears were no longer a concern. After two interminable days of uphill plodding, I convinced Scott and Andy to stop at 12,000 feet to allow my body to return from anaerobic purgatory.

On the summit day Andy went into high gear, forging a trail all the way up, dragging us breathlessly in his wake. I staggered up to the top, kicked my ski tails into the snow, and flopped onto my pack to enjoy the cloudless view. I gazed across hundreds of miles of tundra and forest to Denali, then imagined the Kichatnas to the west. To the north, beyond the earth's gentle curve and far from sight, lay the Brooks Range, dipping its vast north slope to the Beaufort Sea. I could see more mountains than one could ski or climb in several life-times, but the High One—shimmering with white heat, speckled with pink granite ribs, as compelling as the ocean—commanded my attention. There is no other place on earth where the unique combination of high mountains and low plains allows you to discern mountains more than two hundred miles away. Alaska and its highest peak are phenomena of geography.

The finest days of my life were committed to that alp on the horizon. How many people could say that they had built a career around a mountain? How many lifelong friendships had I made in air as inviolate as sapphire, where no bird sings, where dozens of corpses lurk beneath the snow? Would the mountain ever loose its hold on me?

While I lounged on the summit, contemplating a distant Denali, the ultimate rule in ski mountaineering dawned on us: What goes up must come down. As one, my companions and I stood. We stowed the rope, battened the packs, and locked heels into bindings. In tight departmental formation we pushed off into knee-deep powder, aiming our tips toward the tundra, 10,000 feet below, and Denali, 230 miles away.

7

THE MOUNTAIN BY ANOTHER MEANS

There was spring in the air. A few bare spots here and there and ptarmigan cackling all around us. It was if we were starting a new life with only summer and sun and as if the last days and nights were the end of everything hard, cold and sad in this world. Never had we felt so happy to be alive.

—ERLING STROM, ON THE
TUNDRA, WRITING IN HIS
JOURNAL AFTER COMPLETING THE
1932 MULDROW GLACIER SKI
ASCENT

WHILE TENDING TO PAPERWORK IN THE TALKEETNA RANGER STAtion, my feet propped on the government-gray desk, I grimaced about our patrol up Denali. I was out of shape, and lately salmon fishing seemed much more appealing than climbing.

But even rescues, cleaning up feces, and advising countless climbers seemed a holiday compared to office work. Most of all, I ached for the velvety slip of skis sliding under my feet, the wind biting my face, and a descent down the Muldrow Glacier.

Bob Gerhard had directed me to hire some responsible climbers to accompany this patrol. I said that I knew hundreds of climbers but no responsible ones. The boss, desiring not to be distracted by trivial matters, left this personnel decision up to me. I invited Dave Wood and the husband-and-wife team of Jeff and Kellie Rhoades. We set out in mid-May from the Denali landing strip, planning the first cross-country ski descent and traverse of Denali. The evolution of mountain climbing follows a simple enough formula: The first time, you just get up the mountain however you can; then you climb a harder route; then perhaps you climb it in winter; and finally, you ski it. But we were not the first to use skis.

In 1928 the Norwegian Erling Strom first laid eyes on Denali and became engrossed by the idea of skiing off it. Four years later he was joined by Alfred Lindley, Park Service superintendent Harry Liek, and Ranger Grant Pearson—who had never skied a day in his life. In 1932, just approaching the mountain was an epic, but thanks to dogsleds, the team set up camp beneath the Muldrow Glacier within a week, then strapped on their skis. "These things," Pearson wrote after numerous faceplants, "are just a fad."

Skiing all of the knife-edged Karstens Ridge was not an option. They did succeed in climbing both the north and the south summits, even though skiing off the summit was not feasible on wooden skis with leather bindings.

On July 5, 1970, with modern alpine skis and boots that would have made the 1932 ski expedition blush with envy, Tsuyoshi Ueki and Kazuo Hoshikawa became the first to ski down the entire mountain. They were filmed by a Japanese television crew, and like a few dozen skiers who followed over the coming decades, their greatest difficulty was rasping enough oxygen into their lungs while jumping off the 20,320-foot summit.

In 1972, the Swiss skier Sylvan Saudan hired six porters to carry his gear and cook for him. One of Saudan's disgruntled American porters, Steve Hackett, told an Anchorage reporter that Saudan was too unfit and harried from the snowstorms to make it to the top. Indeed, two hours below the summit,

Saudan ordered a halt. Saudan even had the audacity to market his film, *Skiing MacKinley* [sic], which shows Hackett helping the Swiss star into his boots "at the top" (clearly the plateau 1,000 feet below the summit), while Saudan begins whacking Hackett for pushing on the frozen boots too hard. Soon enough, with a radically tilted camera, Saudan starts windshield-wiper turns down the 5,000-foot couloir. Although his descent was briefly known as the Saudan Couloir, it was later named the Messner Couloir after the man who first climbed it and went to the summit in 1976. During his U.S. video tour in 1992, Saudan still insisted that he skied off the summit.

In 1982, French extreme skier Patrick Vallencant mushed to the base of the Wickersham Wall on a dogsled. Vallencant's coral-colored jumpsuit made his more plainly dressed entourage of camera boys, cooks, and aides-de-camp blush with a peculiar Gallic jealousy and rage. Although Vallencant had skied the 26,400-foot Broad Peak in the Himalaya, he took one look up Denali's 14,000-foot wall, cloaked beneath its usual storm, and said, "It is not right." Never mind the several-hundred-thousand-dollar film budget. Vallencant swallowed his pride and caught the first plane out—never mind the plan to kayak 100 miles out to the ocean after the descent.

When I interviewed Vallencant in Talkeetna, he was ordering a hamburger with all the trimmings. He told me in broken English that he simply could have climbed up, then skied the West Buttress Route if he wanted to, and with a shrug of his shoulders, he said, *"Est très facile, comprenez-vous?"*

On our own 1983 ski trip, Dave Wood was selfless. He was also strong as a bull and cursed in a Canadian-burred joking eloquence that was inimitable. His impatience was like mine, so during the first day on Kahiltna Glacier, I understood his rambunctious energy.

Jeff Rhoades balanced our restlessness with a casual, almost lazy style. Beneath the surface throbbed a steady-pulsed excellence in everything he did. A few years earlier, Jeff had skied Grand Teton, a precipitous 13,766-foot peak in Wyoming, his jumpturns sweeping the snow with the precision of a Swiss watch.

Kellie Rhoades skied with 5-feet, 2-inches of finesse, etching telemarks with all the rhyming longevity of a Robert Service poem. Otherwise, this tenacious young fireplug imparted manners to what otherwise would have been a team of barbarians. The first night out, Kellie got sick, although she wasn't complaining. If it had been possible, Dave, Jeff, or I would have traded places with her. In the morning she felt fine, so we packed up camp.

At 11,000 feet we were trapped by a storm that howled for three days. We took shifts shoveling out the tent. After one evening of negligence, we awoke completely drifted over by a wall of snow. Jeff wormed his way out the side portal and dug us out.

In the morning we found several rips in the tent fly and one pole bent grotesquely. And we all took turns with "tent fever," despondent and depressed from the lack of action. During a lull in the wind, we broke out of our trances and climbed up Motorcycle Hill, then skied 1,000 feet of powder snow. I thought relaxing was the key as I faceplanted, then watched Jeff, seemingly born with size 210-centimeter feet, then Kellie, tucking cautiously into her turns, and finally Dave, fast, hard, and sure—the same way he broke trail with a big pack. And it was fun again, laughing at the storm, stomping our feet to stay warm, and savoring the fullhearted happiness of powder skiing.

On the seventh morning the 11,000-foot camp came alive

with whipped climbers, baying their retreats after the windstorm. To my relief, an unfit Swiss climber who asked for a rescue had "recovered" and started down with a Norwegian.

I passed out plastic crapper bags to French, British, Italian, and American teams, disappointed that they didn't follow the "clean climbing" talk we regularly gave at the ranger station. Snow for cooking had to be chosen carefully from the wasteland of brown turds.

Bowed over in the wind, we hustled up to the 14,300-foot camp. I felt sanguine because the 60-mile-per-hour breeze at Windy Corner didn't seem to upset anyone; we were rolling with Denali's punches. When we arrived at 14,300 feet, Brian Okonek and Dr. Peter Hackett grilled us halibut inside their heated medical camp wall tent.

Hackett is a world authority on high-altitude sickness. For years he has been the principal investigator at this medical camp, along with a redoubtable team of climbers, doctors, and researchers. Their primary goal, research, was often performed on sick climbers in exchange for a night of oxygen— or for saving their lives. Despite the gourmet cuisine, I politely refused Hackett's various admonitions to test a new drug, have a bronchostomy tube stuck into my lung, or allow them to do a spinal tap.

Unfortunately, the medical camp's presence seems to encourage a lack of self-sufficiency among those climbers who are inexperienced on Denali. Word had gotten out that if you were in trouble on Denali—cold, scared, or sick—you could just check into the "medical clinic." Nonetheless, Hackett, Brian Okonek, and their colleagues had rescued many climbers.

We took it slow the next day, acclimatizing and getting to know the other climbers. That night it snowed without wind, and the skiers in camp could barely contain themselves. In the morning we broke trail up to 15,000 feet. The first ski run was glorious, with new velvety snow spraying over our heads and caressing our faces. Still acclimatizing in the thin air, we finished the run blue in the face, wheezing over our ski poles.

Skiing is perhaps the easiest way to introduce your body to high altitude, so our days were filled with the breathless rush of skis beneath our feet. Climbers bound for the summit tramped by us in endless, solemn-faced lines, laden with heavy packs, while we simply lugged our skis up and soared down the slope like raptors testing our wings.

Between ski forays I fulfilled my official duties by wandering around camp with plastic bags in my pockets, delicately broaching the subject of waste disposal. My pitch started with the usual weather commentary and then a bit of idle gossip. This logically segued into my question "So, by the way, where do you shit?" I would then launch into a field briefing on how to dig the proper latrine and line it with the bag. I finished explaining that this receptacle was to be disposed of in the nearest large crevasse.

Demonstrating the toilet training scenario was easy, if tedious; the real work lay in trying to improve my skiing. My frustration centered on some undefined kink in my technique —maybe it was a lack of technique altogether—and I wondered if I was forever destined to boost group morale with spectacular faceplants. Meanwhile, the sun parboiled my face until I discovered that I'd accidentally put dish soap in the film canister labeled as sunscreen.

On day eleven we carried loads to 16,200 feet. The following day, at the medical camp, Dave tried to shake his bronchitis, while Jeff and Kellie volunteered for medical sleep studies. I got a jump on my janitorial duties and spent two days alone at 17,200 feet, chopping out feces from the ice and cleaning up trash. When the wind blows this high basin free of snow, human feces dot the ice like an overused cow pasture. Snowcaves and unused tent sites are rife with leftover food and packaging.

Back at headquarters, the Park Service paid $20 an hour to bearded men in large suction trucks for performing a similar mission at dozens of outhouses. I worked for less than half the pay and no small loss of face if other climbers caught me in the act of "burly chipping." It entailed locating my quarry, not unlike misshapen Baby Ruth candy bars in the snow. Then I would tighten the wrist strap on my ice ax and proceed to chop around, but not on, the frozen objects. Finally I would open up the large plastic bag and herd each turd inside with a shovel. At the end of each day I would march to the crevasse field, then, with a banshee scream, fling my findings into the very bowels of the mountain.

By noon on the twelfth day I had hauled several sledloads of abandoned garbage and frozen feces to a crevasse. While sorting through this refuse like a derelict picking through the city dump, I watched Brian Becker and Rolf Graage stagger down into camp.

Graage's toes were frozen, swollen, and purple. With help from Okonek we lowered him to 14,300 feet. Although these climbers had completed a daring new route on the southwest face, their climb was diminished by their need for a rescue and their complete dependence on the doctors below. After Hackett dressed the frostbitten climber's toes, the duo soon began eating everything in sight. To the great relief of the medical camp, Lowell Thomas, Jr., flew the thankless Graage out to the hospital.

The next afternoon Okonek and Hackett arrived to report a Japanese man with a broken leg at 19,500 feet. Hackett broke trail at a demonic pace, but since his fly was unzipped, he frostnipped a vital organ. Although Okonek and I considered ourselves compassionate people, we let Hackett perform the rewarming by his own ingenuity.

We stumbled upon Chiba, the victim, at midnight, stuffed him into my sleeping bag inside a haul sack, sealed him up, tied him off, and spent the entire morning lowering him to 17,200 feet.

It was a rough ride for Chiba, bumping over small cliffs, crevasses, and rough ice. During our frequent rest stops, we occasionally leaned on the haul sack, quickly jumping off when the tiny man blurted out his sole words of polite English: "Rescue, preeze."

Time slipped by, and dawn lit the sky in a tenuously linked spectrum of colors, more serene than any meadow of wildflowers. I watched Hackett fall asleep from exhaustion, then joined him slumped over on the rock-hard glacier, rime bearding our faces, spittle freezing on our chins.

Then Okonek arrived. "Gee," he said, "what a neat evening, huh, guys?"

At 6:00 A.M. we floundered across the 17,000-foot plateau. Kellie and Dave handed us hot drinks, and we slept in the tent until afternoon. Hackett rebandaged Chiba's leg, then left with Okonek to tend to other medical camp emergencies. I spent the day sleeping off my twenty-seventh birthday.

The next morning two passing climbers volunteered to help me lower Chiba. To his credit, he smiled the whole time. And he never complained unless someone sat on him—the perfect victim. When he was finally unwrapped, still smiling, he hugged and kissed the nearest rescuer.

Meanwhile, as Dave descended, debilitated by bronchitis, Jeff reached the summit and plugged his boots into telemark ski bindings. Some climbers walked by, knackered by the rarefied air, shaking their heads in disbelief. Jeff took several deep breaths and jumped off the summit headwall, skinny skis chattering on the concrete snow, his legs burning from the turns. He finished the several-hundred-foot-high headwall doubled over his poles, gasping for air. Kellie walked behind, watching carefully, amazed at her brazen husband.

At Denali Pass, several hundred turns later, he took one long look down the thousand feet of ice known as the Autobahn and wisely took off his skis. When husband and wife came back to the tent they were wobbly-legged, happy drunks, exhausted and elated from their day. It had been a dream come true for Kellie—attaining the summit of North America—and for Jeff—skiing off it. That night the snow pattered soft as cottonseed against the nylon tent walls.

At noon the next day we lashed ourselves under monster packs in front of compromising sled-drag bags. We reached the 18,200-foot Denali Pass after three thankless hours of trailbreaking and consoled ourselves with the promise of skiing down the other side. The recalcitrant sleds caught on rock-hard snow mushrooms, so we strapped on our crampons —at least it was downhill.

That night after eating crunchy tuna noodle casserole, we drank quarts of hot tea. For dessert, we called the ranger station on the radiophone. Happy laughter filled the background: Scott Gill was having a party.

"Yeah, guys, it's too bad you're not here," Scott said. "We've got salmon barbecuing, moose steaks, a huge salad, and chocolate cake for dessert."

Kellie and Jeff rolled their eyes. "Thanks, buddy," I said while holding down the transceiver button, "Park Service clear."

Over the next two days we delighted in the isolation and silence of Denali's north side. There was no garbage, no burly chipping, no trail markers, and no people. Routefinding without a trenched trail is indeed a rare privilege on such a crowded mountain.

Although Jeff contemplated skiing the knife-edged, blue-iced Karstens Ridge, like Strom fifty-one years earlier, he knew that losing an edge would equal a four-thousand-foot plunge. After Kellie gave her husband a long warning look, we began cramponing down the ridge in the setting sun, sashaying in and out of the clouds, watching the light go from yellow, to red, then pink.

In the morning Kellie and I had to tear Jeff away from his book, *The Happy Hooker*. Griping about losing fifteen minutes, we waited impatiently for him to pack up, but soon enough we were jumpturning down the Muldrow Glacier, end-running crevasses, then coasting downhill.

While we were circumventing the Lower Icefall, fifty yards ahead of us an avalanche spewed a thunderous wave of rocks and ice blocks a mile across the glacier to the opposite side. Many tons of debris filled large crevasses. After a few minutes the cloud of ice particles settled. We sat on our packs, stunned and shivering. If we had been even fifteen minutes earlier— the amount of time it took Jeff to read about the Happy Hooker servicing a client—we would have been buried forever.

At midnight we skied into a National Outdoor Leadership School camp and were treated to bacon, hash browns, and gritty cowboy coffee. We continued down in slush to an Outward Bound School camp and woke up the instructors by shaking their tents and growling like grizzlies. Lured by the promise of flowers and green grass, we staggered onward, only to stop dead in our tracks beneath McGonagall Pass, too tired to walk the last uphill steps.

In the tent Kellie cooked popcorn and I dropped vast handfuls toward my mouth as I lay half awake on my back. The others laughed at the kernels strewn in my beard and around my neck inside the sleeping bag. I fell asleep smiling and dreamed of a huge wooden table overflowing with platters of fruit and vegetables and meat. Then I was routefinding again, circling indigo crevasses, cutting hundreds of turns, tied in tightly to my companions.

Two friends met us in the morning with fresh fruit and bread. Snow fell on the pass as I stopped to look at the flowers brightening the gray landscape, waking me to a world I had forgotten.

We napped a mile below the pass as snow built on our shoulders. When the squall passed, an arctic ground squirrel approached; I held my breath. The original Athapaskan inhabitants of this land called it *huddaggaza* (it stands erect over an area). In a moment symbolic of our return to the world of rushing streams and wildlife and greenery, the squirrel walked up on my knee and licked the salty sweat from my leg.

We camped that night in a lush meadow. The late sun rambled along the horizon, casting a warm glow over our camp, our sodden sleeping bags, and into our souls. Coming off the mountain onto the tundra, I began to realize the timeless, priceless value of the Alaskan wilderness.

The next day we staggered beneath our crippling packs. Rest stops became mosquito torture stops, so we walked all day through mosquito metropolis with our skitips waving like ten-foot antennae above. Past tundra swales and miles of boot-sucking mud. Balancing over rotted logs. Across Clearwater Creek and down the old rutted horse trail.

Standing above Turtle Hill, we looked out over the McKinley River and back at the mountain and over tundra that stretched as far as eyes could see. We ran down and crossed the river as one, our arms wrapped around one another, giggling against the cold glacial torrent that filled our boots with silt. Then we walked those final miles to the campground at Wonder Lake.

It would have been wise to stay in the backcountry, but we wanted to experience a night of camping in designated tent sites with other people, to reintegrate ourselves into the real world and to shed packs once and for all. We got into the campground just before midnight. Any other night, we would have been tired. Yet this night was our last, and we were giddy from our experiences, beyond exhaustion. We joked about *The Happy Hooker* avalanche; running out of toilet paper; Chiba's "Rescue, preeze"; and Kellie's water-bottle toiletry during bad weather. We would have talked all night, but a lumpy, elderly woman in a plastic raincoat strode over from a nearby campsite. "Shhhh," she hissed. "Quiet down—we're trying to sleep!"

The woman's maternal tone caught us completely off guard. The boom of an avalanche, a crampon crunching in the snow, the wind snapping nylon, or even the howl of a wolf pack we could've coped with. This woman, however, was too much.

We tried to hold it back. At first it was a trickle of giggling, hands over our mouths. Then we could no longer contain it, and the laughter flooded out of our tent and across the entire campground, a tremendous ruckus. We laughed and fell over one another until we cried.

The woman came back and scolded, "Don't you have any respect? My husband and I have to get up early in the morning and we'd appreciate it if you quieted down in there. Otherwise we'll have to call a ranger!"

We burst into laughter immediately. Wiping the tears from my face, I wished I could somehow explain where we had been and what we had done together and why we needed this release. I managed to get everyone quieted down and hoped the straight-backed Wonder Lake rangers wouldn't come and bust us for disturbing the peace—no one would have believed I was a ranger.

Several hours later I woke up to the red-orbed sun caressing my face through the tent doorway. A loon cried from Wonder Lake, a cry that was at first comparable to talking, immediately followed by a louder and lower-pitched wail, followed by yodeling laughter. The common loon is identified from other loons by a white necklace around a black throat and head, and a black and white checkered back.

Athapaskan legends tell of the ancient man who became *dodzina* (the common loon), restoring another man's vision. In return, *dodzina* was given a cape with a black and white shell pattern—remaining on the back of the loon until this day.

Its call is described by Athapaskans as "the greatest voice that a human can hear" as well as a significant inspiration for all creative thought. I could no longer sleep. It was 5:00 A.M., and my companions were nestled tight and sound asleep.

I slipped outside with my camera. The mountain stood eighteen thousand feet above, twenty-five miles distant, sparkling in the still air, so clear it seemed I could touch it. I felt close to some truth that morning, as if the wilderness dawn held something, some secret, and if I only looked hard enough, I might find it, even though the loon had vanished. I set out with my camera and promptly ran into the elderly couple packing their car.

The man began reprimanding me for our evening of indiscretion, our rudeness to his wife. He looked me over from head to toe. "You couldn't possibly be a lover of wilderness," said the man.

My heart fairly leapt, for he had hit it all and I knew he would understand me. I stood back because there were no showers on the mountain, then asked, "Do you know where we've just come from?"

He seemed taken aback. "No."

I pointed to Denali, a brilliant ghost spilling over the sky and across the horizon. "We've just come over the mountain. We've rescued some people and we've been out a long time together."

He smiled. The gap was bridged. We talked about the

places he had been, the wilderness, and how nothing compared to this. I wished him and his wife well. We shook hands. Then I started down the road, not certain of any destination, just walking aimlessly and trying to put everything in perspective. When they drove past we smiled and waved to one another. As the car disappeared and dust settled on the road, I held my breath to avoid breathing their exhaust.

I turned to study the mesmerizing white wall, the High One, rising out of the tundra hills with more vertical relief than any mountain in the world. I sat down. Some juncos flew by and faded into the distances surrounding me. What was I doing here in this great shadow, chasing Denali like a lunatic with a butterfly net? I wondered if being with Denali was the remedy for my life, if I was squandering my youth by running around this subarctic, high-latitude piece of inanimate geography.

In the end the mountain gives no quarter to our banal interrogations, only an existential beauty so deep and wild and stunning that you can lose all self-absorption if you just accept Denali for what it is. I breathed deeply, closed my eyes, and lay back on the spongy tundra, losing time and space and all my petty cares.

8

IN THE SHADOW OF DENALI

The early people who lived around the mountain spoke in riddles (initiated by "Wait, I see something:") rich with metaphor. "Stars," for instance, also meant birds because both lived in the sky; great flocks of birds would perish after hitting the High One.

> Wait, I see something:
> The stars are rotting on my sides.
> Answer: Denali.
>
> —EARLY ATHAPASKAN RIDDLE

HERB ATWATER WAS AN ATHAPASKAN WHO LIVED ACROSS THE RAIL-road tracks from the Talkeetna ranger station. His Fu Manchu mustache and his broad-cheeked face made him appear a lot older than his twenty-four years.

Herb and his father's father's fathers passed on oral stories about their beginnings, dating from the ancient "Distant Time," when "Raven" created the earth and all its beings. Rather than fictional legends or myths, Athapaskans consider the ancient stories to hold more evolutionary truth than, say, Darwin's *Origin of Species* and the Bible combined.

In the Distant Time, when all the humans died, they were transformed into the animals and plants of today. The respect that Herb Atwater felt, but could not articulate, explained his love of the wild game he shot, the salmon he hooked, and the beauty of the mountain.

In 1908, his people's story of Denali's creation was first documented by Jette, a Jesuit priest:

> When Raven was a man he paddled across an expanse of water to marry a woman. When the woman refused his hand, Raven made her disappear, incurring the mother's wrath. Two brown bears were asked to drown Raven, but using his magic, he managed to calm a path through huge waves sent by the bears ripping up the shore.
>
> Eventually Raven grew exhausted, threw a harpoon, and fainted. When he awoke, the waters had changed into a great forest; the wave that his harpoon stuck on had solidified into Denali.

Nowadays this tale has been forgotten and ignored, although Herb had heard it as a child. He was always curious about the mountain and asked many questions. Each time I took it to the next stage and hinted at inviting him on a ranger patrol, he begged off. Herb was clearly afraid of the mountain, and although he did not consciously admit that the mountain held great spiritual power, his blood coursed with the genes of respectful ancestors.

One morning during salmon season, I found a freshly caught coho salmon, still silver and untarnished from its long swim, mysteriously sprawled on the kitchen counter and waiting to be eaten. Athapaskans called coho or "silver" salmon *saan laagha* (summer swimmer), prized for its fat and richness. Herb was the only one who could have left it.

In the afternoons, Herb would wait quietly in the ranger station for the climbers to depart; then Scott and I fixed peanut butter sandwiches and a thermos of coffee and walked out with fishing rods. You had to run to keep up as Herb strode to Whiskey Slough; Denali stood fifty miles off like a brilliant and cloud-drenched sentinel. Herb would stop suddenly, pull off his ragged rucksack, and yank out a bag full of cured salmon eggs. Brandishing a gleaming six-inch knife, Herb deftly skewered the salmon roe, passed me a golf ball-sized hunk with the tip of his blade, and silently directed me to bait my hook.

Herb smiled a lot when he was fishing and hunting. He never used any high-tech fishing accouterments—polarized glasses or hip waders or Gore-Tex raingear. Yet he always knew where to find the fish, and where he saw crimson, black-spotted underwater life, Scott and I saw only rocks or swirling patterns on the streambed.

In certain years, during the big spawns, the waters coursed with red, writhing fish. Or as an Athapaskan riddle goes:

> Wait, I see something:
> We come upstream in red canoes.
> Answer: The migrating salmon.

After Herb pulled his salmon ashore, he killed them immediately by smashing his knife handle against their foreheads. He then pushed his blade into the fish vent and slit the belly up to the gills. If the fish was a female, Herb would cup one hand, pull out two coral-colored clusters of eggs, and carefully slide them into a canvas satchel. He popped stray eggs into his mouth like caviar.

There in the shadow of Denali, Herb taught me everything I know about salmon. He showed me how to cut the head off tight above the neck and tighter still with the fillet knife along the spines, wasting no meat and always flinging the innards back into the fast-moving river whence they came. At the time, I thought Herb was simply cleaning the house he lived in. But age-old traditions, instituted long before the modern environmental movement, mandated that all animals be treated with respect. Even after fish were killed, their remains had to be cared for properly. The spirits of animals could linger for days around their dead bodies.

Back at the Atwater house, we filleted the orange meat and hung the strips up in Herb's smoke shed, or cut the big fish crosswise, wrapped the steaks in newspapers, and set them gently into the six-foot-long freezer. Wild meat was never lacking here, and Herb's mother, Nellie, would grill us fresh salmon or moose steaks. As we drank cup after cup of acrid coffee, Herb shared his fantasy about moose hunting with his eight-inch handgun, or landing a salmon bigger than his 150 pounds.

In turn, Scott and I often spoke about our rescue work on Denali. Herb clearly preferred his ancestors' name for the mountain, and although he was too timorous to speak disdainfully of the white men who renamed the mountain McKinley in 1896, he sat up in his chair, put down his cigarette, and beamed when I first pronounced the Athapaskan name. While being up on Denali defined my own life, hunting and fishing defined Herb's. We tried hard to understand one another.

Herb had fished in the waters of Denali since he was a child, and he wasn't about to stop when the authorities closed the fishing. Once, while flying a helicopter up the mile-wide Susitna River, the fish and game cops spied Herb standing blithely up to his ankles in mud, dabbing his line in the tannin-colored waters of Birch Creek. Since the area was closed to fishing, the authorities immediately landed their Bell 101 helicopter between Athapaskan angler and birch forest. Herb, clutching his halibut fishing rod, jumped directly into the slough. As the "fish cops" screamed "Hey, you! Stop!" Herb surfaced beside a game trail into the thick alder on the opposite bank and disappeared as cleanly as a wolf.

He had been chased again by the fish cops, and he had been caught three times, but he refused to repent by informing on other illegal anglers—a common practice served upon Alaska's fishing criminals. When his license was revoked, Herb simply fished at night. He explained that you should never pay the fines because the fish belonged to everyone and as long as you respected and lived off whatever you killed, that was *real* law and order.

Herb would not talk about his work. Every fall, after he finished jarring salmon and butchering a moose, he traveled north to work at the Prudhoe Bay "oil patch," or south to an Anchorage construction site. He fit pipes and pounded nails for union wages that made our ranger salary appear a pittance; the rest of the year he collected fat unemployment checks. But Herb was diffident about money: It meant nothing to him. Nor was he meant to live in the modern working world. Herb was truly, as the cliché says, born a hundred years too late.

I always thought Herb wanted to come when we were called off on rescues. One Friday in August, we were asked to join a search for a missing hiker in Denali National Park; the Atwaters told us to be careful. Scott, Roger, Bob Seibert, Randy Waitman, and I immediately drove north to headquarters.

Gretta Berglund, twenty years old, had backpacked with her family in California and spent five weeks as a student in a wilderness educators' course in Wyoming. Although Gretta was one of a legion of wilderness connoisseurs who frequent the parklands, like most tourists she had more love for the out-of-doors than hands-on skill. Camping out in Wyoming under the tutelage of several instructors would provide most people with just enough knowledge to kill themselves in unforgiving Alaska.

My partners and I had learned that our backyard was vastly more rugged and unpredictable than that of the lower forty-eight. For instance, passing through a mile of dense alder and willow thickets can cost you five hours, and possibly a good mauling if you surprise a sleeping bruin.

Avoiding grizzly bears is sometimes feasible by day, but by night the bears often wreak havoc while you try to sleep. And while grizzlies might run off with all of your food or crack your skull like a walnut, a cloud of bloodthirsty buzzing mosquitoes can slowly drive you insane. I had witnessed otherwise gentle alpinists—people steeped in the art of suffering stoically—who stooped to petty vengeance by sitting behind tent bug screens for hours at a time, luring mosquitoes to the screen, then plucking out their tormentors' proboscises with tweezers. But Gretta came during a snowstorm that killed off the mosquitoes.

There was one more Alaskan difficulty about which Gretta had learned only the bare rudiments. When Gretta confronted a stream in the Wind River Mountains of Wyoming, she had simply grabbed a stout wading stick, pulled on a pair of sneakers, and unbuckled her pack waistbelt in case she fell in. She then waded up to her knees in crystalline water as fat trout flashed by. But in Denali National Park the glacial rivers are clouded with particles of rock called glacial till, preventing you from gauging either the next foothold or the depth of the water. Trout would perish here.

Most sensible backpackers consider Alaskan river crossings —in 36-degree-Fahrenheit, thigh-deep water—to be the most difficult part of every outing. By the time you arrive on the far shore, linked arm-in-arm with your companions, your body is clenched in a form of rigor mortis, your teeth are chattering like castanets, and your brain is locked in a severe ice cream headache.

Taking a solo trip into the Alaskan wilderness was something that my ranger colleagues and I had all undertaken once, but not twice. Clearly you needed a companion to share the route-finding decisions or to link arms with on river crossings. And stumbling too far into the wilderness of your own undiscovered psyche was dangerous stuff. As the northern lights lick the celestial palate above, the deafening silence of uninhabited open spaces preys on your mind with a ringing so loud that you feel compelled to scurry back for the trailhead—but here the only trails are meandering muddy ruts from flighty bands of caribou. As our backcountry ranger brethren were fond of saying, "Denali Park backpackers should be comfortable getting lost."

Gretta had chosen a solo overnight hike over to, then alongside the steep, three-mile Sanctuary River canyon. If you were accustomed to this kind of subarctic canyoneering, you could travel along the river by circumspect balance moves over polished river boulders, some short but technical scrambles over rotten cliffs, and hopping over metamorphosed scree that slides away beneath your feet.

When a ranger called the Berglund family in California to tell them that Gretta was overdue, Greg Berglund said that his sister was "high on life" when she left for Alaska. But he confessed that she had poor balance and a bad sense of direction and was overconfident from her Wyoming wilderness course.

Scott, Roger, Randy, and I spent the first two days beating the bushes while performing line searches: walking ten yards apart and canvassing less than a square mile per day for signs of Gretta. Snow frosted the ground, and at night we huddled around a campfire and watched our breath cloud the air. By the time Gretta's backpack washed up below the Sanctuary River canyon and a bloodhound had picked up her scent leading into the canyon, we all knew that we were wasting our time out in the forest. Gretta was in the canyon.

By Sunday morning we had become part of a fifty-five-member search team. Planes and helicopters shredded the air overhead. Wildlife had long since departed the area. Because the canyon was considered hazardous, and the mountaineering rangers were considered gullible, we four were assigned to comb the river canyon with grappling hooks and poles. Everyone else continued beating the bushes below the canyon.

At first the work was entertaining and we played like otters in the river, checked by our climbing ropes as we waded out into the torrent. We poked into backwaters and eddies with the poles, then dragged hard-to-reach pools with the hooks. Anything was better, we agreed, than monotonous line searches in tight willow and forest. Nonetheless, by midday our work turned repetitive and we grew chilled from wading chest deep in the glacial water.

Roger had become the self-appointed communications man. Whenever we rounded a bend in the river or checked out a new riffle, Roger excitedly plucked the radio out of his holster and barked out a progress report. Every rescue has its "radio rapper," and in a search this big, there were several other egomaniacs in the air above and combing the willows below. These men couldn't resist keying their radio every few minutes and proclaiming in long-winded ten-code lingo that they had heard Roger's message, as well as whatever else crossed their minds. "Ahh, ten-four [okay] on that, we're ten-eight [in service] and our ten-twenty [location] is about five miles east of the canyon, we're about to proceed with the next grid. We'll ten-five [relay] your message to base." Scott and Randy and I simply turned our radio volumes down and concentrated on the river, quickly losing patience with Roger and the radio rappers.

As Roger walked around a tower of crumbling basalt on the opposite side of the river, I found a leg bone stuck three feet under the water. I yanked it out, and after careful scrutiny, discovered that I was holding the decaying two-foot leg of a Dall sheep. By the time Roger reappeared on the opposite side, I lofted the bone, festooned with chunks of flesh, and yelled across the river, "Roger, look what we've found!" Roger's hand flashed to his hip, whipped out the radio, and he began shouting his discovery of Gretta's body; Scott keyed his transceiver button and blocked the call until Roger calmed down.

That evening, when the helicopter brought us back to our staging camp, Scott lifted his eight-foot pole toward the overhead rotor, and only the frantic gesturing of the pilot prevented that week's second mishap on the Sanctuary River. After that, the helicopter pilot treated us just like everyone else: turkeys looking for a decapitation.

As we changed into dry clothes, a support plane landed beside the river. When the blur at the nose of the plane reappeared as a propeller and the engine coughed shut, the pilot pitched out dozens of foam containers of freshly barbecued halibut and salmon. The pilot also handed out a discreetly wrapped package marked "Talkeetna Rangers." Once opened in the privacy of our tent, we found a bottle of whiskey wrapped in a note from our boss, Bob: "Find her *safely* you guys, then let's go home."

The night sky blushed deeper than ebony, and from somewhere far beyond, a wolf howled at our intrusion. Drizzle, then snow, pattered softly on the nylon walls. While Roger spoke of how much he missed his lovely wife, I thought how it would feel if I were Gretta. Even if you *knew* the backcountry here, a solo traverse of the canyon in flood conditions would offer all the edgy pleasure of a curfewed Zulu tiptoeing the midnight streets of Johannesburg.

Certainly, Gretta followed the correct river crossing protocol, unbuckling her waistbelt and wriggling out of her shoulder straps before getting pulled under. Although she somehow clambered out of the river, walking out must have been a futile act of desperation. She was soaking wet, shivering with cold, and her food, tent, and dry clothes had washed away. Her only chance was to try to hoof it upriver and out of the canyon. Somewhere, though, the river took her again.

Was she so cold that it didn't matter anymore, that everything became a blur? Or did she pray to see her new boyfriend and her family again? A starless night like this could last far longer than you planned, so my cohorts Scott and Randy and Roger and I drank the whiskey instead of talking about Gretta. We all knew that we would find her. By midnight we resorted to the mockery that substitutes for grown men expressing their love for one another:

"God, your boots are ripe."

"Move over, asshole, you're hogging the whole tent."

This banter mostly muted our fears about finding the body. But before falling to sleep, I promised myself not to look in Gretta's eyes when we found her.

Monday was our second full day probing the river canyon. Scott wore a neoprene wetsuit to insulate himself from the ice water, while the chief ranger lent me his windsurfing shell, more suited to the Caribbean than Alaska. Randy and Roger lowered us into the river, and each time we finished probing pools for a submerged body, we pulled up our legs and let the current sweep us back to shore. We moved quick and efficiently, signaling by hand who would cover each section of river.

A surliness came over all of us as black clouds scudded past like warships in the vast sky above. Even Randy—who normally brightened our days with a disarming smile—frowned. And Roger stopped talking on his radio.

By five o'clock I was shivering and my lips were blue. After a long argument across the roaring, frothing waters with Scott—who would have searched all night—I convinced him I was hypothermic: I was shivering, my lips were blue, and I could barely bend my fingers. Scott argued that we had to be close.

Finally we agreed to call in our pickup and quit until tomorrow. Randy and I found a narrow spot where a running jump and a bit of a swim got us to Scott and Roger's side of the river. But as the chopper hovered in above a hillock, the search captain urged us back downhill by pointing urgently at the river. Twenty yards from where we had quit, an arm waved up and down in the current. Call it adrenaline or fear, but suddenly I stopped shivering.

Scott and I spent an hour up to our necks in icy water, trying to girth-hitch that waving arm. Her hand felt alive, and my heart galloped at the thought of the disembodied hand grabbing me back; mostly I wanted to get the job over with as quickly as possible. Every time I looped the webbing past the knuckles, the slippery, bloated flesh greased out of my own hands and back down into the depths. Through the murky waters I could make out a head of long, brown hair suspended in the current. Maybe I *was* hypothermic and tired, but there in that icy river there was the recurring impression that, if you got too close, this underwater Medusa would snatch you down and pull you under for company. Scott diagnosed, more rationally, that getting too close to the body would trap one of us—despite the roped belay—in the same rock crack that held Gretta fast.

Randy, his hair down to his waist, smiled like a knowing Buddhist and said, "Hey, she's dead, you guys, mellow out." So we threw the grappling hook. After snagging a leg and yanking, dreading that we might separate a limb, the body came free like a champagne cork and shot down the rapids. We ran pell-mell until the corpse finally caught on a shoal a hundred yards downstream.

Scott swam out with the rope and secured the body. When we pulled it ashore, I made the mistake of looking too long.

Her hazel eyes leaked light, not water, and her pink face seemed frozen in a wan smile. Roger muttered that she still looked alive.

"She's too young," I said, "much, much too young."

Someone passed me the body bag, I looked away, and then it was done. No one spoke. We shivered beneath the rotor wash. My closest friends stood surrounding me, and I was thankful for that. We had enough respect not to try to lighten things with a joke. We all held hands over our ears, and the helicopter labored up the dark canyon. The orange body bag drew lazy, spinning circles against the sky.

On the bus back to headquarters I didn't know whether I was hot or cold. Fifty other rescuers sat jubilantly relieved. I put my pile jacket on, then took it off ten times before a woman across the aisle smiled. When she turned toward the front I thought for an instant that I was looking at Gretta. I closed my eyes and wiped my hands again and again and again on my pants legs.

At the rescue debriefing, I walked out because there was nothing to be learned. Moreover, one of the law enforcement rangers at headquarters had examined the naked body and made a lewd remark that left me and my partners filled with revulsion. I craved a hot shower.

While driving back to Talkeetna, we stared at pavement as dark as the night and discussed what kind of political pull the Berglund family had to put together a search that would cost the taxpayers more than $60,000. I tried to get our boss to stop for whiskey in Cantwell, but no one had any money. Bob drove all three hours, and no one spoke as water rinsed through the wheel wells like a broken washing machine. The mountain hid beneath the sorry black curtain that covered all of Alaska.

During that long, wordless drive, I realized that life beneath the mountain moved quicker than anywhere else, like a series of departures. Spring fell into summer, which bled into fall, but the darkened winter, as the joke goes, is the only true season in Alaska.

Finding tranquillity amid this landscape of perpetual change was tough. All was constant transition: Salmon were spawning and dying in the streams, wolves stalked the ungulates, and rivers flooded their banks. Life was short here. Although several climbers died every year up on the mountain, *off* the mountain, death seemed as constant as Denali, holding a dazzling white vigil above all of its dominion.

Back at our creaky-floored ranger station, home to a family of mice and colonies of mildew, we were all too tired to talk, so I walked to the back bedroom. I laid down on my bed and hoped the rain would stop by dawn. Sleep stole me away.

In the small hours of that morning, Gretta arrived outside and began scratching her fingernails against the window. I fought to wake up and end the nightmare, to no avail. So I forced myself to look in her wide hazel eyes again, and that placid pink face from the river was now a death mask of terror and unhappiness. If this was a dream, and if dreams can offer a glimmer of reality, Gretta Berglund was even more frightened than I because her destination was somewhere that no one should go until they're good and ready. Athapaskan stories tell of dead spirits walking down either an easy trail or a trail of suffering; Gretta's path was obvious.

When I finally forced myself awake and lunged for the window, she was gone. I sat up and turned on the light. During the long black hours before dawn the rain hammered the roof.

I lay awake thinking about Gretta. I was certain she had visited.

Although Gretta had now left the window, I could not put her out of my mind. Athapaskans also believe that spirits have a very long journey to make into their afterlife. Spirits were considered dangerous, and in the instance of violent death, they often lingered in the place where they had been killed; I was not anxious to return to the Sanctuary River. Spirits, the stories said, were most active at night.

Life around Denali seemed constantly shaded by such death. Perhaps I had just reached an age when everyone confronts these issues. Indeed, no one lives forever. My friends would die and I would die—perhaps even tomorrow.

While living elsewhere, it seemed a lot easier to "use your fun tickets" and become so preoccupied that you could avoid this nagging tug of mortality. But around the mountain the nature of rescue work—moreover, the immutable raw power of the primal landscape—left me with a new impression of how fragile life really is. Sooner or later, anyone living on the mountain or in its checkered shadow would be forced to confront the inexorable cycle of death.

The talk around town held that Herb had become a binge drinker. It had rained most of that summer, and locals wondered aloud if this was the year that Talkeetna—Athapaskan for "three rivers"—would flood.

Scott and I were ticketed at Montana Creek for fishing in a poorly signed closed area by a zealous fish and game cop. As he wrote us up, I entertained punting the potbellied, gun-slinging fish cop into the river, which Herb would have appreciated. Instead I let justice take its own slow course. The ticket read "fishing in a closed area"—which we thought was open—and we were to appear in court a month later.

Near the end of the salmon season, while fishing out on the Susitna River with Herb and Scott, I hooked a king salmon (*ggaal* in Athapaskan) that pulled like a whalish sixty-pounder. It exploded two feet out of the water as a blur of red-backed quicksilver, and after it splashed back into the milk-colored current, every angler on the shore pulled in their lines. The boat nearly tipped over when I stood up and "the king" surged downriver.

Of course, Herb, and even Scott, had landed the richest and biggest salmon. I had not. So it had become ritual for Scott to tease me that "I was not man enough" to bring in a king—naturally he was jesting, but Herb interpreted Scott's banter as condemnation; I didn't know why.

I had hooked kings before in this seven-mile-per-hour current, but they always turned downriver, and before Herb could pull the anchor and give chase, they broke my line. This time, though, Herb had changed my line to a sturdier ten-pound test, and I was playing the fish slowly, letting it run. Then winding it in slowly, letting it run, winding it in slowly.

I succeeded in coaxing the fish to the boat in fifteen minutes. As Scott reached toward it too quickly with the net, the king spooked and ran: My lightweight fiberglass pole snapped in two with the resounding crack of a sapling split by winter; now the king bolted downriver. Herb tried to smile. Scott laughed. I slammed the pole on the gunwale, then pulled the anchor. Nobody spoke as Herb yanked the engine to a roar and took us downriver, cupping his cigarette and steering the Envinrude tiller. He watched the ubiquitous and dazzling white mountain as if maybe fulfillment could be found up there in the clouds.

The next morning in the kitchen I found a brand-new, stout halibut fishing pole, guaranteed for hauling up hundred-pound monsters. The etiquette of lightweight fly rods did not impress Herb, and I would no sooner proselytize about sportsmanship in fishing than he would tell me how to climb Denali. Anyway, the rod was the same brand as Herb's, and it balanced on the counter where the salmon gifts had been placed. Herb was sitting on the couch drinking coffee—he clutched the cup tightly with both hands—nervously, it seemed, because he could not smoke in the ranger station. I picked up my gift carefully; tools of the hunt were infused with spiritual power and must be treated with respect. Herb flashed me that guileless smile of a man innocent of the complex world outside.

"That telephone pole," he said, "ain't gonna break. Let's get you a king."

Herb began his own passage toward the mountain during a rainy September night. In the middle of a dinner party at the ranger station, Nellie Atwater burst in and shouted, "Come quick, Herb's trying to kill his father!"

Scott and I sprinted across the railroad tracks and found Herb incoherent, his breath stinking sweeter than gin, his normally affable brown eyes filled with red rage at a world in which he could not belong, and inadvertently aimed at his father, Ted. When Ted's face appeared at the locked door, Herb bolted forward screaming murderous thoughts and threw his fist as Ted jumped away from the flying glass. Herb raked his arm back through the jagged shards of the door.

Blood covered his shirt. Scott and I tried to inspect his arm, but he pushed us off and warned us to leave as more blood spurted from his biceps. "You'll bleed out," Scott pleaded. "Let us help you!" But Herb only turned with slitted eyes toward the house, his blue jeans blackening with blood.

Scott's lips were clenched tightly, and we glanced at one another with eyes as wide as deer caught in headlights. I clenched my fist—never doubting my friendship with Herb—drew back my arm, and swung in an urgent, precise arc until my fist connected with the point of Herb's jaw. He dropped backward like a chainsawed tree. I jumped onto him and pinned his elbows with my knees while Scott held pressure on the three-inch laceration on the soft flesh of Herb's arm. Nellie called for an ambulance.

It was only an hour's ride to the Palmer hospital, but the

oily, starless night stretched on and on as Herb struggled against the restraining straps, alternately whispering in my ear so his mother wouldn't hear, "Kill me, Jon, please kill me tonight, go ahead and do it, oh, please, kill me kill me kill me." I touched him softly on the shoulder, then clenched his hand as Nellie told him that we all loved him. At the hospital the doctor gave him a sedative, and everyone tried to erase the night from their memories.

A week later, Scott and I faced the judge. He announced to the courtroom of drunk drivers, bitter divorcees, and common criminals that we were federal rangers, no less, fishing in a closed area. We explained that the fine print on the fishing sign at Montana Creek was ambiguous, but the judge fined us each $100 anyway. Scott wrote out his check immediately so he would not jeopardize his ranger career; I just waved goodbye to the court clerk. If the bureaucrats who managed the Alaska Fish and Game Department ever issued a warrant for my arrest, I never knew about it.

At dawn of the first day of moose season, Herb took his four-teen-hundred-pound bull moose with the big pistol. Scott and I helped carry in the ribs, then the legs, then the haunches. It took all three of us to carry in the majestic antlered head. My pants were dappled with sticky blood; my back would ache for days.

Herb was sheepish at dinner, and although I whispered to him that nothing had changed for Scott or me, the smile had faded from Herb's face and his eyes lacked their usual luster. An unspoken shame wedged between father and son because Herb had not taken a career. He wanted to spend his time knocking the heads of grouse and stalking the waters for salmon and admiring moose prancing in the forest. He was an instinctive hunter and woodsman plunged into a world ignorant of the truth of the Distant Time. If the analogy of Raven holds true, Herb had also been turned down by a woman, but unlike Raven, Herb had no magic with which to calm the waters.

Nonetheless, the ritual of our moose feast made everyone lighthearted and happy. Instead of saying grace, Nellie passed the nostril *(bintsiyh)*. It fell apart between my teeth like putrid gray gelatin, and I caught Herb smiling so beautifully from across the table that I laughed instead of gagging and thought that the taking of the moose had somehow restored my kindhearted friend. But I was wrong.

That winter Herb accepted a job pounding nails in Anchorage, far from the salmon streams that sustained him—Athapaskan legends tell of the salmon's ability to protect people from bad spirits. But Herb wore no dried salmon around his neck. And Herb had no one to marry, not even a girlfriend.

In the blackest part of winter, Herb began drinking again and concluded that he had no place in the modern world anymore. He had not fished for six months. His life seemed so distant from the wild country that made him whole that he unholstered his eight-inch pistol, lifted it deliberately to his head, and pulled the trigger.

Wait, I see something:
It is spreading softly on the surface of the water.
Answer: Blood from the king salmon, clubbed in the water so it will not upset the canoe when it is pulled inside.

When Herb was alive, fishing and hunting sustained him just as Denali's glacial melt returned the salmon from the sea, just as the mountain's rich river sustained the moose.

On my wall there is a photograph of Herb, Scott, and me each holding up forty- to fifty-pound salmon. I had caught my first king all because of Herb. It was more than his kind patience and the "telephone pole"; it was his gift of intuition for the spirit of life that would make even sonar seem obsolete.

In the background of my photograph are a lush green meadow and thick leafy woods where a family of feral cats waited for scraps. Scott and I jostled one another about whose fish was bigger; Herb stood just beside us so serene with his broad cheekbones, holding the most silver-skinned fish of them all.

I do not know if he went down the trail of suffering or the easy trail. I am sure that either way, like Gretta, he haunts his river.

Now I know that "to hunt" literally translated from the Athapaskan tongue means "to be a man." And I will never forget that Herb and his father's father's fathers named the mountain Denali.

9

REQUIEM FOR THE BEARS

A bear loped before me
on a narrow, wooded road;
with a sound like a sudden
shifting of ashes, he turned
and plunged into his own blackness.

—JOHN HAINES

OUR ATHAPASKAN NEIGHBOR TED ATWATER BERATED RANGER *Scott Gill and me for taking patrols through bear country around Denali without a gun. After all, the bear of Athapaskan folklore,* ghonoy tlaaga *(bad animal), has the most powerful spirit of all animals.*

Most Alaskan backpackers, even pacifists, prefer guns for bear protection. However, backpackers from the lower forty-eight—or, as Ted would say, "outside the country"—believe that carrying a gun is an aggressive act that will provoke bears to attack. Scott and I wore bells on our packs so we wouldn't surprise a bear in the brush, we carried an air horn to frighten bears away, and we had cans of Mace to spray in a charging bear's face.

Naturally, Ted regaled us with stories of human remains found in the Alaskan bush beside chewed-up bells and aerosol cans of Mace and air horns punctured by ample teeth. Scott quipped that it was against federal statutes for bears to eat a ranger.

"There ain't a bear in Alaska," Ted would reply, "that won't run away if you fire your gun straight up in the air. Bears are smarter than people."

I finally took Ted's large-magnum handgun with its metal bluing worn seashell white around the chamber. Although Scott and I couldn't hit many targets beyond ten yards, the .41 Smith & Wesson was capable of six disturbing explosions between reloads.

In July of 1985 we were flown into the Dall Glacier beneath Mount Russell, a satellite peak of the thirty-five-mile-distant Denali. With a week of food, Scott and I began marching over glacial rubble and through thick alders, bearing toward Chelatna Lake. After five days of clomping mindlessly across rock and ice, we bivouacked on a white sand beach at the confluence of a milk-colored stream and a clear, glittering brook. Fresh bear tracks crisscrossed the sand we slept on; spawned out, reddened salmon flopped in the eddies. Where all was inert behind us in the glaciated mountains, in front of us, it seemed, lay the very nucleus of living, breathing creatures and lush green flora. It was the loveliest confluence we had ever visited.

At dawn Scott began scrambling up a granite pinnacle several thousand feet above camp, while I bushwhacked up the stream of remarkable white sand. That morning I was absorbed by a fantasy that Shangri-la lay at the headwaters. My progress, however, was limited to holding in my elbows and thrashing through tight alder bushes until I found a well-traveled game trail. Then I discovered pawprints an inch bigger than my own hands and lacking claw indentations: sign of a large black bear.

I walked another mile up the valley before clambering onto a steep boulder field and trying to catch sight of Denali. When I finally located it, the mountain lofted high above the stream, high above all other peaks, high above the clouds even. I sat down to admire this earthly paradise of pink capillaried granite and blinding white glacier, then promptly fell asleep.

When I awoke, I was amused to see a large black bear ambling down the valley on the trail below; if the bear had come an hour earlier, we would have collided. When "blackie" reached the place where I had veered off the trail, it stood up over five feet tall, began sniffing the air, and sprinted up the boulder field, following my scent like a bloodhound.

Knowing that bears are somewhat myopic, I immediately jogged toward a cliff where I could climb to safety; somehow the bear perceived my strategy and cut me off by sprinting across the boulders and tightening its line of approach. With the bear forty yards away and closing, I waved my arms and shouted "Go away, bear!" trying to convince it that I was not a moose calf—but blackie continued its charge.

At last I remembered the gun on my hip. I swept the magnum skyward and squeezed thunder into my ears. The bear straightened its forearms onto a boulder and froze as if freshly mounted by a taxidermist, then soundlessly loosed its bowels; the ringing in my ears blocked all noise except for the hammering of my heart. I sniffed the air just as the black bear did. Then we came to a unanimous and wordless agreement: The bear and I simultaneously turned in opposite directions and ran as fast as our legs could carry us. Scott and I traveled a lot more carefully on our way out the salmon stream to Lake Chelatna.

For me, bears symbolized all that was wild and undeveloped in Denali National Park. Certainly bears cannot coexist with people, and without wilderness, bears are doomed.

I thought a lot about bears after a month of living high during my last ranger patrol on Denali in the summer of 1985. Getting to know the park wildlife, forests, and rivers is a natural progression for anyone who spends too much time up on the mountain. When I descended to Kahiltna Pass, at 10,320 feet, I began thinking about a bear that had become legend among some Park Service rangers.

A male grizzly had been convicted of raiding garbage dumps and tourists' tents on the north side of the park. The resource management team tranquilized the bear, bundled it up in a cargo net beneath their helicopter, and flew it over

Denali. Several hundred feet above sea level, on the south side of the park, close to Chelatna Lake, they landed near an uninhabited forest and unleashed the sleeping bear.

Upon waking, that bruin began walking up the sixty-mile-long Kahiltna Glacier, avoiding hundreds of crevasses until it reached the pass I stood on. Given a grizzly's metabolic needs for constant forage, this bear probably walked over a hundred miles to get to the pass, dodging unpredictable icefalls and jumping deep crevasses, guided by some inexplicable natal radar. The ever-shifting glaciers of Denali are anything but safe, and with the exception of a few wiry, summer climbers like myself, there is nothing to eat.

I looked down the crevassed glacier and tried to imagine a bear winding through this labyrinth. From where I stood, getting out from the avalanche-bombarded Peters Glacier and onto the nourishing tundra was another thirty miles; getting back to the garbage on the north side of the park was another hundred miles. One hundred thirty miles as the raven flies would be several hundred miles for a meandering grizzly.

Home again, the bear must have dipped its nose into more packs and tents, or maybe even bluff-charged a tourist or two. No one ever says what really happened to the Kahiltna Pass bear, but the Park Service did not make the effort to transport it again. And the Kahiltna Pass bear is only one of hundreds of curious bears in the park.

After I skied back down to the seven-thousand-foot Southeast Fork of the Kahiltna airplane strip, I slept and dreamed about grizzlies. Finally, Jim Okonek landed, shut his propeller down, and spindrift sifted through the air lazily, a sparkling fly hatch. I lifted hands from my ears. As my friend Sandy Eldredge stepped out of the skiplane, her chestnut eyes reminded me of warm earth and green trees and birdcalls.

After too much time on Denali, climbers often become icy-eyed and deprived of vital sensory input. A plane then plucks them off the glacier and deposits them, dazed, in Talkeetna. They wander past the woods, smelling flowers, then are blasted back into catatonic reality by cars, the tinny jukebox, the cigarette smoke, and the beer-induced stupor of the Fairview Inn. Not me, though.

I needed to get out, but gradually—via the wilderness instead of a skiplane. We planned to drift down the Tokositna River and let the very glaciers I had come to abhor wash me home on their meltwater. The prospect of bears, gurgling water, green trees, bird carols, and warm breezes titillated me.

In 1980 the Alaska National Interest Lands Claims Act had added several million acres of monument and preserve lands, which bulged toward our destination. The 5.5 million acres of Denali National Park and Preserve hold close to 300 grizzlies, 2,000 moose, 2,500 Dall sheep, and 200 wolves.

But there are storm clouds on the horizon of this wilderness. Denali State Park and Denali National Park and Preserve plan to develop the south side of the park, a vision no less absurd than smashing Michelangelo's marble, pissing on the Tabernacle steps, or snowmobiling up Denali. So Sandy and I were going down the Tokositna just in case the surveyors, bulldozers, and asphalt do come. We wanted to see Denali's wilderness untouched, untorn, and untarred while it was still possible.

Our route encompassed ninety miles of glaciers, gravelbars, and rivers. The same itinerary performed in Rhode Island, where I was born, would have shot me into neighboring Connecticut, past the homes of millions of people; here in Alaska, we would pass only one seasonal cabin. We would ski down the huge Kahiltna Glacier, tracing the route of the Kahiltna Pass grizzly, swing onto a side glacier, then coast out of the Alaska Range via the Kanikula Glacier. We would then walk five miles to a prearranged raft cache and float to Talkeetna. Our sojourn would be one of climatic transition, from the frozen, icelocked mountains into a world teeming with bears, moose, and birdlife.

We would see the wilderness—or "monument," in Park Service officialese—as untrammeled as Belmore Browne and Herschel Parker had seen it in 1906. These men boated up the Tokositna River, then bushwhacked through alders and picked through the glaciers, searching for a route up Denali.

To climb the mountain, Browne and Parker logged months in the wilderness. If they couldn't scare off marauding grizzlies or quarter a caribou, they didn't stand a chance of even reaching their mountain. Moreover, these early suitors of Denali came to understand the wilderness with an intimacy that their grandchildren would miss in a forty-minute skiplane flight. But in return for his suffering, Browne was rewarded with the big picture: He understood that Denali, its surrounding landscape, wildlife, and rivers are one cohesive and interdependent system. Browne dedicated six years of his life to climbing Denali, coming within five minutes of its summit in 1912.

More importantly, Browne spent a decade badgering the lawmakers of Washington, D.C., to set aside an unprecedented amount of wilderness land. In 1916, standing beside the conservationist Charles Sheldon in Washington, D.C., Browne told a Senate committee:

> . . . at any time the powerful form of the grizzly bear may give the crowning touch to the wilderness of the picture. But while the Mount McKinley region is the fountainhead from which come the herds of game that supply the huge expanse of south-central Alaska, that fountainhead is menaced. Slowly but surely the white man's civilization is closing in, and already sled loads of dead animals from the McKinley region have reached the Fairbanks market. Unless a refuge is set aside, in which the animals that remain

can breed and rear their young unmolested, they will soon follow the buffalo.

Because of Sheldon and Browne's efforts, President Wilson signed a bill in 1917 that created Mount McKinley National Park. Hunters could no longer ravage Dall sheep, migrating caribou, and grizzly bears. Sheep populations stabilized. But for reasons unclear even to biologists, whereas thirty thousand caribou once roamed the park, there are now only three thousand. And like the caribou and the buffalo, the future of Denali National Park's bears is also precarious.

These thoughts weighed heavy on my mind as Sandy and I skied around Mount Hunter, its summit plateau rimmed with ice cliffs glistening like a grizzly's teeth. Okonek roared by and bombed us with a half gallon of ice cream, ten yards to my side. I packed snow around the carton in my sled.

We turned the Kahiltna Icefall on a ramp down the side. Sandy and I sped like rockets next to the glacier—thousands of tons of buckled and writhing ice whose movement down a steep hill can be perceived only in the microseconds of geologic time that equal decades of our lives. We skied uncontested past hundreds of gaping crevasses. And I found no sign of bears.

Below six thousand feet the Kahiltna is pocked with turquoise meltpools. Everything was dripping, melting, and collapsing (including the chocolate ice cream in my sled). Multiton ice blocks—barely attached to their tenuous aeries halfway up the mountainsides—thundered and dove like wingless pterodactyls, smashing into the glacier, briefly regaining flight as massive clouds of vaporized snow. We screamed at one another, first paranoid, then delighted as our safety was evidenced, needlessly pointing to the cataclysm. Our hearts pounded, and seconds seemed to slow into minutes as the ice blocks finished grinding across the glacier and the localized snowstorm settled into silence.

Down on the Kanikula Glacier, a bevy of sparrows flitted by, which brought a bounce back to my stride. Plants waved in the distance. It's easy to take the simple smell of green for granted until you spend too much time up high in the cold. When you come down from this mountain, it is like stumbling into a warm kitchen when you're starving. Whiffs of alder and cottonwood caught the back of my nose with a subtle sweetness, full and lime-rich after the stale emptiness of glacier air.

The glacier sloped gently downhill, and we carved rounded telemark turns on our skis as the sleds clipped our heels. We camped at the edge of greenness near a waterfall and watched a slate-colored dipper wheel and twirl in the spray. It dove underwater, chased a bug, popped out like a cork, shot into the air, then dove in again downstream.

The Tokositna area shelters many black bears, who prefer the cover and forage of forest, unlike the larger and more versatile brownish-colored grizzlies. We spied a black bear with two cubs pawing the snow, sliding, playing, and romping on the cool moraine. Amid the abundant browse of the Tokositna Valley, black bears often settle for salad instead of hard-to-run-down prey, as evidenced by the boneless scats around our tent. As the sow and cubs disappeared into a thick curtain of alders, I was too excited to sleep.

Even the next morning's rain and gray fog couldn't conceal the lushness of the valley. As we tramped over streams and threaded through miles of snowless moraine, there was a clicking hum of insects, the spill and splash of water, the whirring of wings, and everywhere the effervescent emerald glow of life.

Waterfalls frothed and disappeared under the rocky and compressed ice at the Kanikula Glacier's toe. The river emerged in a torrent from beneath the glacier, roaring and carrying away the Alaska Range as pulverized silt. The glacier offered boulders to the river with a final "KA-WOOMF." Sandy and I flinched fearfully, then jumped back when the entire glacier shifted, boomed, and surged several inches beneath us.

Our feet fit inside grizzly tracks in the silt. We sang out loud to drive off any lurking bruins. Then we bumbled upon a moose-kill, its coarse brown hide and yellowed bones scattered in a large circle. I reconstructed the kill scene: the old graying cow shuffling through deep drifts with the grizzly in pursuit, slim and hungry after a winter's fast.

By early afternoon we found our raft on a barren gravelbar next to the Tokositna—we were lucky that bears had not pillaged it—and spread out our gear to dry in the sun. The scene became like a Third World flea market, with tattered, faded mountain clothes strewn everywhere. We celebrated by eating freeze-dried lasagna. At home we would heap abuse on these crisp rubber band-like noodles impregnated with catsup and moldy cheese; out in the wilderness, it was delicious. We were ravenous.

We had fifty-five miles of river to float back to Talkeetna. Yet we were in no rush, for we wanted to watch the country carefully and catch all of its textures. That night a porcupine, bristling at my approach, waddled around a mud puddle. A coyote loped by, pursued by two shrieking jaegers—birds with long forked tails that wintered in the southern hemisphere. We laughed as the coyote slunk into the cottonwoods. Finally, an unnamed peak blushed pink in the dying sun. Although the mountain had been attempted several times, it was unclimbed—real wilderness always has several mountains greater than men. As we nodded off, a great horned owl hooted at the night.

The next morning we crashed our raft into a logjam while

trying to avoid the channel next to a 350-pound grizzly. As soon as the bear smelled us, it sprinted up a steep hill without looking back. The barren-ground grizzly can survive in the wilderness for almost thirty years, eating 80 to 85 percent vegetation (berries, roots, grasses) and 15 to 20 percent meat (moose, caribou, squirrels, fish). Standing as high as seven feet tall, *Ursus arctos horribilis* is not as horrifying as its thousand-pound-plus brown-bear brothers, who stand ten feet tall and grow fat on rich salmon and other prolific food sources along Alaska's coast. Nonetheless, whether three hundred or thirteen hundred pounds, grizzlies demand respect, as I had once learned while walking alone through prime grizzly habitat for three days.

Up on the spine of the Alaska Range that summer I had come to an abrupt impasse: a thousand feet of unmapped steep glacier that called for an ice ax—mine was fifty miles away, at the ranger station. I took out the magnum and unloaded six shells into my pocket. I held the barrel into the snow, lay face down, and started sliding, braking my speed by poking the gun deeper into the snowpack. In five minutes I reached tundra and gravel.

When I came to the icy Toklat River, I crossed and recrossed the knee-deep channels, shivering as I sang out every song I knew in order not to surprise a grizzly. Their signs were everywhere: torn up ground-squirrel holes three feet deep and five feet wide; berry-speckled droppings as ample as horse pies; acres of paw-sized trenches where they had chewed up peavine roots.

Below a riverbank and out of the wind, it seemed that no bears were around, so I took off my pack and knelt down. I began field-stripping the magnum with a pocket knife, spreading the parts over my pack. At first I dried the metal with a cotton towel; then I dabbed sweet-smelling gun oil over all the moving parts and let them sit in the sun to dry.

It was then that I looked up to confront a large cinnamon-colored grizzly, walking toward me and staring down at me while wrinkling its softball-sized nose, its hair standing on end. I grabbed the pack as if it were a tray, and while backing across the river and up the opposite bank like a harried waiter, I tried not to spill the disassembled hors d'oeuvres. The bear sauntered after me, matching my strides. I kept my movements deliberate and flowing, as if I wasn't scared of this big bruin, and when I got to the top of the hill, I shouted at the top of my lungs: "GO AWAY, BEAR!" Just then the bear seemed to lose interest. The bear meandered down the riverbar, sniffing, pawing, poking. My fingers shook as I reassembled the gun.

Wilderness without fearsome leviathans would be tame and limp country indeed. And, for that matter, what good are "safe" mountains? Climbers and wilderness lovers alike need hanging glaciers, avalanches, stonefall—and big beasts with halitosis that can knock us from our feet with one flick of a hairy paw. I would rather sleep uneasily in grizzly territory than see its game trails paved over; I would rather run for my life up the Valley of Death beneath Denali than ride a tram above its hanging glaciers. I profess that risk-taking—scaring ourselves silly as an infrequent antidote to the banality of nine-to-five living—teaches us humility and respect and shows us that we are no greater or lesser than any mountain or beast of the wilds.

On the Tokositna River, five miles below the glacier, Sandy and I paddled into a broad floodplain with dozens of tundra swans surrounding their young. Like the bear of Athapaskan lore, the swan, *tobaa*, has more spiritual significance than any other waterfowl. It is also one of the smartest, always knowing which rivers have the richest food and always knowing when it is time to flee winter.

As we drew closer, they slapped the water with their wings,

lurched forward, then gained the air. For brief minutes that will stretch eternally in my memory, the sky clouded with pearly white, grunting, wing-whistling birds. They honked and beat the air and circled our raft until we grew dizzy. The swans flew in pairs and remain paired; unlike *Homo sapiens*, these birds keep their wedding vows. As they faded into the distance, I stared long and hard at Sandy. If she was a swan, I was surely more kin to the transient terns pecking along the riverbanks, unlikely to settle down anywhere between Tierra del Fuego and Alaska.

The Tokositna River has been designated (by biologists employed by prodevelopment bureaucracies) as an "invaluable nesting habitat." The Park Management Plan, determining the fate of the area, has been redrafted numerous times by both state and federal planners. It claims that swans or bears won't be displaced by development.

We could see the site of the proposed road, helicopter pad, and backcountry "facility" up on the north side of Peters Hills. This jungle of impenetrable alders is enough to stop most city-dwelling developers and ill-conditioned tourists, at least on foot. But astride their powerful bulldozers (and later in their heated, four-wheel-drives), developers and tourists will see an area resembling a mowed-down rain forest. Meanwhile, the facilities (proposed both here and out on the eastern edge of the park) will keep the bears at bay.

Behind the nesting area we saw moose browsing in the river or on the alder banks, always watchful lest they be surprised by a grizzly. Beavers raced beside us, slapping their tails and frolicking in the current with peculiar humming noises. Athapaskan elders tell stories of a beaver (*ggaaggateeya*) as big as a bear, but when it was shot at, the bullets bounced off.

The omnipresent Denali hung in the distance. The mountain grew pale and ghostly above the world of cold-biting rivers, toothy critters, and thorny devil's club.

While thinking about the climbers on high, their axes pitched in battle, I breathed a sigh of relief; I was once again glad to be down. I had overlooked the wilderness too long now, and as the pioneers had learned many years ago, mountains are integral with the surrounding tundra, forests, and rivers. The real danger of mountain climbing is in "conquering," an arcane notion that seems lately to have resurfaced. "Conquering" boulders, crags, and mountains means climbers are presiding over and above nature—the same philosophy behind the development of Denali National Park and the destruction of its bears.

I feathered the water with my paddle, disheartened and at a loss with the manner in which I used to climb. We need to watch mountains as much as we stand on them. Otherwise we are no better than the wilderness developer clutching blueprints, the bulldozer driver clearing out the alders, or the hunter sighting in on a grizzly. We need to retreat as often as we summit, to tremble with awe, whether it be in the teeth of a storm or in front of a big bruin.

At a bend in the river we came upon a grizzly backpaddling in the water fifteen yards away. It lifted a huge paw to the banks, turned in our direction, and snuffled the air with a huge black nose; when the bear smelled us, it burst out of the water like a breaching whale, exploded up a steep bank, and slammed through a tight alder thicket. Wrist-sized branches snapped, broke, and parted for a hundred yards before I breathed again.

Another bend revealed a large black bear displaying a white, half-moon-shaped scar on its back. We drifted within twenty yards; as our cameras clicked, the bear folded its nose strangely, shuffled closer—then just as unpredictably, ambled.

The mudbanks held tracks: striding cat claws and loping

fox pads and plodding hooves of a cow moose shadowed by calves. There were gnawed trees and webbed feet tracks with fat-tail drag marks; or as an Athapaskan riddle is told:

> Wait, I see something:
> I drag my shovel along the trail.
> Answer: A beaver, with its broad, bare tail.

And there were bears sauntering the riverbanks like Parisians along the Seine. This is the essence of Denali's southern wilderness, a wildlife cornucopia, a culture and artwork read by the tracks on the bank, the colors of the sunset, and the renewing flow of the steel-gray river. This is the Louvre.

We passed a bald eagle's nest, huge sticks like a messy hairdo in the cottonwood tree; we passed a family of anxious goldeneye ducks; we passed more cavorting beavers.

Dark clouds swooped in front of a north wind, and the sun set prematurely into the blackening sky. There is no escaping the mountain. We not only floated by the grace of the melting glaciers whence we skied, but the weather was also determined by that 20,320-foot bulk of snow and ice catching every bit of moisture wafting through the atmosphere. Surely the mountain, the river, and the weather are one.

We two were going to get soaked, so we pulled the raft up onto the sandy confluence of the Ruth River as water unfolded from the sky in prodigious waving sheets. We scurried into the tent and cooked our last dinner, catching our leaky tent's raindrops with our tongues.

As a bitter dessert, Sandy and I pondered the pending development, which would unalterably change this immense wilderness museum. A visitor center is planned just downriver from where we lay, drawn into both Alaskan and federal plans, for the state park and the national park abut one another. Denali National Park claims that south side development will ease the crush of tourist visitation on the fragile tundra of its northern region. Yet any tourist who travels all the way to Alaska is most likely going to visit and unknowingly impact both sides of the park. Garbage will draw the bears; rangers will be forced to shoot the bears.

I wished the bureaucrats and planners could come with us on the raft, away from the road, away from their helicopters, where the tent could drip on them and they could shiver and laugh with us among the bears and beavers. Wilderness wields a subtle power that tourists would be hard-pressed to understand from an automobile, helicopter, or jetboat; wilderness must be earned through sweat and muscles and fear. Wilderness does not have buildings, roads, interpretive naturalists, trail systems, trash cans, or outhouses. Nor does wilderness need guidebooks, helipads, or ranger stations.

"Leave it as it is," Teddy Roosevelt once said, speaking of the wilderness of the Grand Canyon, soon to become another national park. "You cannot improve on it, the ages have been at work on it, and man can only mar it."

I slept restlessly. Morning dawned soggy and the sky was tinged with sooty clouds as we continued to bump our way downriver. My mood further darkened when we confronted the homesteading cabin of the Neil family. It didn't take long to be invited in for cups of tea next to their crackling woodstove. Although I was taken by the genuine warmth of their hospitality, I was saddened, for seeing this cabin clearly signaled that we had reached the end of our sojourn. I knew that wilderness can't exist where people build their homes, because civilization inevitably steals wildness.

John Neil told us about the time he stopped his raft under a riverbank to photograph a black bear with a half-moon-shaped scar on its back. As John's shutter clicked, scarback crinkled its nose, then lunged into the river to attack; the family barely outpaddled it. But the Neils also told stories about bears they had to kill. Sandy and I exchanged a long look, thanked our hosts, and excused ourselves.

As we floated to the Tokositna's end, into the vast waters of the Chulitna River, civilization loomed closer and closer. We could see the traffic on the Parks Highway until we were pulled under the Chulitna Bridge like sticks of flotsam. Automobile rubber and metal vibrated against concrete and prestressed girders at sixty miles per hour, echoing everywhere; I put hands over my ears.

Sandy deftly steered us away from standing waves as I balanced the stove on the bouncing gunwale. I cooked popcorn, then brewed coffee. I was grateful for my companion's river expertise, and although we hotly debated where to turn, she was the rightful captain of our little ship. She pivoted the boat as silt-choked water pattered on the rubber sides like drizzle on a tin roof.

A fly hatch speckled the river, a thrush's notes flowed like moving water, a propeller droned closer. Sandy's sunglasses reflected warm earth and green trees. Our raft pointed toward Talkeetna, a dry bed, hot showers, and fresh food. I was eager for comforts long denied, but I couldn't help greeting civilization with mixed emotions. I turned back to look for the mountain, but it had already faded into the vast space that is Alaska.

After my patrol, a mountaineering ranger was requisitioned to work with the resource management team on a "bear conditioning" program on the northern side of the park. I volunteered immediately, and in early August I drove for two and a half hours to headquarters.

At Broad Pass, the tundra was already flushed with autumn. Berry-pickers stooped over vast fields of wild blueberry and mountain cranberry. The only bear in sight was propped up six feet tall in the willows near Cantwell—an authentically painted metal grizzly that nearsighted hunters had ventilated with bullet holes.

At the park I met Doug Waring, a twenty-five-year-old Alaskan turned park employee. He wore a blue wig, his cheek ballooned out with chewing tobacco, and he was plucking a Hendrix tune on his electric guitar; a neighbor screamed at Doug to turn the volume down. In lieu of a handshake he offered me a half-empty fifth of Jack Daniel's.

The favorite joke among Denali National Park employees was that Doug had fathered one of the more well-known grizzly cubs. It was true that Doug was more interested in bears than in socializing with the community of naturalists and college dilettantes obsessed with the board game Trivial Pursuit. But I warmed to Doug immediately.

On my first day, we were presented with the carcass of a sow bear run over by a tourist's car. Since bear cubs remain with their mothers for two years, the likelihood that its two four-month-old cubs had survived was nil. An order came down that we were to skin the mother bear for tests; Doug showed me how.

As we scraped back the final hank of fur from the white-sinewed flesh below, we stood back and stared. For a brief moment that showed us what the Athapaskan people had always known about bears, we gazed at the naked body with stark and abject realization: It resembled a human being.

That summer, there were three mischievous bears known as "101," "102," and "103" by the Resource Management higher-ups but called "Snagglepuss," "Yogi," and "Boo-boo" by Doug. All these bears had chased tourists, torn down tents, and eaten backpackers' food. Consequently, instead of being destroyed, "the Three Musketeers" (Doug's collective name for them) were shot with a dart gun and knocked out with a drug called Telazol; PCP had been discontinued because bears were purported to have flashbacks and violent reactions after waking up. As the bears slept, Doug and his coworkers installed neck collars that emanated three different radio signals.

Our job was to baby-sit the bears and to provide regular "negative reinforcement encounters" that would stop *Ursus arctos horribilis* from harassing tourists. Several times a week, Doug and I drove up and down the eighty-mile dead-end dirt road with a radio transceiver, dialing into radio channels 101, 102, or 103 and spinning our hand antennae until we found our bears. Mostly the bears stayed five miles away and out of radio range in the backcountry.

On other days we watched photographers of grizzlies escape near-maulings. We tested backpacker bearproof food canisters by smearing them with fish oil and offering them to hungry-looking bears on the roadside.

We also tried to shoot cans out of the air at the firing range. We were hardly sharpshooters. But we did succeed in emptying the substantial government ammunition cabinet, hoping to improve our shaky marksmanship so we could hit the bears.

The first day that I located a radio-collared bear, we parked the beat-up, bear buster van (decorated with a poster of a smiling bear encircled with a red slash), loaded two shotguns, and marched straight out onto the ocean of tundra surrounding Denali. Doug loved performing in front of tourists. A busload of them had stopped, horrified to see two armed men chasing a bear in a protected national park where firearms were prohibited, but once we plunged into thick willows, no one could stop us.

While I set up the tent—a half mile downwind of Snagglepuss and its fetching spring cub—Doug started the stove and threw on a pot of pork soup: "One of ol' Snagglepuss's favorites," said Doug. We dove into the tent, zippered the door halfway up, and trained our binoculars on the bear. Within a minute, Snagglepuss stood up six feet tall and smelled the pork soup, but playing coy, it laid down and pretended to sleep; baby Snagglepuss napped at its mother's side; Doug turned down the stove and fell asleep.

After half an hour, Snagglepuss began sauntering over, unable to resist the aromas of pork any longer. I shook Doug awake and he scooped a huge wad of Copenhagen past his lower lip and verified that the safety on my shotgun was off. As Snagglepuss ambled toward the simmering soup, its forty-pound cub ran to the door, looked up at Doug, and growled playfully. Their resemblance was plain to see: Drool hung from their lips, the cub smiled broadly with needlelike teeth —not unlike Doug's—and they shared the same hair color. Doug whispered, "Shoo, go away!" and flipped his hand at the blond cub, more interested in Doug than food.

When Snagglepuss came within fifteen yards of our tent door, bending toward another free meal, I aimed my shotgun at the mound of fat on its hindquarters and fired: My rubber bullet bounced off Snagglepuss's huge rear end and it turned in midair and galloped away as if stung by a bumblebee. The cub issued a token growl of farewell and bounded off after its mother.

I spent that August chasing bears and being chased by bears. More than once, the bears outsmarted us, and every day we gained new respect for their regal comportment, their strength, and their catlike agility. One day the collared grizzly "102"—Yogi—pretended to lose interest in our pork soup and walked away behind the willows. Fortunately, one of our partners sitting on a high ridge radioed a warning that Yogi had sprinted two miles in a big circle and was now stalking us from behind. Yogi always proved too sly to meet any rubber bullets.

Apparently the program actually worked. We could no longer entice the Three Musketeers into our camps. Now these bears will not bother anyone until someone turns and runs like a caribou, or until some misbehaving child tries to hand-feed a bear. Shooting bears in their rear ends is not ultimately the answer, but until human and bear contact can be eliminated in Denali National Park, it seemed a temporary and humanitarian solution.

While out on bear patrol we ate a lot of cold cans of Army C rations that Doug had pilfered from the rescue cache. I often closed my eyes as Doug accelerated on the wrong side of the road toward approaching ranger law enforcement vehicles. Many times we forgot we were working.

Sandhill cranes rattled overhead in chevron formation. Migrating caribou fled west with clicking heels. Pink stands of fireweed fell limp into ditches. The bear berry and moss campion and mountain saxifrage bled crimson beneath us, skimming past our nostrils in astringent fermentation; salmon berries dissolved tartly in our mouths. The mountain, with its strange white heat, burned hotter than the meek and distant sun.

I have never loved the earth more. The tundra seemed an infinite bleeding plain where even Doug couldn't remember his foul puns and we ached at the beauty of the autumnal death surrounding us and at the mountain beaming above, brighter than all life itself. From the top of Denali I had seen the land breathe. Now, from below, I watched it die one of the slowest and most radiant deaths I would ever see.

After I departed for Talkeetna, Doug had a real bear problem. And it wasn't Snagglepuss, Yogi, or Boo-boo.

Roberta Ashbrook, who ran the Kantishna Roadhouse, was proud to own land inside park boundaries. She constantly reminded the "feds," as she called Doug and Ranger Brian Swift, to protect her business. But Brian saw his job as protecting bears, too, so he dropped lots of hints to Roberta about cleaning up her garbage dump.

"Shove it," she would reply in typical bush woman dialect. Roberta's dump lies in back of the roadhouse and alongside a bear trail. On a regular basis she loaded her garbage onto the blackened pile, doused it with diesel fuel and motor oil, then lit it with a match. The paper and plastic and synthetics wafted upward in an odoriferous velvet cloud of fluorocarbons. But no matter how much fuel Ashbrook applied, her leftover pork chops, stale bread, and T-bones just became more richly roasted.

After the fire died, every bear within miles perceived the charred and smoked offal as a sumptuous casserole. Since garbage dumps were introduced in Yellowstone National Park over a hundred years ago, few bears have been able to turn down such "free food," particularly since it doesn't exhaustively have to be stalked, chased across hill and dale, then hamstrung before it can be eaten. And more grizzlies have died on garbage dumps than on any other human encroachment.

Roberta liked to brag to Doug that she could drain the brainpan of marauding bears with her .44-magnum handgun "if the rangers don't have the balls." But Doug's only weapons were food canisters, Telazol tranquilizer darts, and 12-gauge shotguns loaded with rubber bullets or bird shot.

Soon enough, Brian began putting the pressure on Roberta, calling regularly and politely asking her to clean up the dump. So Roberta wrote a letter to her congressman, Don Young, and complained about the rangers harassing her on her own private property. From the beginning, the case was destined to be a politician's *cause célèbre*, a mission in which the small-businesswoman can be saved from the bully government. The rights of the grizzly, however, were never considered.

Ranger Brian Swift was a true diplomat, schmoozing with the locals at the roadhouse and buying folks a drink. Each time he visited, though, he reminded Roberta about cleaning up her garbage dump. It was clear that Roberta didn't give a toenail about bears or wilderness. Finally Brian gave an ultimatum: "Clean up the dump or I'll bulldoze it over."

Roberta felt her rights were violated. She immediately phoned Congressman Young—who remembered her earlier letter—and Roberta raised a stink calculated to win support. The Honorable Don Young knew nothing about sensitive bear problems in national parks. He immediately phoned Brian's boss, the park superintendent, who knew a lot about political appointments and forgot what he knew about bears and garbage dumps. His secretary typed a memo, which was shuffled into the chief ranger's overstuffed "IN" box, and after the passage of several days, the message trickled down to Brian that he should lay off Roberta. Period.

There was only one person who could effectively lobby for the bears. By September, Doug had succeeded in exasperating all the rangers with his foul cigars, loud guitar playing, excessive speeding in the "bear busters" van, and games of "chicken" with oncoming ranger vehicles. But Doug was the only park employee who could work around the myriad of red tape and rules; he didn't care if they fired him.

Several years earlier, he had been forced to shoot and kill a black bear that had charged tourists at another park garbage dump. Doug did not brag about this qualification for his job. Before working for the National Park Service, he had lived off the land for several years, and like most Alaskan trappers, Doug used to have no compunction about killing bears. Although he delighted in "conditioning" bears to stay out of campgrounds with rubber bullets, after he shot the black bear, he swore that he'd never fire a lead slug into a bear's chest again.

Doug and his new trainee, Kenny, knew all about the roadhouse dump. Earlier that summer, as Doug inhaled a canful of cold meatball C rations, he had watched a blond-colored bear scarfing garbage from the smoldering pile. The only thing that Doug liked better than eating was to watch bears eat, but at the roadhouse garbage dump, Doug smelled trouble because this big male bear had become a regular.

So Doug became a regular at the roadhouse. He pulled the protesting Kenny along and they played Roberta in a completely unorthodox and unauthorized manner. Even if Brian hadn't been unplugged by the superintendent, all of the bulldozers, free rounds, and canned good-ol'-boy talk wouldn't have allowed Brian to follow Doug's act.

Doug instructed Kenny to practice plenty of Earl Scruggs and Jerry Jeff Walker on his twelve-string. Then, every Friday night, Kenny strummed his guitar and wailed in a talented twang at Roberta's bar; Doug sucked cigars, ate Roberta's leftovers, and pumped beer with the locals, shooting the bull, but not the bear, with Roberta.

He had nearly convinced Roberta to compromise. *À cheval* a barstool, eye to eye with Roberta (silently lamenting the blond bear's fate), Doug promised her a truck, which Doug would "borrow" from the rangers once a week to haul out all her leftovers and garbage.

Doug knew that he was just a seasonal peon surrounded by seasoned bureaucrats. He knew that he couldn't guard the blond bear forever, because he had to leave soon. Somehow Roberta decided that if she accepted Doug's garbage-hauling offer, she would only lose face. So there in the smoke-filled barroom, she told Doug to "go shove it."

When Doug returned to college in Anchorage, the blond bear started dining even more regularly at Roberta's dump. The rangers told Kenny to scare the bear off with bird shot, and if that didn't work, the bear could be tranquilized and transported.

Young Kenny loaded up the van—now missing its "bear busters" poster—and in deference to the rangers who are trained to look for speeders rather than bears, he drove fifteen miles an hour under the speed limit for eighty miles to the roadhouse dump. He was relieved to be holding the wheel because Doug had tormented him with games of chicken and ditch driving.

Several hours later, he found the blond bear on top of the still-smoking pile of refuse. Kenny nervously grabbed the shotgun and marched a little closer, forgetting that he had loaded a round of the larger-grained and more powerful buckshot behind two rounds of birdshot. Kenny pumped and pulled the trigger of the Winchester three times: The third unexpected blast of buckshot blew Kenny backward and walloped the bear's rear end, knocking down the four-hundred-pound bundle of fur, fat, and muscle. The bear still refused to leave; maybe it was expressing territorial dominance, or maybe it was too dazed by the buckshot.

Even Kenny realized that if the bear didn't eventually menace tourists, it might end up underfoot from Ashbrook as a huge blond rug. So Kenny fired a dart of Telazol into the bear's furry flank. The bear fell into a deep sleep and, just like the Kahiltna Pass bear, it was helicoptered in a cargo net toward a remote corner of the northern parklands.

Roberta had won. Now she smiles more smugly at the rangers; the superintendent added one more congressional buddy to his Christmas card list; and, in theory, wilderness lovers can travel through a tamer park.

But what about the bear? Does anyone really care about a wild beast with four-inch claws and bad breath that has been shot at, hunted after, and driven from every wild landscape except parklands? If nothing else, it is an animal that strikes humility into the hearts of grown men and women, forcing them to swagger with loaded firearms and recite boundless tall maul tales.

Of course, the newspapers never picked up the story:

Kenny felt too guilty to breathe a word, and a clerk buried it all in a file amid hundreds of other files. Even the unflappable Doug grew morose after dragging the news out of his former trainee. So Doug quit the Park Service and pursued a career in engineering.

The same day that Kenny tranquilized the blond bear, it was lowered groundward; blade wash ruffled its fur like wind quaking the aspen leaves. Denali rose three vertical miles above. When the helicopter shut down, everyone stood still in the deafening silence so peculiar to this vast wilderness.

The Athapaskans who once frequented this tundra knew an unequaled respect and awe for bears. While hunting they never pointed at bears or referred to them except obliquely. Women were not permitted to speak of *ghonoy tlaaga* at any time, let alone look directly at a bear or eat it. When a bear was killed, all bones had to be burned so the spirit was not desecrated. Hides could only be hung up, because stepping on a bear rug would be great sacrilege to its spirit.

According to the shamans of modern-day resource management, bears normally regain consciousness from such dart-induced sleeps quite slowly, wallowing around like winos. But this time the stress of the mistakenly fired buckshot, or maybe one excess milliliter of Telazol, proved too much. Whatever the cause, this bear would suffer the same fate as the Kahiltna Pass bear.

Kenny watched its fierce brown eyes go dull. He watched its chest stop moving and its limbs stiffen. As Kenny ran his fingers through its silken fur and smelled one last fetid breath of pork chops, stale bread, and T-bones, he felt a need to cry.

10

DELIVERANCE FOR FOOLS

They catched are in an entangled net,
'Cause they good counsel lightly did forget:
'Tis true they rescued were; but yet, you see,
They're scourged to boot. Let this your caution be.
— JOHN BUNYAN

I FIRST CONNECTED WITH MUGS STUMP IN 1981 AT THE SOUTH-east fork of the Kahiltna Glacier. Between composing poetry in his tent, he gazed out the door at Mount Hunter; the Athapaskan name for his peak, Begguya, meant "the child of Denali." Mugs stared longingly at what he would later name the "Moonflower Buttress"—a five-thousand-foot prow of granite and ice. The route had attracted dozens of suitors over the years. Cracking the buttress would signify a quantum leap in technical difficulty for Alaska Range climbing.

A lot of climbers spent time in Mugs's palatial tent. He generously shared graham crackers, filterless Camel ciga-rettes, and pipes of caustic hashish. Mugs often sat as passive as an abbot, legs folded beneath him as he listened to his wind chimes or lit another stick of incense. I liked to watch him reach out to other climbers with a smile, a few words of kind encouragement about their proposed climbs, and a gentleness that seemed antithetical for a professional football player turned climber. He said that he climbed mountains because of deep religious convictions; balancing on handholds and hang-ing off steep ice were more spiritual fulfillment than physical satiation. Mugs was on some sort of a metaphysical quest, and I immediately identified with him.

In a more urbane place, he might have been perceived as an everyday jock: His ungainly nose sprawled across an almost simian face; his short, clipped syntax could easily be mistaken for locker room colloquy. In this mountain arena, however, Mugs fulfilled the image of a cerebral Greek Adonis: stomach muscles rippling under the broad shoulders of an athlete; the alabaster skin below his neck contrasting vividly with his bronzed and bearded face; his mahogany eyes radiating intelligence and seeking direct eye contact with everyone he spoke to.

In 1981, Jim Bridwell and Mugs climbed the coveted east face of the Moose's Tooth, rising like an abrupt granite chimera from the Ruth Gorge. Jim, renowned as the best big rock wall climber in the world, wrote that "Mugs was a true climber. It was etched in his face, expressed in every movement of his body and apparent with his every thought. The words we spoke made our blood rage with excitement for the same lover . . . a lover with cold, hard, ruthless indiscrimination. Oh, how he loved this mistress of high places!"

But most climbers would never suspect that Mugs did virtually all of the hard leading. The "wall master" became Mugs's "belay slave." In the subzero treachery of the Alaska Range—pinching a handhold with two fingers and levering an ax in his other hand—Mugs knew no peer.

Under subzero conditions, they barely survived their ascent. Short on both gear and food, Jim was forced to rappel from a questionable anchor behind a dubious small rock flake. Mugs stood on their small ledge in the middle of a blank wall of granite and began reaching toward the anchor to unclip in case it pulled out under Jim's weight. But Mugs took his hand back, preferring a fast death to the slow starvation that would eventually come to the isolated ledge. That night they ranted and raved about reaching the glacier alive. It took hours of babbling at one another in their tent for their adrenaline to subside.

For hard-core alpinists throughout America, Mugs's greatest contribution was his vision of how to do these hard new routes. Technologically and psychologically there are rarely quantum advancements in climbing. But by coming to the Moose's Tooth in winter conditions and making it an ice climb instead of a rock climb, by bringing very little gear and moving fast, Mugs shared a new vision about intuition, perception, and risk. After the Moose's Tooth, it seemed that Mugs was unstoppable. He had ushered in super alpinism to Denali.

Mugs would guide clients up the Cassin Ridge, solo that route in one incredible day, create more elegant routes in the Ruth Gorge, solo two-mile-high and unclimbed Antarctic faces, and attempt the most difficult routes in the Himalaya. But he always returned to his spiritual home on Denali.

When Mugs recruited a partner for the Moonflower Buttress in 1981, New Zealander Paul Aubrey relinquished the leading, conceding that the climbing would go much faster with Mugs in front, on the "sharp end" of the rope. While following hard pitches, Paul frequently shouted up, "Mugs, you're superman!" At night they perched on half-a-buttock-wide ledges.

The only story Mugs ever published about his many climbs concerned the Moonflower Buttress. To describe the crux—a four-hundred-foot dagger of ice—Mugs wrote:

> Never had concentration made so much noise in my head. I was a simple shell of forces and movement. . . . My excitement was explosive as I screamed to release the fullness; I felt I belonged here.

In the normally staid *American Alpine Journal*, Mugs passionately described the end of the climbing two days later:

> No place to stop, there was no need to stop. Freedom was
> my catalyst as I deliberately and methodically made each
> placement. As I pulled over the top and onto the summit
> slope I was envisioning a crack such as this running for
> days. Where could I find it? I didn't want the feeling to
> stop.

Most climbers in the Denali region hop the first plane out when they finish their climbs. While Mugs's departing peers quaffed down lager in Talkeetna, he remained at the Kahiltna landing strip for two weeks, drinking in the feeling of Denali and admiring his buttress. I, too, had a lot of spare time, so Mugs and I often sat quietly in his spacious tent and listened to Jean Michel Jarre or Vangelis or Michael Oldfield on the tape player, turning it down only to admire the roar of nearby avalanches.

Once we skied over to the Moonflower Buttress. Mugs declined to tie into my rope on the crevassed glacier, and rather than ski along the relative safety of an established trail, Mugs skied, shirtless, over obvious crevasses. His laid-back technique for glacial travel sounded a strange chord because he knew better, particularly since other climbers had died in nearby crevasses.

Mugs finally accepted my rope as we climbed over a couple of crevasses up to the buttress. He tapped my shoulder, smiled softly, and traced an index finger in the air, as if I could share the climb with him. He told me of the shape of ledges, the paucity of handholds here, or the sublimity of the climbing there. He explained the mountain to me slowly, because nothing else assumed such importance in his life. His neck never stopped craning at the route above.

I was mostly looking at Mugs. Across a face that could have been chiseled from stone, crow's-feet held dancing eyes; between a brown beard and a large mole, his lips lifted to reveal yellowing teeth. His expression of undying respect and gratitude showed that Mugs was in love and didn't know how to leave.

For me and many other climbers, Mugs symbolized an approach of self-sufficiency in the mountains. He was a purist, and if most of the hordes on Denali could have found his respect for the mountain, it would be a much safer and saner place today. He laughed at Park Service regulations and made his own rules. He rarely relied on a radio. And accepting a helicopter rescue under any circumstances, even after his own death, would have been anathema to Mugs.

Several years after I met Mugs, sweat beaded on helicopter pilot Jim Porter's forehead as he hovered in toward a pickup at 17,000 feet on Denali. He and I had come for an accident victim who had supposedly broken his neck and now lay in a makeshift litter below us. Porter didn't know that twenty-two years earlier a pilot and rescuer were caught here in a down-draft and killed. No point in telling him now.

Suddenly the Alouette III plummeted like a broken elevator. Porter throttled the engine full and steered for a huge crevasse as we careened past the surprised faces of the ground team, then plunged down into the blurry, cobalt-walled hole, skimming its white floor at 100 miles per hour until we shot out the end of the hanging glacier over 8,000 feet of space. Porter said nothing, his white-knuckled hands clutching the stick, his face an L.A. expressway of sweat. Our night had only begun.

We suspended discussion of the 17,000-foot pickup, because it was obvious that we'd simply try again when conditions were safer. Guided by my finger-traced map on the canopy window, Porter circled to the 14,300-foot medical camp below the west buttress, where a doctor had requested we evacuate two other victims. I tried to joke with Porter, but he was preoccupied and nervous; I told him I'd buy him a beer once we got down safely.

The light was fading as we fell toward the camp. The doctor wind-vaned his arms on the landing site, but we lost him in the whiteout created by our rotor. A tinny-edged scream vibrated through the headphones into my ears as Porter commanded me to open the door and tell him where the glacier was. Just as I shouted "I can't see . . ." we slammed against the snow, rocked forward, and Porter trimmed the power. Spindrift settled on my lap.

I jumped out and escorted the two injured victims to the chopper. We took off immediately but were forced to climb to 18,000 feet, above the cloud layer that had blown in. We sailed above this frothy white ocean with no references except the tip of Denali in the rearview and the instrument panel at our knees. The two victims chatted away in the backseat as if this were an Anchorage taxi.

We flew an easterly course at seventy miles per hour for ten minutes. Figuring that we had passed all the peaks, we descended blind into the clouds. We alternated between gaping at the twirling hands of the altimeter and craning through the canopy for the granite wall that could meet us with all the grace of a speeding car catching a dragonfly. My clothes were sweat-soaked.

I jumped as the low-fuel buzzer wailed and flashed angry red: Ten minutes of fuel remained, and we were twenty minutes from Talkeetna. We looked at one another in horror as we realized that we had burned off too much fuel while flying fully loaded up high. I turned to the victims and told them to snug their seat belts quickly. They complied and, catching the urgency in my voice, the fear in my eyes, they thankfully stopped gossiping. The pilot and I continued staring at the altimeter, alternately searching through the canopy for something, anything other than the all-prevailing whiteness. We didn't know where we were.

After five minutes we finally ducked under the clouds, and the brown terminus of the Ruth Glacier popped into view— our reckoning was dead-on, for we had skipped over the granite walls of the gorge. Then I pointed out the headlights of a car on Parks Highway, several miles away. My heart fairly leapt.

By all rights the ship should have gone down. Finding the highway was sheer luck.

Minutes later we landed on an asphalt pullout. Beneath us leaves trembled on big cottonwoods from the rotor wash; as the skids hit pavement, I murmured "Thank you, God."

Jim radioed for a plane to come rescue us with helicopter fuel as I dug under the seat for flares. The women wanted to get out and stretch their legs, but the anger and fear on my face silenced further requests. I then ran out onto the highway, ripped the paper from the flares, and fired red flames out onto the center line, burning my hand. I made sure the first cars stopped, then ran down to the other side of the pullout and lit two more, stopping southbound traffic.

Five minutes later, Doug Geeting's Super Cub split the night. Skimming the roof of a Volkswagen bus, his fat tundra tires hit the double yellow, and the Super Cub bounced three feet in the air until Doug yanked it screeching into the pullout as if he were driving a Maserati.

Doug was smiling as he opened the door and handed me a five-gallon fuel can. "Having fun t'night, are we?" he said. The plane reeked of gasoline; I was glad Doug wasn't smoking.

Jim and I carried the fuel over and spilled twenty gallons into the chopper (and on ourselves); Doug tinkered with a broken switch inside his plane. In my absorption with getting refueled, I had forgotten about the burned-out flares. A few cars whooshed by, but it seemed best to save the last two flares until Geeting needed to take off again.

Suddenly the sleepy driver of a semitruck saw the helicopter, and thinking we needed help, he yanked his rig into the pullout just past us and then slammed on his brakes when he saw the dimly lit Super Cub. Geeting vaulted from his plane and ran; the truck skidded to a halt several feet from the wing. Porter and I looked at one another and loosed adrenaline-provoked guffaws of relief.

The truck driver walked over to apologize, but we were too wild-eyed to hold a normal conversation, so we simply thanked him. He jumped in his rig and left. Before I could light the flares, Geeting gunned his own engine, checked for oncoming headlights, and taxied into the southbound lane. He was airborne within forty yards.

Our helicopter flight back to Talkeetna seemed a mere boring cruise in comparison. Porter and I entrusted the care of the two women to another bush pilot in Talkeetna. The victims were flown to Anchorage. On the drive from the airport to the hospital, they convinced their next taxi driver to stop at a fast-food restaurant for dinner. This act hit the newspapers the next day, when they were both released—one with minor frostbite, the other with a bruised hip. Someone complained to my boss that we were too slow, despite the bad weather. And no one thanked us.

Several days later, during the next window in the storm, we picked up the "broken neck" victim from seventeen thousand feet (he was later diagnosed with a wrist fracture and facial cuts). The taxpayer picked up the $12,512 bill. My adrenaline subsided three days afterward. I finally drank that beer with Porter in the Fairview Inn. Mugs was there drinking tea and talking to his clients.

Porter ran his fingers through his beard and stared at the portraits of dead pilots and climbers on the wall. This is a wall that Talkeetna climbers do not bandy about much because joking about portraits of dead brethren is bad karma. Suddenly Porter set down his beer and confided that the rescue was just like his combat flying in Vietnam.

The Park Service cannot be held responsible for preventing deaths. Throughout the many rescues I became involved in, it had become apparent that many Denali climbers were lacking in self-sufficiency. Some groups were not trained in emergency care and rescue practices. Others, if they got hurt, picked up their radio and called for a helicopter instead of fixing things themselves; Mugs often bemoaned this trend. His philosophy was not only that parties should rescue themselves, but also that you should avoid calling for a rescue at all costs, short of dying. "After all," Mugs said, "why should some pilot risk his life for me?"

Mugs was a rescuer as well. In 1979, Ken Currens took a long fall and badly broke his leg on a Denali route called the Isis Face. His partner, Jack Tackle, made Currens comfortable in a snowcave. Jack rappelled down to the Ruth Glacier, skied out through crevasses, and just before noon, caught a skiplane out to Talkeetna.

Jack had problems. One bush pilot was a stringer for a television news station and badgered Jack about filming some spectacular rescue footage. The only ranger was three hours away and tried to convince Jack that he should wait until morning for a military helicopter to pluck Currens off the face. In the midst of all this, Mugs and Jim Logan poked their heads in the doorway and said, "We'll help."

Mugs had been mounting the first of many attempts on the unclimbed Moose's Tooth. Volunteering to help rescue Currens could easily have jeopardized one of Mugs's longtime dreams. Certainly most Alaskan climbers with "new route" fever would not have been psychologically prepared to shift gears and rescue Currens.

When they were flown back onto the glacier at 6:00 P.M., they confronted miles of trailbreaking. Mugs grabbed seventy pounds of rescue gear and started dragging the litter and breaking trail in an unconsolidated foot of snow. Neither Jim nor Jack could keep up. Jack looked at Jim, who said, "I can never fucking keep up to Mugs anywhere we go."

They reached the face at midnight and started climbing. Jack was impressed by Mugs's skill on snow and ice—always straight up the slope with a highly efficient and flowing economy of movement, known to devout ice climbers as "French techniquing."

After chatting with the comfortably dazed Currens, Mugs lowered the victim, attached to Jim and Jack. They reached the glacier just after dawn. From the safety of the flat glacier, it was an easy helicopter pickup.

Jack would never forget Mugs's calm under pressure, his serene composure. Moreover, Mugs became an exemplar of self-sufficiency.

In 1985 an event on the north face of Mount Hunter (directly above the landing strip and beside Mugs's Moonflower Buttress) showed how different most climbers are from Mugs.

A pair of Colorado climbers, Jeff and Dick, spent two days climbing the face. On their second night a storm inundated the route with new snow and avalanches. The next day Jeff and Dick began rappelling down, but they got lost. Snow continued to fall, and they began yelling for help as if they were hurt; climbers below radioed the ranger station.

Geeting and I flew by and air-dropped food and a radio from a belly hatch in the plane, but the radio missed their site and was lost. Eventually Jeff held his arms straight up in the air, showing that they wanted to be evacuated. Even though they appeared safe, we could not question their decision.

At six the next morning, Chris Soloy lifted them off in a tricky helicopter pickup, balancing the starboard skid next to the tent and risking everything for two climbers who had cried wolf. Jeff and Dick later volunteered to pay for their rescue costs, but told us that if the Park Service had required climbers to carry radios, their rescue could have been avoided. A hefty bill was given to the taxpayer, while paltry thanks went to the rescuers.

I never banked on "thank yous" because rescues were my job. In some deviant way I might have been hooked on the adrenaline of bumpy, storm-washed helicopter rides in the same way I was hooked on climbing. Neither did I expect the scorn rendered by many victims. Maybe our victims were shamefaced to have resorted to the indignity of rescue by the bureaucratic Park Service. Perhaps it was our uniforms and badges; we parodied ourselves by hanging up magazine ads of uniformed rescuers—smoking Salem cigarettes with perfectly blow-dried hair—above our rescue radio.

After my boss wrote Mugs a $300 citation for guiding without a permit, he began avoiding the ranger station. He had once spent a few days in jail for smoking grass, and all of a sudden the Talkeetna rangers made Mugs feel like a criminal again. But we had more pressing matters than mollycoddling Mugs or convincing him that we were there to help climbers.

My ranger confreres Scott Gill, Roger Robinson, and I often stayed up late at the ranger station and fantasized about dynamic new regulations to minimize the risks for the deliverance of fools from Denali to the hospital. We imagined obligatory helicopter winching loops built into all climbers' harnesses, and mandatory radiotelemetry neck collars (used on troublesome Denali Park grizzlies) to reduce search time. Roger, recently married, became even more discerning. If the mission seemed at all risky—which is implied any time you ride choppers at high altitude—he stayed in the station and operated the radio. We didn't blame him. As gluttons for thrills, Scott and I eagerly jockeyed for Roger's seat on the helicopter.

The next year our jobs would become permanent, replete with pay raises, health benefits, lateral job rights anywhere in the national parks, and elevated GS ratings. But the mountain takes everything you have. I was fried and knew that this fourth year would be my last. Scott held out another two years and got married; although Roger lost a kidney, he still might endure until retirement.

During one cloud-hung evening I went too far—it was the same week that a state trooper had cited me for driving ninety miles per hour in the Park Service truck while racing the helicopter to an Anchorage hospital. Maybe it was my frustration mixing with exhaustion, but on this cloudy evening the helicopter couldn't fly and there was an injured climber lying at seventeen thousand feet, impatiently awaiting our services because he lacked the sense to carry an ice ax. In that mildewed, tilting Park Service trailer that served as home during the richest years of my life, I turned to the government-issue IBM and typed a midnight memo on Department of the Interior letterhead. When the clouds cleared and the chopper could fly again, I wanted to air-drop the following message out the door, padding the loaded .41 magnum:

Dear Climber:

Chopper pilot gone fishing, rangers out to lunch, but here is a bullet for you. Otherwise, you are authorized to begin descending.

Sincerely,

The Rangers

P.S.: Never cry wolf.

By 5:00 A.M. the clouds had lifted; Denali burgeoned outside my bedroom window like the blinding light at the end of long, dark tunnel. Skiplane propellers vibrated the tin roof, helicopter rotors beat the air, and an urgent scratchy voice kept repeating "Come in, Talkeetna ranger station, please come in!" I grabbed the rescue pack and a large bottle of oxygen, suddenly realizing that once I left Denali and this rescue work, I would lose a sense of purpose to my life. I seized the radio mike and barked out our ETA. Before running out the doorway, I ripped my note from the typewriter, crumpled the paper, and threw it at the wastebasket.

It is rare to encounter old friends in crowded airports. But during the spring of 1992 in Denver, someone shouted my name from the wall of pay phones: Alan Danson had once traveled the Japanese Ramp on the south buttress of Denali.

"Jon," Alan had once said, "if ever I forget and say that was fun, you can correct me about how much I suffered up there." Alan had spent a lot of time in storm, coming up just shy of the summit. We had no time to talk—he had a business associate on the phone, and I had a plane departing for Utah—but Denali preyed on both of our minds. There is no escaping it.

On that same trip I ran into Mugs at the Salt Lake City airport. He wore an elegant lamb's wool pullover he had brought back from a climb in Patagonia; I was wearing a sport jacket purchased from a clothier in Vail. Mugs's eyes were dreamily fixed at the level that they would meet Denali from the town of Talkeetna. His long brown locks had grayed; the beard was gone. I was happy to see him, but instead of launching off into his usual tales of climbing in Alaska, Antarctica, or some wild western wall, Mugs was lost in a deep blue funk. I tried to get him talking, but his eyes wandered toward some interstellar appointment.

He muttered about getting a Denali guiding permit so he

could guide legitimately. But rather than elaborate on the two clients he was going to guide up Denali's South Buttress ramp for another guide company, he spoke of the house he had just bought in Salt Lake City. I told him about what an effort it was to get a bank loan for my own house in the mountains of Colorado, but Mugs looked at me flat-eyed without his usual direct eye contact and told me that he borrowed all the money from friends and told the banks to go fuck themselves.

This was it, then: just a gruff good-bye from the most inspirational Alaskan climber I knew. We love the same mountain, but the difference between us was that he was still committed to Denali, while I had found another life. I was deeply envious as he stalked off to catch his flight to Alaska.

On May 21, 1992, Mugs came to me in a dream. I woke up wondering why he never got the recognition deserved for his fabulous mountain career. Maybe it was because Mugs never publicized his climbs; maybe it was because climbing was his deeply felt and private ballet.

The real news did not come until several days later in a phone call, but Mugs wasn't the only one. Ten others died. The storm and sorrow of 1992, in fact, surpassed even the eight-man death toll of 1967 on Denali. The summer of 1992 might remain in the history books as the most infamous summer ever on Denali: In addition to all the deaths, there were a record 1,070 climbers on the mountain. And rescues cost the taxpayer $431,345, nearly four times the expense of any previous year. Although more climbers will die on Denali, 1992's events will make most climbers think twice about hanging it out.

At first, the subzero cold prevented most climbers from summiting, an event merely typical of early spring weather on Denali. Then, on May 11, a Fairbanks meteorologist forecasted "the worst storm that'll hit the mountain in 10 years."

Within 30 hours more than 5 feet of snow fell at the 7,000-foot base camp; winds of 110 miles per hour hit the 14,300-foot camp. Over a month's time, 22 climbers would be rescued; 18 of them were foreigners.

There were also dozens of minor accidents and rescues, including the evacuation of a Korean who fell while rappelling from the south face. Two Germans fell below the summit, and although capable of walking down with their minor injuries, they sat apathetically at 18,200 feet until Dr. Colin Grissom came to their rescue.

Meanwhile, a 48-year-old Italian climber, Giovanni Calcagno, had pooh-poohed the rangers' advice and arrogantly stalked out of the ranger station, thinking that no one knew how good a climber he really was. Calcagno then succeeded in climbing most of Cassin Ridge with his thirty-year-old companion Roberto Piombo, but at about the time they would summit, the wind began trumpeting like freight trains on top. On May 15, after receiving reports of a body, the rangers flew in by helicopter and found Calcagno's body hanging at 15,400 feet and Piombo's on the 11,800-foot glacier below Cassin Ridge. Piombo's body was slingloaded out, but Calcagno's body could not be retrieved.

At the same time, the rangers tried to evacuate three Koreans from Cassin Ridge; they had been stranded in a 17,700-foot snowcave for a week, radioing for help after the storm blew their tent and food away. Two days later, after the altitude-sick Koreans were nearly decapitated in the rotor, they were choppered down to 14,300 feet. The last Korean climber hooked three backpacks onto the skid below, but the ranger kicked them loose, explaining to the Korean that the extra weight could make the helicopter crash.

When the ship landed, instead of being thankful, one of the Koreans exploded about their packs—containing money and passports—being abandoned to the mountain. There at

14,300 feet, standing in the prop wash of a second helicopter that would take the Koreans to the hospital, Matt Culberson explained to the Koreans that being safe counts more than anything else. But the most irate Korean refused to board the helicopter until the packs were rescued; Jim Wickwire and John Roskelly wrestled the man aboard.

By May 17, the well-acclimated Swiss climber Alex Von Burgen, 42, had carried two loads above his 14,300-foot camp on the West Buttress. Immediately after sitting up to sip the tea that his wife had prepared for him that morning, he died from cardiac arrhythmia. Will Sayre was there, reliving the events of our winter climb, and even though Sayre knew it was a hopeless gesture, he went into the tent and alternated breathing into the dead man's mouth with hand compressions on the sternum.

Later that afternoon, three Koreans from the Je-Ju University Expedition unknowingly began setting up their tent on top of a crevasse bridge at 15,000 feet on the west buttress. Suddenly the 200-by-40-foot-wide bridge broke. Duk Sang Jang ran down for help.

Roskelly, Wickwire, Matt and Julie Culberson, Ron Johnson, Bruce Blatchley, and Brian Okonek rushed to the rescue. The second Korean, Seong Yu Kang, was buried up to his chest at the bottom of the crevasse; Roskelly and Matt Culberson rappelled 60 feet down and dug him out.

But Dong Choon Seo was hidden somewhere else beneath the collapsed snow bridge blocks. Seo assumed he was going to die slowly, so seeking a quicker end, he began chewing his tongue so he would bleed to death. The blood had clotted until he could barely breathe around the swollen, pulpy flesh that remained in his mouth. The snow around him began reddening. Culberson spied the bloody snow and a foot sticking out; he began sawing apart ice blocks; his shouts elicited a long moan, and finally the Korean's hand reached out and grabbed Culberson's ankle, as Culberson wrote in his journal, "with tremendous force."

After half an hour of working in subzero temperatures, risking another crevasse collapse, Roskelly and Culberson finished digging out Seo, whose arms and legs were pinned by huge blocks of ice. He was quickly evacuated, and in addition to the mess in his mouth, he had a broken back and a myriad of internal injuries.

Of all the rescuers who had seen accidents on the mountain before, Wickwire was doubly relieved about Seo and Kang. Over the past two decades, Wickwire had four partners die at his side. Eleven years earlier, beneath Denali's Wickersham Wall, it was impossible to free Chris Kerrebrock from a similar crevasse, so Wickwire was forced to sit and watch him die from hypothermia.

On the morning of May 20, three other students from the Je-Ju University Expedition radioed from 18,000 feet on the west rib that they would soon descend. At 5:00 P.M., the Culbersons—who were descending on the same route—found a long streak of blood on the snow at about 15,500 feet; below they saw three dark objects. Matt belayed his wife down, and when Julie saw the now discernible Korean bodies, Matt heard her shouting, "Oh, no! Not again! Why do you guys keep doing this?"

Since 1972 there have been eleven other deaths and several serious injuries here, partly because some climbers continue to proceed up in storms, but mostly because of the perennially tricky snow conditions at about 18,000 feet. Guides and rangers now morbidly refer to this chute as the "Orient Express" because of its inordinate number of Korean and Japanese victims.

There was still more. Later that month, four Canadian climbers bivouacked below the summit and became overdue.

While flying in a search plane, Roger Robinson spied them descending near the edge of the Messner Couloir at 19,300 feet. Minutes later, the last person on the rope stumbled and fell, plucking his three partners off; all four plunged 2,500 feet.

Dozens of climbers watched from below. "I saw one black dot going about 50 miles per hour down the slope and then you couldn't see any more from the clouds of snow they were kicking up," said Dr. Colin Grissom. "It gave me a real bad feeling in the pit of my stomach."

"It was horrible," guide Michael Covington was quoted in *Outside* by journalist Jon Krakauer. "They were smashing off rocks, bouncing far into the air, and all we could do was stand there helplessly and watch them die."

Colin finally plowed through dangerous avalanche conditions and reached the four bodies the next morning. "It was very, very obvious that they had died on the way down," he said. "I have to say it was a rough thing to witness."

Then Mugs. After taking his client Nelson Max to the storm-washed summit on hands and knees, he escorted Max and Robert Hoffman back down the seldom-climbed South Buttress Route. At that point in the season, only 9 other climbers out of 420 had reached the summit. It is a testament to Mugs's skill that he had gotten so high while escorting clients up in such sordid weather. He had held everything together perfectly when the going was tough—unlike most victims that summer—but when things became easier, perhaps Mugs let down his guard.

The next day, May 21, at 14,500 feet, the three were route-finding down the "Japanese Ramp," a 4,000-foot shortcut swept by unpredictable avalanches. Hoffman stopped at the edge of a crevasse, and since he was unsure how to proceed, Mugs walked past Max and Hoffman without taking a belay, incurring 15 feet of slack in his rope. Although it was a common mistake, Mugs regularly practiced "casual" glacier travel techniques. He turned around as if to say something, and at that instant a huge crevasse bridge broke with the resounding crack of a rifle shot beneath his feet: Mugs plunged in and dragged Max twenty feet before he could stop. The rope between him and Mugs became slack. For brief seconds everything was silent until the clients begin yelling Mugs's name.

Horrified, they peered into the crevasse, buried by tons of dense snow and ice blocks. After getting no reply to their shouts, they cut the rope, and Max rappelled into the crevasse —more than any guide could ask of a client. He dug for long minutes amid dense blocks of snow and ice. Finally, numb with the realization of what the mountain is capable of, they admitted that Mugs had to be dead.

The two started descending the mountain without stove or radio (buried with Mugs), and when picked up the next day in a helicopter—frostbitten and shaking—they quickly showed the rangers Mugs's grave, more than 25 hours after the accident. Max and Hoffman were dropped off at 7,200 feet and taken by airplane to the hospital; Max had frostbite on both feet.

The helicopter, carrying one of Mugs's former climbing partners, Ranger Renny Jackson, returned to the crevasse. Tons of snow and ice still overhung the area, known to previous South Buttress climbers and avalanche survivors as "a bowling alley." Given the steepness of the slope, the falling ice potential, and the amount of time that had elapsed since the accident, it would have been folly to look. Mugs's parents told Jackson's boss it was okay, and the body was wisely abandoned to the mountain.

Back in Talkeetna, a lot of nonclimbers wanted to know why Renny "didn't do more," not knowing that Mugs was a good friend. Renny hated this. No one really understood how bad the South Buttress Ramp is. So Renny went back up in the helicopter and videoed the dangerous crevasse from the air.

Most people could not believe that Mugs would die so ignobly, guiding such a relatively "easy" climb, particularly after everything he had survived in the Alaska Range.

Ranger Ron Johnson broke down when he heard about Mugs. Johnson knew he needed to get down and get some help. It wasn't any one event. Bundling up bodies below the Orient Express, the dead Swiss climber, dealing with the Koreans in the crevasse, keeping the tents dug out, and just staying warm made Johnson lose sleep and start having stress headaches. "Mugs was the final *coup de grâce*," said Johnson. "It just got out of control."

Talking with the other rangers accomplished nothing. They would all nod their heads, lift another beer, and say, "Well, you know how it is." They all needed help.

A psychologist was flown up from Washington State for a "critical stress incident debriefing." Since the psychologist did not know "how it is," he forced the rescuers to explain everything. "It allowed me to hear that the things we were experiencing were normal," said Johnson, "and they would eventually go away."

Anchorage journalist Craig Medred wrote that Mugs's death "rocked the soul of the climbing community." And Jack Tackle (who Mugs had helped in the Ruth Glacier rescue of 1979) scribbled me a card while en route to Denali: "to go take some 'mental health drugs' by myself. I am so sad about Mugs, one less hero to make all this alpine climbing worthwhile."

Three days after the accident, a memorial service was held for Mugs on the banks of the Susitna River at a cabin owned by Kathy Sullivan (widow of former Denali guide Ray Genet). Forty locals and guides and rangers stood around kicking sand washed down over the millennia from Denali. The sky seemed more infinite than the ocean; everyone watched the mountain. As climbers and friends took turns telling stories about Mugs, the group alternated between tears and laughter. A mother spoke lovingly of how Mugs tenderly fed yogurt instead of baby's milk to her infant. Another climber remembered what an absentminded driver Mugs was and how he crashed several of his friends' cars. A ranger recalled Mugs's illegal guiding on Denali and how he would tell passing climbers that his bumbling companions were "just friends." No one bore any grudges against the High One, fifty miles away, ripping clouds as the most stunning and luminescent tombstone on earth.

The New York Times, *The Anchorage Daily News*, *Newsweek*, *Rock and Ice*, *Climbing*, and *Outside* covered the tragic events of that summer, but no one got it quite right. One journalist suggested a new adventure-travel theme for Alaskan vacations: "Climb Mount McKinley—and die." And the journals mostly referred to the mountain by its Republican name, Mount McKinley, instead of the name that Mugs and Herb Atwater used, the name that most Alaskans continue to use.

"Mountain of death," one journal called it, ignoring the fact that more Americans have died on 6,244-foot Mount Washington in New Hampshire, or in automobile accidents, or in senseless gang wars, or from one of many diseases that can snuff you with none of the quick mercy that climbers have found on Denali.

Newsweek asked if climbing the mountain is sport or a "kind of athletic Russian roulette." The journalist then asserted a timeworn platitude that "the old 'because it's there' romanticism that makes people climb mountains lurches into hyperdrive on McKinley."

But no journalist wrote about the banality of city life or

how easy it is to become yet another automaton paying bills
and working nine to five and being so removed from the primary necessities of life and so far from real fear and natural
beauty and human instinct that when death finally approaches
in some antiseptic white room, just as you have been waiting
for it, you sense that you have already been dead for years.

Mugs knew that climbing Denali is a means of getting in
touch with your life and confronting your own fragility, instead of putting it all off and counting your days as atrophied
decay. Despite his crevasse travel techniques, Mugs, unlike
most of 1992's victims, had a sense of self-sufficiency and
respect for the mountain.

The New York Times, with its impeccably objective report-
ing, referred to "a Utah guide" without even mentioning his
name. The paper brushed the truth with its headline: "In the
Shadow of Mount McKinley, a Town Lives with Death." The
story touched on "the death wall" in the Fairview Inn, but
most readers would not have understood the significance of
any of the portraits hanging there, so they were not described.
Precious few indeed would understand that Ray Genet loved
mountains more than anything else in his life when he died in
a bivouac on Everest; or that the sad-eyed bush pilot Don
Sheldon risked his life innumerable times to rescue others
because he liked doing it, and probably because he sensed his
own crumbling battle with cancer.

Outside magazine also gave it a shot. "Because of his unim-
peachable climbing record," wrote Jon Krakauer, "no one
suggested that Stump's death was anything but a freak accident."

Since Allen Carpé's death in 1932, eleven climbers on
Denali have died in "freak accident" crevasse falls. Nine of
those climbers were of Mugs's caliber and had let down their
guard on low-angled glaciers, traveling without rope, with a

short rope, or with slack ropes. And Mugs? He was weirdly cavalier about proper rope technique on crevassed glaciers.

When the phone call came verifying his death, I was stunned. But there is consolation in thinking that Mugs had finally gone home, smiling at the storm and saved from those wretched silver-haired years when his memory would falter and his strength would slip and he would have been forced to find the patience to eke out the autumn of his life. No journalist suggested that the forty-three-year-old foresaw being shackled by house payments and being forced to find a "real" job and pace an earth flat and dull without the extreme climbing on the mountains he loved.

Mugs's body remains up there along with the bodies of thirty-two others. Undoubtedly future South Buttress climbers will encounter Mugs's spirit there on the Japanese Ramp; at the very least they will share his enthusiasm for a mountain that the 1903 climber Robert Dunn called an "unearthly castle of opalescent glass." Most other climbers will relive Denali as the zenith of their lives. And surely more climbers will entertain staying on the mountain like Allen and Johnny and Dave and Chris and Mugs have all done.

It is no coincidence that, beginning with Allen Carpé, the Alaskan climbing veterans who have died on Denali all treasured, and in some instances even memorized, Robert Service's poem *The Spell of the Yukon*. Mugs knew it well:

> There's a land where the mountains are nameless,
> And the rivers all run God knows where;
> There are lives that are erring and aimless,
> And deaths that just hang by a hair;
> There are hardships that nobody reckons;
> There are valleys unpeopled and still;
> There's a land—oh it beckons and beckons,
> And I want to go back—and I will.

In my dream about Mugs just after he died, he disapproves of my life with its lack of action and my brooding with words on paper as I worry about paying bills while sitting all day in an office. Mugs often appears in my dreams. He is disappointed that I am not going up Denali anymore, and he tries to talk me into a climbing trip that will last forever, with granite rasping our palms and frozen clouds coursing through our lungs, and where we will look out the windows of heaven at an alabaster ripsawed skyline and pink-orange clouds of a thousand shapes.

It is not stretching the imagination to see Mugs watching the green tundra four miles below disappearing into a gentle curve of the earth. He sees the Bering Sea on beyond like bluing infinity and hangs his legs out over the abyss of the south face while contemplating the air rising and falling through the granite gorge of Ruth Amphitheater—knowing that our planet is all one being as it breathes over him with the heat waves shimmering on beyond the blinding white of the glaciers toward Talkeetna and the budding life and rivers and greenery as far as he can see. Nothing up there is too terrible to behold. There on top of North America, Mugs smells that seared cobalt sky and watches the sun wink through passing clouds. He has found happiness beyond all time and ambition and breathing.